CO-ASV-766

3000 800067 06671
St. Louis Community College

Florissant Valley Library
St. Louis Community College
3400 Pershall Road
Ferguson, MO 63135-1408
314-513-4514

That's All Folks?

That's All Folks?

*Ecocritical Readings of
American Animated Features*

Robin L. Murray and Joseph K. Heumann

UNIVERSITY OF NEBRASKA PRESS
LINCOLN AND LONDON

© 2011 by the Board of Regents of the
University of Nebraska

Acknowledgments for the use of copyrighted
material appear on page ix, which constitutes
an extension of the copyright page.

All rights reserved
Manufactured in the United States of America

∞

Library of Congress Cataloging-
in-Publication Data
Murray, Robin L.
That's all folks?: ecocritical readings of
American animated features / Robin L.
Murray and Joseph K. Heumann.
    p. cm.
Summary: "Examines animated films in
the cultural and historical context of
environmental movements"—Provided by
publisher. Includes bibliographical
references and index.
ISBN 978-0-8032-3512-0 (cloth: alk. paper)
1. Environmentalism in motion pictures.
2. Animated films. I. Heumann, Joseph K.
II. Title.
NC1766.5.E58M87 2011
791.4334—dc23   2011021894

Set in Sabon and Cooper.
Designed by Shirley Thornton.

Contents

Illustrations

Acknowledgments

We would first like to thank Heather Lundine and the University of Nebraska Press staff for supporting this project. We would also like to thank Lola Burnham for her helpful commentary on the original manuscript and the Eastern Illinois University Council on Faculty Research for their financial support of this project. Support from our colleagues, including our English department's chair, Dana Ringuette, and our weekly research group has also encouraged us. Most important, we would like to thank our family and friends for their encouragement and understanding throughout this project. Thanks also to Julia Lesage and Chuck Kleinhans, editors of *Jump Cut*, for their unending support for our work.

We also appreciate the professional climate University of Nebraska Press provided us. Our experience with the University of Nebraska Press has been a pleasant one because of editor Heather Lundine's dedication to this project.

Parts of chapter 1 and chapter 2 were published in *Interdisciplinary Studies in Literature and Environment* and are used with permission. Chapter 10 is an expanded and revised version of "*WALL-E*: From Environmental Adaptation to Sentimental Nostalgia" published in *Jump Cut* 51 (Spring 2009) and is used with permission.

That's All Folks?

Lumber Jerks: Goofy Gophers build a home.

Introduction

A Foundation for Contemporary Enviro-toons

The 1955 Warner Brothers' cartoon, Goofy Gophers in *Lumber Jerks*, ends with a line from one of the gophers that illustrates the 1950s lifestyle: "Isn't our house much better than it was before?" he asks his partner as he looks up at a "tree" built of furniture sawed from what had once been their tree home. A television set tops off this house of furniture that stands alone among the stumps— what is left of a forest clear-cut for its lumber. The gophers seem happy with their new home, merely commenting, "It will be better when we have electricity." But after seeing the consequences of "progress" as depicted in the cartoon—devastation of our forests—are we meant to answer "yes" to the gopher's question? Does the cartoon argue that "our house [is] much better than it was before"?

Jaime Weinman argues just the opposite when stating that *Lumber Jerks* is a model "enviro-toon." She claims that it "never preaches. . . . And instead of showing that only evil people harm the environment, it shows that trees are being chopped down in order to make the things we use every day—in other words, we are the ones harming the environment." Unlike cartoons with anthropomorphized animals or plant life alone, what Weinman calls "enviro-toons" not only humanize nature but comment on abuse of nature and the natural, especially by humans.

For us, enviro-toons are animated shorts or feature films that address environmental concerns. Some may preach, but they all embrace an environmental message that responds to their historical and cultural contexts. *That's All Folks? The Ecology of the Animated Feature* rests on the belief that the genre of animation gains power because it challenges expectations of art, film, and narrative. The best animated films "offer the greatest potential for expressing a variety of divergent points of view, while at the same time accommodating a dominant paradigm of established social meaning" (Wells, *Animation and America* 13). Studios may resist or subvert the aesthetic and ideological orthodoxy associated with Disney, but they challenge aesthetic as well as ideological expectations through their negotiated resolutions between dominant and subversive views of social mores. As Wells suggests, a cartoon's "very status as an animation asks an audience to re-perceive supposedly everyday issues, themes, knowledge" (6).

Enviro-toons—animated shorts and feature films with ecology at their center—ask an audience to re-perceive everyday issues, themes, and knowledge related to differing phases of the American environmental movement: human ecology, organismic ecology, economic ecology, and chaotic ecology. The field of ecology, literally the study of homes, as its Greek root *oikos* (which translates as "household") suggests, received its name from German biologist Ernst Haeckel in response to Charles Darwin's work in evolutionary theory in the 1850s. According to environmental historian Annette Kolodny, Haeckel's notion of ecology as the study of homes served as the inspiration for the development of the field of human ecology.

The human ecology movement grew out of the work of

chemist Ellen Swallow Richards, who translated Haeckel's work from its original German and, according to Robert Clarke, introduced the concept of ecology in the United States. Richards defined human ecology as "the study of the surroundings of human beings in the effects they produce on the lives of men" (1910). Since she viewed humans as part of nature, she considered urban problems like air and water pollution as products of human activity imposed on the environment and, subsequently, best resolved by humans. The human ecology movement eventually evolved into home economics, but its grounding in conservation had lasting effects. A 1948 *New York Times* editorial, for example, endorsed a smoke abatement protest by "urg[ing] housewives and others to take this opportunity" to join the anti-pollution campaign (Kovarik).

Organismic ecology is based on Frederic Clements's view of a plant community as a living organism that evolves through succession. According to Clements, as a living organism, a plant community changes over time: "The unit of vegetation, the climax formation is an organic entity. As an organism, the formation arises, grows, matures, and dies. . . . The climax formation is the adult organism, the fully developed community" (Clements 124–25 qtd. in Merchant 182). This process of succession paralleled both the life cycle and the developmental history of the United States, with pioneer species invading ecosystems until climax communities of species were established: the deciduous forest climax, the prairie-plains climax, the mountain range climaxes of the Rocky Mountains, and the desert climaxes of the Southwest. A plant community is also vulnerable to disruption or death by technologies such as those that caused the Dust Bowl, however, when humans as pioneer species "had not appreciated or understood the grassland biome native to the Plains" (Merchant 184).

The *organismic school* of ecology "rejected Social Darwinist assumptions of a nature characterized by Thomas Henry Huxley as 'red in tooth and claw,' for a nature of cooperation among individuals in animal and human communities" (Merchant 184). Warder C. Allee and Alfred E. Emerson, organismic ecologists at the University of Chicago after World War I, saw the workings of the natural world as a model for healing societal problems. Organismic ecologist Aldo Leopold, on the other hand, applied human ethics to the natural world, constructing a manifesto, "The Land Ethic," which encouraged an ecologically centered view of the land as a biotic pyramid in which humans were a part. In Leopold's view, humans had "the scientific and ethical tools to follow nature and heal it" (Merchant 185).

Whereas the organismic approach to ecology encouraged preservationist policies toward the environment, the economic approach, in which ecosystems were seen as sums of their parts, not living organisms, encouraged fairuse politics that called for the exploitation of resources for human gain. Such an approach valorized humans as managers who were "above nature and able to control it" (Merchant 186) and who used environmental resources for human benefit. Economic ecologist Kenneth Watt asserts, for example, that human beings are economic animals, and "economic ecology's goal is to maximize the productivity of each type of ecosystem and each level of that ecosystem for human benefit" (qtd. in Merchant 188). Although ecologist Eugene Odum connected the tenets of organismic ecology with those of the economic to demonstrate ways humans can repair the natural world, the ultimate goal of economic ecology—maximizing benefits of nature for humans—serves as more of a disruption than a tool for healing. Human ecology, organismic ecology, and economic ecology, however, are all products of

Haeckel's development of ecology as a field in his 1866 work, *Generelle Morphologie der Organsmen*, and developed from at least the late 1910s forward.

The last approach, *chaotic ecology*, did not emerge in its current form until the 1970s, when chaos theory was developed. Chaotic ecology views nature as a potential disruptor of its own ecosystems through natural disasters such as hurricanes and tornadoes. Since both human and nonhuman nature disrupt nature, this theory suggests that "both can work in partnership to restore it" (Merchant 190). Yet chaotic ecology's premise that nature disrupts its own ecosystems also parallels an ancient view of the natural world as a powerful force that sometimes overwhelms human nature.

Although these four approaches are sometimes seen as linear phases, they are rooted in Haeckel's definitions of ecology and continue to influence environmental policy. They also continue to influence media responses to nature and the natural world, at least in the world of the short or feature-length animated film.

We assert, then, that American enviro-toons from the 1930s forward reveal three narrative and aesthetic patterns in relation to the historical and cultural context and approach to ecology underpinning them: the power of nature over the human world, the need for controlling human intervention and nurturing the natural world in order to strengthen their interdependence, and criticism of human exploitation of the natural world. Animated feature films emphasizing the power of nature over the human world draw on the worldview reflected in both economic and chaotic ecology. Films encouraging interdependence between human and nonhuman nature seem grounded in human and organismic ecology. Animated films criticizing humans' exploitation of the natural world reflect all four approaches. Variations depend primarily on the historical context of the films and the studio and/or director that produced them. Ultimately, however, animated features primarily serve as moneymakers on multiple levels, especially as broad-based family entertainment and conveyors of consumer products. Only Ralph Bakshi's adult-centered animated features, X-rated *Fritz the Cat* (1972), R-rated *Heavy Traffic* (1973), and R-rated *Coonskin* (1975), with their violent, dystopic representation of urban environments avoid this total immersion in an anti-environmental consumer market and counter the messages most animated films deliver.

If, as Norman Klein argues, "cartoons [are] ever the barometer of changes in entertainment" (211), these enviro-toons also serve as representations of America's changing attitudes toward the environment. Unlike cartoons that either maintain the nature/culture binary, or those that seek to reconcile the binary through the intervention of a controlling agent, animated shorts and features that critique our treatment of the natural world respond explicitly to changes in the American cultural context and illustrate an ambivalence toward modernism and its ramifications. All three categories of cartoons we have highlighted, however, serve as enviro-toons that do more than present nature or a landscape. They confront the natural in increasingly complex ways in response to the ideologies of studio and director and the cartoons' respective historical and cultural contexts. They also debunk the myth that the environmental movement started with Rachel Carson's *Silent Spring*. In fact, the environmental movement has been a formal movement in the United States since the nineteenth century, with nods to conservation and animal rights beginning with Plato and Aristotle. If Wells and Klein are right, enviro-toons do engage with repercussions of progress in the modern and postmodern world. The environmental movement as we know it did not begin with Richard Nixon's creation of the Environmental Protection Agency. Because of conservationists such as Ellen Swallow Richards, Frederic Clements, Aldo Leopold, and even Eugene Odum, environmentalism was a growing concern before, during, and after World War II, at least in the world of animated film.

The Contexts of Environmentalism

With the critical and popular acclaim a film such as WALL-E (2008) has received, it seems clear that the environmental movement has influenced the content of the animated film. What may be missing from discussion of environmental cartoons, however, is the filmic history behind recent animated enviro-toons such as *Avatar* (2009), WALL-E, *Happy Feet* (2007), and *Bee Movie* (2007). When we began our study of enviro-toons, we examined more than five hundred animated shorts from the 1930s, '40s, and '50s, decades prior to the burgeoning environmental movement of the 1960s, '70s, '80s, '90s, and 2000s, and found that although such enviro-toons were rare and, as a group, were not attributable to a particular studio or director, cartoons such as *Lumber Jerks*, *Porky Chops* (1949), and other enviro-toon shorts from the classical era of Hollywood animation serve as potentially powerful cultural productions. For animators such as Friz Freleng, environmental devastation and negative consequences of progress may serve as comic plot devices, but they also contribute a cultural critique. Warner Brothers offered a challenge to the orthodoxy of Disney, and United Productions of America (UPA), for example, conveyed explicitly embedded liberal and radical messages in its cartoons. These and other enviro-toons also paved the way for feature-length enviro-toons from *Mr. Bug Goes to Town* (1941) to *Avatar*. They are also rooted in environmental history.

The period before, during, and after World War II is

commonly associated with a drive for technological advancement, from constructing needed military equipment during the war to building highways and freeways and entering the space race after it ended (see Rothman and Shabecoff). Still, there were noteworthy exceptions, such as Teddy Roosevelt's creation of the national park system and Franklin Delano Roosevelt's New Deal programs. In 1933, for example, the Civilian Conservation Corps was formed and opened two thousand camps, planting trees, and building bridges, roads, and fire towers. That same year, the Dust Bowl storms began in the Midwest, but Roosevelt's Tennessee Valley Authority and Soil Conservation Service helped offset the storms' disastrous consequences. Aldo Leopold and Arthur Carhardt founded the Wilderness Society in 1935, from which Leopold's land ethic stemmed. And the Federal Aid in Wildlife Restoration Act passed in the U.S. Congress in 1937, the same year *Snow White and the Seven Dwarves* was released, creating a federal tax on sporting arms and ammunition that supported wildlife management and research programs across the country. Walt Disney's *Bambi* was released in 1942 as a blatant critique of hunting practices. Rachel Carson had published her first environmental treatise, *Under the Sea-Wind,* the previous year.

Even during World War II the environmental movement continued its work. The Audubon nature center opened in 1943 in Greenwich, Connecticut, and became a model for future nature centers, and the Soil Conservation Society was formed by Hugh Bennett in 1944. Much has been written about DDT use during World War II and its exploitation after the war, one of the reasons Carson published *Silent Spring.*

After the war the environmental movement burgeoned. In 1946 the U.S. Bureau of Land Management and the International Whaling Commission were established.

The Defenders of Wildlife and Everglades National Park were established in 1947. In 1948 the Federal Water Pollution Control Act was passed, the same year as William Vogt's best-selling conservation book, *Road to Survival*, and Fairfield Osborn's *Our Plundered Planet* were published. Aldo Leopold's *Sand County Almanac*, one of the most influential eco-works ever written, was published in 1949, a year after Leopold's death. Leopold's work had a positive influence on both Supreme Court justice William O. Douglas and Secretary of the Interior Bruce Babbitt. Douglas began protesting what he saw as exploitation of nature as early as 1954, when he successfully opposed the building of a proposed highway that would destroy the Chesapeake and Ohio Canal and its towpath. Bruce Babbitt, who served under President Clinton, is still a tireless advocate of environmental issues. In a preface to the 2000 edition of *Sand County Almanac* written in memory of Leopold and in honor of Leopold's conservation work, Babbitt traces the origin of his stances to Leopold's book.

The 1950s were a particularly active time in American environmentalism. In 1951 the Nature Conservancy was formed, the Animal Welfare Institute was founded, and Rachel Carson's *The Sea around Us* was published. Eugene Odum's *Fundamentals of Ecology*, a synthesis of organismic and economic approaches, was published in 1953. In 1954 the Humane Society of the United States was formed; in 1955 Congress passed the Air Pollution Control Act; in 1956 Congress passed the Water Pollution Control Act. In 1957 the Committee for a Sane Nuclear Policy was formed; in 1958 the Campaign for Nuclear Disarmament in the United Kingdom and the United States was formed; in 1959 California set the first automobile emissions standards.

These environmental gains stood in conflict to the mainstream responses to progress in the post–World War II industrialized world. After the war Americans had gained enough economic stability not only to purchase cars in record numbers but also to use them for traveling on cross-country highways such as Routes 40 and 66. According to Rothman, Americans after 1945 increasingly vacationed in national parks and forests. And "as more of them vacationed, exemplified by record numbers of visitors at Grand Canyon National Park each month after August 1945, they had an impact on the natural world that soon caused them to take notice" (85–86). Rothman claims that "what Americans found in many of their national parks and forests shocked them: decrepit and outdated campgrounds, garbage piled high and a lack of facilities and staff to manage them" (86). Americans took to the road, towing trailers behind them, so they could experience some of the nature they had left behind when they moved to the cities and the concrete suburbs surrounding them.

Vacationing Americans noticed the devastation in national parks and forests, but the Wilderness Act that served to protect and preserve them was not passed until 1964, almost twenty years after the end of the war. Alexander Wilson claims that Americans in the late 1940s and 1950s saw "the open road [as] a metaphor for progress in the U.S. and for the cultural taming of the American Wilderness" (34). Wilson even suggests, "What we saw out the window of a speeding car . . . was the future itself" (34). These views of nature through the window of a car—or even the window of a camper in a national park—skewed Americans' vision of the natural world. Such confusion between seeking pristine nature and embracing progress at any cost complicated ideological views of the environment and environmentalism. In "Conservation Esthetic," a section of his *Sand County Almanac*, Aldo Leopold describes late 1940's views of nature and wildlife recreation well: "To him who seeks in the woods and mountains only those things obtainable from travel or golf, the present situation is tolerable. But to him who seeks something more, recreation has become a self-destructive process of seeking, but never quite finding, a major frustration of mechanized society" (165–66). Yet the Americans Leopold describes are only part of the story. The environmental movement had strong roots in place after World War II, from seeds sown by the human ecology, organismic ecology, and, to a certain extent, economic ecology movements. These environmental movements made a mark on animated children's television and film.

Enviro-toons and Environmental History: Crossing Studios, Crossing Approaches to Ecology

The genre of animation (and animated shorts) gains power because it challenges expectations of art, film, and narrative. The best animated films "offer the greatest potential for expressing a variety of divergent points of view, while at the same time accommodating a dominant paradigm of established social meaning" (Wells, *Animation and America* 13). Studios may resist or subvert the aesthetic and ideological orthodoxy associated with Disney, but the cartoons challenge aesthetic as well as ideological expectations through their negotiated resolutions between dominant and subversive views of social mores. The following brief analysis discusses representative animated shorts and demonstrates the often subtle but nonetheless powerful ecological messages conveyed within them from the 1930s to the 1950s. Keeping in mind that the historical and cultural contexts in which these cartoons were produced vary, we argue that, ultimately, beliefs about technology, consumerism, and the natural are reflected in, and sometimes critiqued by, enviro-toons.

Of the enviro-toons we viewed, most demonstrate the power of nature over the human world, a perspective rooted in economic and chaotic approaches to ecology. These more traditional cartoons seem to be a by-product of the ongoing conflict between "the machine and the natural" (Klein 79) and may have their roots in economic and chaotic approaches to ecology. As Klein argues, cartoons are a product of technology and seem also to glorify it (76). Klein compares technology behind cartoons to the *machina versatilis*, which appeared in Italy in the 17th century and, as Ben Jonson suggests, harkened in a "Mechanick Age" (qtd. in Klein 76), an industrial age in which industries were causing massive deforestation in England.

Industrialization widened the gap between nature and culture, between humans and the natural world. Nature, then, was seen as either a resource to be exploited or an "enemy" to be controlled. Carolyn Merchant's study of changes in representations of nature in New England and Annette Kolodny's examination of American literary representations of women and nature demonstrate the ramification of this historical change. Eco-critics such as Lynn White Jr. and Frederick W. Turner historicized these representations in useful ways, concluding, too, that the nature/culture binary widened after industrialization in the West.

Some early Felix the Cat cartoons foreground this re-emphasized nature/culture binary when they show how stormy weather can spoil a picnic. *April Maze* (1930) seems to anticipate New Deal programs that saw nature as a powerful force needing both respect and taming. Tennessee Valley Authority projects, for example, promoted a system of dams to control flooding on big rivers—and to bring electricity to the rural poor. Michael Barrier explains that Otto Messmer, the cartoon's director, "never let his audience forget that Felix was as artificial as his environment" (*Hollywood Cartoons* 45), but in *April Maze* nature is effectively portrayed as a powerful force that the more humanlike Felix cannot conquer.

Cartoons from the 1940s, too, reflected this conflict between humans and the natural world. Perhaps as a reaction to World War II, however, superheroes like Superman fought natural elements and won. Norman Klein concurs, suggesting that the world war had just as much of an impact on cartoons as film noir and screwball comedies from Hollywood (183). The Superman series from this period seems to reflect this impact most visibly. Superman cartoons also exaggerate the *machina versatilis*, "updat[ing] an old theme of theirs, the film screen as machine" (Klein 86). According to Klein, "The entire screen seems to be made of steel, like a machine housed in black, corrugated metal, with gray canyons beneath skyscrapers, and diabolical machines instead of ghouls" (86).

In this mechanized context, the cartoons place Superman as superior to elements in the natural world. In the opening to most of the cartoons, Superman masters lightning and other elements such as those in *April Maze*. And in *Volcano* (1942) Superman stops a volcanic eruption to save Lois Lane and the town below. Superman always comes out victorious, expressing hope for the Allies' own victory over the Germans. Klein argues, "From 1942 to the end of the war, about half of the cartoons produced were 'war related,' and at some studios for a time the proportion ran as high as 70 percent" (186). The war provided the industrial background of a modernist world in which technologies (and humans) triumph over nature.

Several Walt Disney cartoons from the 1930s, 1940s, and 1950s highlight this sustained conflict between humans (or anthropomorphized animal figures) and the natural world—unsurprising coming from this more conservative studio. *Flowers and Trees* (1932) foregrounds idyllic nature's triumph over an evil anthropomorphized tree stump. As the first color short from Disney, *Flowers and Trees* won an Academy Award with its Technicolor dancing trees and flowers, romantic tree love story, and jealousy. But the tree stump's jealous rage is thwarted by birds, who literally put out his fire. The tree stump clearly represents the evil human world, since his tongue is a snake and his goal is to destroy the tree lovers and their forest. In the end, the stump destroys himself and reinforces his non-flora status, since vultures encircle his corpse.

Four Disney cartoons that feature Donald Duck and Chip an' Dale highlight the power of nature over the human world—or at least the humanlike world of Donald Duck, all in relation to the chipmunks saving their nuts: *Chip an' Dale* (1947), *Out on a Limb* (1950), *Out of Scale* (1951), and *Dragon Around* (1954). This approach to ecology continues in feature-length films from Disney and other studios, from *Alice in Wonderland* (1951) to *The Daydreamer* (1966), *The Many Adventures of Winnie the Pooh* (1977), *The Little Mermaid* (1989), and *Lilo and Stitch* (2002). All of these cartoons emphasize the power of nature over the human (or anthropomorphized animal) world and suggest that economic approaches to ecology blossomed during this pre– and post–World War II industrial era and continued into the late twentieth and early twenty-first centuries.

Other cartoons, however, demonstrate the need for controlling human intervention and nurturing the natural world to strengthen their interdependence, a perspective grounded in human and organismic approaches to ecology. Many shorts taking this approach were distributed in the 1930s during the height of the New Deal and suggest that an equal relationship is possible, even in the modern world, where technology and industry threaten nature. But they also do demonstrate awareness that humans can negatively affect their natural environments. With one exception, *The Seapreme Court* (1954), all of the cartoons we noted that follow this pattern come from the 1930s, primarily after the Hays Code became more stringently enforced. The Hays Code, or Motion Picture Production Code, governed what was morally acceptable or unacceptable content for motion pictures produced for a public audience in the United States. In comparison to cartoons before and after this period, cartoon story lines between 1934 and 1938 seemed more affected by the Hays Office agenda (Klein 46). Klein states that the "controller persona" in each cartoon "increasingly had to speak for justice and perseverance" (47), even in relation to elements of the natural world. Klein even suggests that Mighty Mouse saved the day "like a cartoon New Dealer damming a flooding river" (47). Four of the five cartoons highlighting interdependence seem to follow this narrative structure.

Another Felix the Cat cartoon, *Neptune Nonsense* (1936); *Seapreme Court*, *Molly Moo Cow and the Butterflies* (1935); and the Warner Brothers Bosco cartoon *Tree's Knees* (1931) seem to encourage interdependence between species, both in the wild and in captivity. *Neptune Nonsense* excludes "human" figures, but it includes some very humanlike institutions—under the sea. Neptune acts as the controlling persona here, saving the day for his fish and for Felix and his pet fish, Anabelle. Neptune controls the natural order of things, but he also promotes an interdependent relationship between his sea world and Felix's anthropomorphized land.

The Little Audrey cartoon *The Seapreme Court* includes some of the same strategies to negotiate compromise that come up in *Neptune Nonsense*—as well as elements from its plotline. A dream teaches Audrey a lesson about sea creatures, again in the presence of Neptune, the controller. Because of her dream trial beneath the sea, Audrey throws a hooked fish back and wins an "offishal pardon." Having learned about the value of animal life, Audrey changes her ways, throwing away her fishing pole and choosing to view sea life as important as her own.

Molly Moo Cow and the Butterflies shows us what happens when a more humanlike figure—a dog professor who collects butterflies—enters an idyllic "natural" world in which butterflies entertain Molly in a vibrant Technicolor stage show. Once Molly chases the professor away, nature is restored to "paradise," and Molly, the heroine, wears a robe of butterflies in celebration.

The Tree's Knees also stresses interdependence between Bosco and the natural world. This Bosco cartoon stands out because it harmonizes technology (as in a scene in which slices from a tree become records played by animals) and nature (when the trees and forest creatures dance to the song). Whereas in other Bosco cartoons an anthropomorphized Bosco runs from natural wild creatures, in *The Tree's Knees* Bosco spares the life of a tree he nearly chops down after it begs for its life and the life of its smaller tree children. The object of *The Tree's Knees* is musical, but the lesson—to encourage an interdependent relationship with nature—comes through, even including tree families with more anthropomorphized animals. This focus on interdependence continues in animated features, including *Mr. Bug Goes to Town* (1941), *Sleeping Beauty* (1959), *The Incredible Mr. Limpet* (1964), *The Aristocats* (1970), *The Fox and the Hound* (1981), *Who Framed Roger Rabbit* (1988), and *Bee Movie* (2007).

Other cartoons respond to human, organismic, and economic approaches to ecology by critiquing human exploitation of the natural world and illustrating the consequences of rampant consumerism that serves as a sign of progress—devastation of the natural world. Instead of looking at nature from the skewed perspective of a speeding car, enviro-toons from the post–World War II era, including *Porky Chops* and *Lumber Jerks*, show us what is wrong with what Alexander Wilson calls "the cultural taming of the American Wilderness" (34) and provide real reasons for embracing Aldo Leopold's conservation aesthetic.

For example, *Hare Conditioned* (1945) seems to illustrate Aldo Leopold's view of recreation gone wrong. *Hare Conditioned* takes the artificiality of outdoor recreation to an extreme, when a camp scene turns into a department-store window display. Here outdoor recreation is not only mechanized (as Leopold argues). It is an illusion. As in other Bugs Bunny cartoons, in *Hare Conditioned* Bugs ends up outsmarting his opponent—this time, the store manager—and avoiding a more deadly artificial display of nature: the manager attempts (and fails) to add Bugs to his stuffed-animal display in the taxidermy department. Putting nature on display here highlights what Dana Phillips calls representation rather than presence. *Hare Conditioned* shows us nature—and outdoor recreation—in a showroom like the living room where Carl Hiaasen's protagonist, Dennis Gault, in the novel *Double Whammy* lays out his bass tackle. According to Phillips, the display window and the stuffed woods animals in *Double Whammy* act as "monuments to a disappearing natural world" (209), just like those on display in the taxidermy section of Bugs Bunny's department store. These two examples seem to spring directly from Leopold's aesthetic philosophy.

A few of these cartoons do come from the wartime era, as well. In the midst of what Klein calls "The Anarchy of Wartime Chase Cartoons" in a chapter highlighting *Coal Black and de Sebben Dwarfs* (1943), several envirocartoons from Warner Brothers Studio and one feature-length film from the Fleischer Brothers stand out as critiques of environmental degradation. According to Klein, "Anarchic gags developed during the war, [to] address . . . the moods of the audience—not simply the patriotism, but also the anxieties and prejudices" (189).

In reaction to the tastes of the GIs as well as the excess in live-action genre films, cartoons such as *Fox Pop* (1942) are less sentimental than those from the later 1930s. They satirize popular Hollywood genres while (unconsciously, perhaps) transmitting environmentally conscious messages. Even though *Fox Pop* came out during World War II, it critiques both advertising and consumerism. The cartoon seems to say that it is not the silver-fox farm or even the executioner bearing an ax who is at fault. It is a manipulative advertising campaign that creates a market for silver foxes. The cartoon seems to say that neither the silver-fox farm nor even the executioner bearing an ax is at fault. Instead, blame is laid on a manipulative advertising campaign that creates the market for silver-fox fur. *Fox Pop* critiques consumerism, especially when it destroys animal life.

Post–World War II optimism faded quickly because of similar binaries—this time those that strengthened the Cold War and skepticism toward "progress" that diminished the power of individuals. These changing attitudes in the United States had an impact on cartoons after World War II, as well as on the cartoon industry itself. In 1948, according to Klein, the studio system changed. Studios were no longer allowed to maintain vertical monopolies so their theater chains were sold off, and film (and cartoon) distribution was transferred to "independent jobbers" (206).

By 1953 Jack Warner had "ordered the animation units [temporarily] to close down, to make way for 3D movies" (Klein 206). Television became a new dominant media, and fewer movie screens were available for audiences. All of these factors led to what Klein calls a "stripped-down" version of cartoons. Klein argues that a "mixture of ebullience and paranoia can be seen very clearly in fifties cartoons, in the stories and the graphics" (207). According to Klein, this mixture "is particularly evident in cartoons about consumer life" (207). The conflict between humans and machines that consumerism has bred is explored in cartoons such as *Porky Chops*, *Boobs in the Woods* (1950), and *Lumber Jerks* and extended to include the natural resources necessary to create consumer goods.

Porky Chops, featuring Porky Pig, focuses on destruction of a forest caused by need for lumber resources. In *Porky Chops*, the less anthropomorphized animal—a bear that appears first on all four legs in a hollow log—takes control and ends the clear-cutting of a forest by Porky Pig. The bear's college-letter sweater, however, suggests that human intervention both potentially destroys and domesticates wild nature. *Boobs in the Woods* critiques outdoor recreation in more subtle ways than *Hare Conditioned*, while also making a statement about the loss of wild nature. In *Boobs in the Woods*, Daffy disrupts Porky Pig (as usual), but Daffy's aim seems to be to stop Porky from painting a natural landscape. Porky camps out in his trailer in a "wilderness" so tamed that it looks more like a golf course than a wild forest, but he fails to capture the scene on canvas. A simple critique, perhaps, of increasing outdoor recreation after World War II, but here the conflict is unresolved.

Of the cartoons from the 1930s, '40s and '50s we viewed, however, the one most clearly an enviro-toon is Goofy Gophers and the *Lumber Jerks*. *Lumber Jerks* seems to emanate from an attitude in 1950s' America that Klein calls "Consumer Cubism" (210), "an obsession with the efficient, angular plan." The faster a consumer could gain access to goods, the better. Klein claims "individualism and democracy were being redefined in terms of consumer desire. The homogeneous surface, open and 'free,' came to stand in for America's imperium" (210). These attitudes were reflected in both narrative and aesthetics of cartoons after 1954.

Like *Porky Chops* and the Donald Duck/Chip an' Dale cartoons, *Lumber Jerks* first focuses on saving one tree in a forest—but the conclusion differs dramatically. Two cheerful gophers scurry toward their home tree, but when they go up into the hollow of the tree they find it has been cut down and carried away. The two gophers take steps to retrieve their tree—what they call their property—tracking it to a river and then picking it out of the hundreds of logs floating on the water. They climb on their tree and row away but cannot fight the current and nearly go over a waterfall. Once they escape, one gopher exclaims, "I'm bushed," and the two fall asleep, waking up only after entering a lumber mill. They survive a saw blade that cuts their tree trunk in two.

After seeing the devastation around them, the gophers state the obvious about the repercussions of consumerism. One of the gophers explains, "It looks like they are bent on the destruction of our forests," and the scene shifts to the mill's workings. One "shot" shows trees, ground into sawdust, being made into artificial fireplace logs. Another shows an entire tree being "sharpened" to produce one toothpick. Then the gophers discover what had happened to their own tree: "They're going to make furniture out of our tree," states one.

But the idea of ownership of consumer goods extends to the gophers and their tree home. They wish to reclaim their property, their own possession, so the other gopher exclaims, "That is definitely our property. We must think of a way to repossess it." The gophers siphon the gas out of the furniture truck and, when it breaks down, "steal" their tree's furniture from the truck. They build a tree house with the furniture, adding branches for good measure and topping the tree off with a television set. The cartoon ends with one of the gophers telling the other, "Isn't our home much better than it was before. . . . [We have] television . . . and just think how much better it will be with electricity!" Because the gophers view their tree home as a possession not unlike the furniture produced from its wood, they seem pleased with their "repossession." But the enviro-toon leaves viewers feeling ambivalent about the price of progress.

Lumber Jerks combines a critique of consumerism with a statement about its source—natural wilderness—but seems also to endorse interdependence between humans and the natural world (and between progress and conservation), at least to the extent that furniture built from a tree trunk can return to the forest as the Goofy Gophers' home. With its overt focus on consumerism, however, the 'toon goes further than the other shorts we examined here. It leaves viewers questioning the Goofy Gopher's conclusion stated in this chapter's opening: "Isn't our house much better than it was before?"

As Klein asserts in his discussion of Tex Avery's *Car of Tomorrow* and *The Farm of Tomorrow*, consumers may become "victimized by the very machines that promise an easier, more extravagant life" (211). After all, the consumer goods that make up the trunk of one tree were built from the trees of an entire forest. *Lumber Jerks*, especially, reflects an increasing ambivalence toward technology and post–World War II progress in an increasingly more complex (and anxiety-ridden) nuclear age. In this cartoon the Goofy Gophers successfully negotiate between the wonders of modernism and its impact on both natural and human worlds that Paul Wells discusses. But it is a negotiation impossible in the world outside cartoons.

Still, Klein's argument that "cartoons [are] ever the barometer of changes in entertainment" may also include changes in mainstream American culture. Unlike cartoons that either maintain the nature/culture binary or seek to reconcile it through the intervention of a controller, enviro-toons that critique our treatment of the natural world respond explicitly to changes in the American cultural context and illustrate ambivalence toward modernism and its ramifications. All three categories of cartoons we highlight here, however, serve as enviro-toons that do more than present nature or a landscape; they confront the natural in increasingly complex ways in relation to their historical and cultural contexts. Enviro-toons from *Snow White and the Seven Dwarfs* (1937) to *Bambi* (1941), *One Hundred and One Dalmatians* (1961), *Mary Poppins* (1964), *The Rescuers* (1977), *The Fox and the Hound* (1981), *Beauty and the Beast* (1993), and WALL-E (2008) attest to the continuing power of ecology and environmental critique in the world of the animated feature.

That's All Folks? fills what we see as a gap in film studies, animation studies, and ecocriticism. Until recently, work in animation studies was seen as separate from film studies. Changes in editions from 1986 (second edition) to the present (ninth edition) in the popular and influential *Film Art: An Introduction* from David Bordwell and Kristin Thompson show how discussions of the animated film have evolved from mere nods to chapter sections that indicate how much animation has distinguished itself as a valid filmic form. Texts centering on animated film are now included in cinema series from publishers such as Wallflower and Rutgers University Press. We see this text as continuing that trend with its focus on animated feature films read from a focused cultural studies perspective.

Although the field of animation studies has grown in recent years, we believe our text opens up a new research direction for the field: ecocriticism. Texts such as Leonard Maltin's *Of Mice and Magic* (1980) have laid the groundwork for Paul Wells's examinations of animation in its American context, including *Animation: Genre and Authorship* (2002) and *Animation and America* (2002). Animation studies' texts such as *Seven Minutes* by Norman M. Klein (1993), *Animating Culture* by Eric Smoodin (1993), as well as Giannalberto Bendazzi's *One Hundred Years of Cinema Animation* (1995, 1999), Karl F. Cohen's *Forbidden Animation* (1997), Leonard Maltin's *Reading the Rabbit* (1998), and Michael Barrier's *Hollywood Cartoons* (1999), along with *Animation Journal*, attest to the growth of the field. But even though animation studies integrates and applies a variety of theoretical and filmic perspectives, from genre theory and neoformalist approaches to cultural studies and auteur theory, it rarely focuses on ecocritical readings of animated films. Our text builds on the work begun in cultural studies–driven texts such as Norman Klein's *Seven Minutes*, in which Klein asserts that cartoons are a product of technology and seem also to glorify it (76).

The work also fills a gap in ecocriticism, which, until recently, focused exclusively on literature—defined as nature writing, poetry, fiction, and drama. Now with the move toward ecocritical film studies, there is a place for work on the animated feature film. Our work begins filling that space, building on work started in David Ingram's *Green Screen: Environmentalism and Hollywood Cinema*, Scott MacDonald's *The Garden in the Machine: A Field Guide to Independent Films about Place*, the present authors' *Ecology and Popular Film: Cinema on the Edge*, and parts of Deborah Carmichael's *The Landscape of Hollywood Westerns: Ecocriticism in an American Film Genre* and Michael Dana Bennet and David W. Teague's *The Nature of Cities: Ecocriticism and Urban Environments*. These works include ecocritical approaches to film, but they do not examine animated shorts or features from an ecocritical perspective.

Our study of feature-length enviro-toons expands on the categories and ecological approaches outlined for classic animated shorts, beginning to fill gaps in both film studies and ecocriticism. In chapter 1, "*Bambi* and *Mr. Bug Goes to Town*: Nature with or without Us," we assert that in spite of the films' close release dates, they exalt conflicting philosophies regarding our relationship to the natural world, not only because they come from different studios with opposing values but also because they respond differently to their cultural, historical, and political contexts.

In chapter 2, "Animal Liberation in the 1940s and 1950s: What Disney Does for the Animal Rights Movement," we begin with *Bambi*, a film that vilifies hunting and the human hunters who burn down the animals' forest. We then demonstrate, through our readings of *Snow White and the Seven Dwarfs* (1937), *Dumbo* (1941), *The Adventures of Ichabod and Mister Toad* (1949), *Cinderella* (1950), *Alice in Wonderland* (1951), and *Lady and the Tramp* (1955), that the tenets of the animal liberation movement, especially in Disney animated films, were well in place before the 1970s, when Peter Singer published his groundbreaking work on the philosophy and ethics of animal rights.

Chapter 3, "The UPA and the Environment: A Modernist Look at Urban Nature," examines how a small independent animation studio responded to cultural changes and attitudes of the late 1950s and early 1960s. This chapter provides a historically and culturally situated reading of *Gay Purr-ee* (1962) that reveals how technology and the urban industrial turn affected humans' relationship to the natural world.

In chapter 4, "Animation and Live Action: A Demonstration of Interdependence?" we explore what happens when animation is integrated into a selection of live-action films. Juxtaposing nonhuman animated characters with live-action figures in itself seems to illustrate an interdependent state between human and nonhuman nature, but the films we viewed take this demonstration of interdependence further. We examine the range and borders of this interdependence in relation to *Anchors Aweigh* (1945), *Two Guys from Texas* (1948), *Dangerous When Wet* (1953), and especially *The Girl Next Door* (1953), *The Incredible Mr. Limpet* (1964), *Who Framed Roger Rabbit* (1988), and *Enchanted* (2007).

Chapter 5, "Rankin/Bass Studios, Nature, and the Supernatural: Where Technology Serves and Destroys," offers a space in which to examine how the environment is addressed in the worlds of animated fantasy and horror. In films from the Rankin studio, technology is interrogated as either a dream maker or a machine that disrupts the garden. We explore these conflicting visions in relation to *The Daydreamer* (1966), *Mad Monster Party* (1967), and *The Last Unicorn* (1982).

In Chapter 6, "Disney in the 1960s and 1970s: Blurring Boundaries between Human and Nonhuman Nature," we look at the evolution of the Disney studio from a clear need for separation between wild nature and the human world toward one that begins to blur these boundaries. Although many films from the period maintain Disney's orthodoxy, other films, including *The Aristocats*, *The Many Adventures of Winnie the Pooh*, *The Rescuers*, and *The Fox and the Hound*, illustrate this changing view.

In chapter 7, "Dinosaurs Return: Evolution Outplays Disney's Binaries," we contrast two Amblin Entertainment films, *Jurassic Park* (1993) and *The Land before Time* (1988). The Amblin films provide a different vision of evolution that may provide a way to break down binaries between humans and the natural world.

In chapter 8, "DreamWorks and Human and Nonhuman Ecology: Escape or Interdependence in *Over the Hedge* and *Bee Movie*," we investigate how a studio other

Lumber Jerks: Television would be better with electricity.

than Disney explores the binary between human and non-human nature, either perpetuating (as in *Over the Hedge*) or offering an interdependent resolution to its conflict (as in *Bee Movie*).

Chapter 9, "Pixar and the Case of WALL-E: Moving between Environmental Adaptation and Sentimental Nostalgia," examines Pixar through a reading of WALL-E as an enviro-toon that merges nostalgia with dystopia and builds a narrative of environmental adaptation that embraces and critiques living nature. Up until the film's end, the film provides a dystopic and mechanistic perspective in which WALL-E acts as a comic hero who empowers an apathetic human race, transforming a hell on Earth into a home by following a narrative of environmental adaptation.

In chapter 10, "*The Simpsons Movie, Happy Feet*, and *Avatar*: The Continuing Influence of Human, Organismic,

Economic, and Chaotic Approaches to Ecology," we address how changes in cultural context have affected the content of enviro-toons, especially in relation to the enduring impact of twentieth-century approaches to ecology.

Our conclusion explores some of the trends discussed throughout the book in relation to their cultural and historical contexts by answering some fundamental questions: Has the content of feature-length animated films changed in response to changes in the environmental movement (see, for example, *Avatar*)? Have these films had an impact on viewers, changing their views on environmental issues as did Al Gore's *An Inconvenient Truth* (2006)? And has the environmental movement affected how animated features are produced? We hope our text offers compelling illustrations of both the questions and their possible answers.

Bambi: Bambi's offspring in a pristine forest.

ONE

Bambi and Mr. Bug Goes to Town

Nature with or without Us

In *Of Mice and Magic* Leonard Maltin asserts that *Bambi* (1942) presents "a visual poem extolling the glory of nature, as seen in the cycle of seasons, and the unchanging pattern of life for the forest animals, from birth to maturity" (66). For Maltin, *Bambi*'s "visual evocation of nature is a tasteful compromise between an artist's fancy and a naturalist's authenticity" (66). For us, however, that compromise translates into an animated world in which the culture of humans and nonhuman nature remain in conflict. In the Fleischer Brothers' *Mr. Bug (Hoppity) Goes to Town* (1941), a film released a few months before *Bambi*, on the other hand, nature and culture negotiate a way to interact interdependently when the lowland bugs build a home in a human couple's literal urban garden, a solution to what a 1942 *New York Times* review calls "Man's relentless encroachment upon the domain of the insect world" (T.M.P. 21). Although both films comment on humans' exploitation of the natural world, they offer conflicting solutions to the human destruction. Building on economic and organismic approaches to ecology, *Bambi* proposes that humans and nature remain separate. Taking a more human-ecology approach, *Mr. Bug* asserts that at least some humans can build interdependent relationships with the natural world.

The films exalt conflicting philosophies regarding our relationship to the natural world because they come from different studios with different approaches to filmmaking and because they draw on different artistic and ideological visions. Although both *Bambi* and *Mr. Bug Goes to Town* are environmental cartoons that illustrate the need for controlling human intervention and nurturing the natural world, only *Mr. Bug Goes to Town* stresses the need to strengthen the interdependence between human and nonhuman forces.

Bambi valorizes nature but maintains a powerful conflict between the human and natural worlds. Here the bifurcations remain—there is no move toward interdependence. Such an overly romantic film had a powerful effect on its viewers, causing hunters to protest such an inaccurate representation of nature and children to object to killing deer that could be a Bambi or a Bambi's mother. Ralph H. Lutts, for example, talks at length about "the Bambi Factor" and the "Anti-Bambi Backlash" (162). According to Lutts, "The 'Bambi complex,' 'Bambi factor,' and 'Bambi syndrome' are three terms used interchangeably for sentimental, sympathetic attitudes toward wildlife, especially deer. They are usually used derogatorily and reflect a backlash against the humane, anti-hunting, and preservationist values, and the excessive sentimentality that Bambi has often come to symbolize" (50).

Mr. Bug Goes to Town presents humans as destructive

and constructive, oblivious to and engaged with the natural world. Carefully rotoscoped human figures—traced frame by frame over live-action film—trample over grass in a vacant lot, thoughtlessly toss matches and cigars, kick cans across the Bugville yard, and, in the process, destroy bugs and their homes. But they also construct impressive skyscrapers and inner-city gardens, matching a modernist urban setting with a planned and controlled piece of the natural world where flowers and grasses provide safe havens for insects. One reason for this environmental difference between the films rests on the studio philosophies driving *Bambi*, a Disney film, and *Mr. Bug*, a Fleischer Brothers production. These differences stand out because the two features, first of all, are products of similar historical contexts and foreground similar hyper-realistic aesthetics.

Bambi and Mr. Bug's Shared Contexts
Hundreds of seven-minute cartoons were made by a variety of studios between the release of the first animated feature, *Snow White and the Seven Dwarfs* (1937), and the first releases of *Bambi* and *Mr. Bug Goes to Town*. By 1942, however, only seven animated features had been released, five from Disney and two from the Fleischer Brothers. Because of America's entry into World War II, between 1942 and 1945 studios had no mandate to produce animated features. Instead, they produced films for the war effort. If studios still produced other animated films, they were shorts rather than features. *Song of the South* (1946) was the first animated feature after *Bambi* and ushered in a period in which Disney dominated the animated-feature industry. *Bambi* and *Mr. Bug Goes to Town* not only shared similar release dates, then, but also were the last two feature-length animated films until a year after the end of World War II.

The United States' entry into World War II had an economic effect on both *Bambi* and *Mr. Bug*. Although neither film could predict when America would enter the war, they could predict Americans' overwhelming fear of it. Both *Mr. Bug Goes to Town* and *Bambi* draw on the atmosphere just prior to America's entry into the war. The United States declared war against Japan on December 8, 1941, but the war had been going on in earnest since the Japanese invasion of China in 1937 and the European conflagration beginning September 1, 1939. By December 1941, Germany's military had neared Moscow and controlled much of continental Western Europe.

Mr. Bug Goes to Town was released immediately after December 7 and the Pearl Harbor attacks, a release date that may explain its small audience when coupled with Paramount's refusal to adequately promote the film. Disney first released *Bambi* during 1942, the first year of the United States' entrance into the war, and its "rental receipts ultimately fell short of the film's cost by $60,000" (Barrier, *The Animated Man* 180). The fact that both films highlight the loss of innocence and the threat of the loss of a safe home was amplified by the early disasters suffered on land and sea by Americans in the first six months of the war. It is important to note, though, that the films come from studios with very different cultures, which affected the films' differing perspectives on the environment.

The period from 1933 to 1942 were also years in which the Civilian Conservation Corps, a Roosevelt New Deal program that served both the unemployment emergency and environmental crises of the Depression era, remained active. Like Gifford Pinchot, a utilitarian conservationist, Roosevelt supported wise-use policies based in sustainable development and natural-resource conservation rather than the preservationist policies of John Muir, founder of the Sierra Club, and "people's forester" Bob Marshall, founder of the Wilderness Society (see Gottlieb). During this Progressive Era, Muir's "preservationist philosophy and Pinchot's utilitarian vision existed side by side in an uneasy alliance" (Maher 26), an alliance that combined organismic and economic approaches to ecology, as did Eugene Odum. Human ecologists (or progressive environmentalists) such as Alice Hamilton of the 1920s and Frederick Law Olmsted of the 1930s and '40s also supported better city planning, housing reform, and urban sanitation—urban environmental issues that could enhance quality of life.

The period before, during, and immediately after World War II, then, focused on preservation and conservation as ways humans construct the idea of "wilderness," an idea, according to William Cronon, rooted in representations of nature as either the sublime or a frontier. The idea was manifested in Disney's preservationist bent and in its hyperrealistic rendering of backgrounds in *Bambi* and in the Fleischers' more utilitarian but equally hyperrealistic approach in *Mr. Bug Goes to Town*. Their differing studio practices, rather than their aesthetic similarities and ideological differences, had a greater influence on the films' varied financial success.

Conflicting Studio Practices at Disney and Fleischer

The Fleischers were unable to compete with Disney once they followed Disney's lead and began making feature films. Instead of maintaining the financial control Disney was able to achieve, chiefly because of the success of *Snow White*, the Fleischer Brothers failed because they signed on Paramount as a partner, giving Paramount financial and production control of the studio. When the Fleischer

Brothers' foray into feature films failed, they lost their studio. Walt Disney, on the other hand, succeeded with the financial gamble he made with *Snow White*, a success that allowed him to expand his studio, maintain control, and produce shorts as well as feature films. Because he made distribution and theatrical arrangements with RKO and other companies, he further ensured that control.

By being forced to tell a feature-length story, the Fleischer Brothers needed in *Gulliver's Travels* (1939) to abandon creative animation for a coherent long narrative. They also needed Paramount's partnership, which ultimately led to the financial failure of their studio. Although *Mr. Bug Goes to Town* returned the studio to its original hierarchy—with the animation department at the top—the Fleischer Studio crumbled when Paramount failed to promote *Mr. Bug Goes to Town*. The film failed financially, so Paramount forced the Fleischers to repay a $100,000 loan. When they could not pay, Paramount refused to renew their contract, and the Fleischers lost their studio.

Disney, on the other hand, placed story at the top of its hierarchy from the beginning. Walt Disney is often accused of being "backward-looking, quintessentially hyper-realist and, ultimately, 'orthodox,'" but "the studio *consolidated* the process of modernity pioneered by McCay, Iwerks, and Messmer by ensuring that the vocabulary of animation was predicated on the folkloric flux and mythical metaphor of oral story-telling traditions" (Wells, *Animation and America* 43–44, emphasis in original). Disney used the modernist tools of animation to retell the stories that in Western culture have become archetypal, especially by animating fairy tales such as *Cinderella*, *Snow White*, and *Sleeping Beauty*. Disney also adapted children's novels and stories that shared the same values reinforced by these tales: the triumph of good over evil, the superiority

34

of small-town and rural values, the value of youth and innocence, the preeminence of female domesticity and masculine power, and the beauty of either wild or domesticated nonhuman nature.

Bambi and Mr. Bug's Similar Aesthetic Visions

In spite of their differing studio practices, both films foreground a hyperrealistic aesthetic based in the ideology each studio embraced. As Robin Allan asserts, the Disney aesthetic has "all-pervasive iconographic power" (xv). The Disney aesthetic influenced every animation studio either to offer an alternative vision or to replicate or surpass the optimal realism to which Walt Disney aspired. Maureen Furniss sees this vision as so pervasive that "in no other medium has a single *company's* practices been able to dominate aesthetic norms to the extent that Disney's has" (109, emphasis in original).

Disney overshadowed every other early animation studio because its aesthetic served as a negotiation between the modern world and orthodox ideology, all in support of traditional narrative, a reconciliation that attracted viewers seeking to make sense of modernity. Disney's traditional narratives drew on folk and fairy tales to appeal to broad audiences, but they also were rendered using the technology and media of contemporary culture. *Bambi*, for example, was a retelling of Felix Salten's novel *Bambi: A Forest Life* from a Disney perspective. The retelling maintained bifurcations between human and nonhuman nature missing from the novel. According to Matthew Cartmill's "The Bambi Syndrome":

> The Bambi myth was the creation of an ambitious young Hungarian writer named Siegmund Salzmann, who came to Vienna in the mid-1880s in search of fame and fortune. . . . A pillar of Establishment pro-

priety on the surface, he was also the secret author of a notorious pornographic novel, *The Memoirs of Josephine Mutzenbacher*. . . . He liked to go hunting with Hapsburg aristocrats and even owned a private hunting preserve of his own just outside of Vienna. But he was also an ardent animal lover, and his hunting experiences led him to produce a masterpiece of anti-hunting sentiment. (7)

Unlike the film version of *Bambi*, Cartmill notes:

> "Death is the central theme of Bambi," writes sports-man-conservationist George Reiger. "Something fears dying, or does die in terrible agony, in almost every chapter." The forest world that Salten describes in sometimes exquisitely poetic prose provides a backdrop of intense color and beauty in front of which his animal characters suffer and bleed and limp and die awful, uncomprehending deaths. (8)

But the worship Bambi and his relatives feel toward humans is eradicated by the end of the novel: "At the end of the book, this delusion is dispelled for Bambi when his dying father takes him to view the corpse of a murdered poacher. Bambi thereby learns the great secret: Homo sapiens is only another dying animal, and the governance of the world lies elsewhere" (Cartmill, "The Bambi Syndrome," 8).

Disney, on the other hand, puts death only in the hands of human hunters, whose guns and fire erupt in a forest where even predators play with prey. This orthodox ideology, however, limited the extent to which Disney could move beyond an idealized view of nature and strive for interdependence between human and nonhuman nature.

Disney faced stiff competition from the Fleischer Brothers, since they also "sought to pioneer technological innovation, and nearly succeeded in their experiences with sound, their own studio system and their commercially oriented interests, but all of their films were still in the service of animation as a radical form aesthetically *and* socially" (Wells, *Animation and America* 38, emphasis in original). The Fleishers developed the rotoscope, a technique in which live-action figures are traced over to create hyperrealistic animated forms, including a Betty Boop–driven *Snow-White* (1933) that came out four years before Disney's version.

The Fleischers' *Mr. Bug Goes to Town* combines Disney's emphasis on story with the Fleischer Brothers' emphasis on graphic narrative. According to Norman M. Klein, unlike Disney, "the Fleischers went for a Hollywood narrative film, scripted like a child's-eye version of Frank Capra. . . . The animated effects were remarkable, if uneven, without a graphic center" (86). Klein asserts that the strongest moments in the film relate to animation and graphic narrative rather than traditional story. Klein notes scenes, for example, where machines with steel claws "disembowel the bugs' neighborhood" (135).

The Film Society of Lincoln Center agrees and asserts that the film's "most compelling imagery . . . is seen in certain establishment shots and in the spectacular, literally riveting finale that shows the hastened construction of a huge skyscraper." According to the Lincoln Center review, the scenes strike "a perfect visual balance between layout and animation to achieve a convincingly microcosmic insect's-eye-view of things, anticipating by decades the CGI-animated Pixar hit *A Bug's Life*."

Time magazine's review from 1941, however, calls the film "no menace to King Disney" and is instead "a workmanlike effort designed for youngsters." But the *Time* review praises the film's choice to imitate the drama of Hollywood instead of the orthodoxy of Disney. Although, as

Klein suggests, the Fleischers' Disney-fied *Gulliver's Travels* and *Mr. Bug Goes to Town* (86), the return to the studio's original hierarchy—with the animation department holding more power than the story department—seems to have complicated the film's ultrarealistic aesthetic, adding technologically driven special effects. For example, the film included neon psychedelic treatments of Hoppity being electrocuted on a nightclub stage and Hollywood-driven extreme low- and high-angle shots, elements that are absent from the Disney aesthetic. Dave Fleischer's rotoscoping of human figures adds to this hyperrealistic aesthetic.

Bambi, on the other hand, serves as a symbol for the Disney philosophy, embracing all of its characteristics. *Bambi* changed the Disney system, as did the Fleischers' feature-length attempts, moving from casting animators by character "in favor of casting by sequence" (Barrier, *Hollywood Cartoons* 315). This change, according to Michael Barrier, had its drawbacks. Barrier asserts that although "most of the drawing and animation in *Bambi* is unfailingly expert . . . there is in the way that *Bambi*'s animals look and move no caricature at all—only mere prettiness of the kind bought by giving them graceful movements and large, liquid eyes" (*Hollywood Cartoons* 317). In his biography of Disney, Barrier further explains that the deer in *Bambi* were not "cartoony." Barrier asserts that Milt Kahl "drew the fawn Bambi and other young animals . . . in a way that maximized their cuteness, their resemblance to human children, by giving them large heads and wide eyes. Such designs would presumably enhance the characters' immediate appeal to the audience" (*The Animated Man* 150). That hyperrealism, however, is countered by the anthropomorphism and idealization of the woodland animals on display, animals who coinhabit a forest whether predator or prey.

Both films establish their settings in similar ways, but unlike *Mr. Bug Goes to Town*, *Bambi* constructs an idyllic vision of the natural world, a hyperrealistic view that looks to the past and obscures a future in which humans infiltrate Paradise. As Theresa J. May explains, "Both a myth and a trope, Bambi is an aggregate of cultural memory, a signifier ripe with ideology. When deployed, Bambi shores up a particular construction of the human/nature relationship." May sees that construction as "an assurance that we also are tame, civilized, and worthy of the biblical role of master" (96). In the context of Disney's filmic version of *Bambi*, however, humans are constructed as shadowy harbingers of death disrupting a well-drawn idealized paradise, a human construction of wilderness, perhaps.

Although visions of animal life in the film fail to replicate reality, backgrounds in the scenes look like Audubon drawings, a connection Matthew Cartmill implies in *A View to a Death in the Morning: Hunting and Nature through History* when analyzing a 1942 *Audubon Magazine* defense of the film's realism. According to Cartmill, the *Audubon* writer "hotly denies" that *Bambi* "misrepresented anything" (179). Only Man disrupts this pristine view of nature. When we hear a gunshot, the animals run. "Why did we all run?" Bambi asks. "Man was in the forest," his mother replies.

Mr. Bug Goes to Town, on the other hand, encourages interdependence between humans and the natural world both in the film's narrative and its aesthetic, a point noticed by the 1942 *New York Times* review. The review illustrates the contemporaneous reactions to the film's environmental appeal:

> It is a disturbing thought, but every time a steam shovel gobbles up a spoonful of earth, or a bunch of boys play kick-the-can in the corner lot or park, life

becomes more complex for the bees, ladybugs, grass hoppers and others of the insect family who take refuge behind blades of grass or build their homes in discarded match boxes. Man's relentless encroachment upon the domain of the insect world is to its inhabitants every bit as real and cruel as is man's disregard for his neighbor's rights. (21)

According to the narrative, Bugville had thrived until Dick and Mary, the homeowners, are unable to maintain their lower gardens. The lowland's fence breaks, allowing other humans to tramp through the yard and smash the bugs' homes and shops. Dick and Mary illustrate a more complex representation of humans that is unlike the universally negative portrayal of humans in *Bambi*. *Mr. Bug Goes to Town* uses hyperrealistic constructions of humanlike insects to critique overdevelopment and stress interdependence between humans and the natural world. The narrative of *Mr. Bug Goes to Town* builds on this goal toward hyperrealism, drawing on melodramas, including Frank Capra's *Mr. Deeds Goes to Town* (1936), its namesake, and accurate depictions of urban settings and characters. This blending of genres also points to blurred boundaries between human and nonhuman nature that illustrate their interdependence.

Both *Mr. Bug Goes to Town* and *Bambi* embrace a hyperrealistic aesthetic. And both Disney and the Fleischer Brothers took great pains to achieve it. According to Ralph H. Lutts in "The Trouble with Bambi," "in an effort to ensure accuracy in the film's backgrounds, [Disney] had an artist spend months sketching forest scenes in Maine's Baxter State Park. A pair of fawns, named Bambi and Faline of course, was shipped from Maine to Disney's California studios where they become models for his artists, who underwent special training in drawing wildlife"

(163). Lutts explains that "the film set a new standard for naturalistic realism in animated films" by noting that the ripples in the "April Showers" segment "radiat[e] from the last raindrops to fall on a pool of water. The splash of the raindrops is accurate even to the momentary central pillar that rises when the drop hits the water" (163). Barrier's *The Animated Man* and Watts's *The Magic Kingdom* also see *Bambi* setting the standard for naturalistic animation from the 1940s forward.

The film was also lauded by environmentalists at the time of its release. When *Bambi* came out in 1942, it was celebrated by wildlife conservationists and denounced by hunters. In fact, the National Audubon Society compared its consciousness-raising power about the environment to *Uncle Tom's Cabin*. In *The Idea of Nature in Disney Animation*, David Whitley asserts that Disney movies such as *Bambi* helped to inspire new generations of environmentalists. Patricia Cohen of *The New York Times* agrees, explaining, "The loving depiction of the woods and animals, particularly Bambi with those big soulful eyes and long lashes, was hailed by wildlife conservationists and denounced by hunters when it was released in 1942." According to Lutts, "In 1943, the year after the film was released, Aldo Leopold pressed for an antlerless deer season to control an overpopulated Wisconsin herd by reducing both its size and its rate of reproduction. Public opposition killed the proposal."

The Fleischer Brothers were equally concerned with accuracy on the screen, this time accurate representation of an urban setting and a bug's-eye view of both "the human ones" and the landscape. According to Leslie Cabarga, the opening shots panning down toward the city reveal "a three-dimensional setback of Manhattan" (186). Cabarga explains, "This was built in distorted perspective with over 16,000 tiny panes of glass in the wood and plastic skyscrapers. The set took four months to build, yet it is seen for no more than a couple of minutes in the film" (186). These efforts to establish a hyperrealistic aesthetic in the film extended to the figures, as well. According to Cabarga, human figures are rotoscoped and "drawn in a cold, art deco manner reminiscent of illustrator Rockwell Kent. They appear to the viewer very much as they must have seemed to the bugs" (186).

The villains in the film look like stock henchmen from Hollywood. The chief villain's henchmen, Swat the Fly (Jack Mercer) and Smack the Mosquito (Carl Meyer), talk and dress like "Brooklyn" criminals. Swat and Smack tell C. Bagley Beetle (Tedd Pierce) about "the trouble in the lowlands," so he can use his upland home as bait when he asks Mr. Bumble (Jack Mercer) for his daughter Honey's (Pauline Loth) hand in marriage, a direct attack on Hoppity (Stan Freed), Honey's boyfriend.

The final scenes are the most effectively constructed images of realism in the film. The bugs all go up toward the top of a skyscraper. The beams carry them ever closer to the top, and humans and their machinery erect the bricks and rivets that serve as the bugs' ladder to the top, where Buzz sees the garden, colorful and well constructed, and hears Dick's music floating from their cottage. The song he composes and sells is a hit. The bugs now live in harmony with "the human ones" in a rooftop garden while Beetle, Swat, and Smack look on from a barred entry. While looking over the edge of the skyscraper, Buzz exclaims, "Look at all the humans down there. They look just like a lot of little bugs."

Yet whereas *Bambi* "effectively spoke to modes of change that viewed modernity as a projection into the future at the cost of a potentially stable and substantive view of the past" (Wells, *Animation and America* 43), in *Mr. Bug Goes to Town* "the fortunes of Bugville are largely tied to the fate of a human songwriter who lives nearby" ("Mr. Bug Goes to Town," The Film Society of Lincoln Center). *Bambi* and other Disney films, in other words, sought to counter a modern world that threatened stability. They highlighted the need for nonhuman nature to separate from humankind and the modern world to survive, harking back to a more stable, naturalistic past. *Mr. Bug Goes to Town* emphasizes a future in which interdependence and distribution of wealth across classes and species prevail, rather than the separation, extermination, or banishment Disney's *Bambi* shows us.

Bambi's Narrative of Nature: A Pristine Garden Kept Safe Only without Man

Bambi makes conflicts between humans and the natural world a serious concern. —The male hunters'— infiltration of Bambi and his mother's safe home in nature shatters the animals' paradise and forces Bambi to mature and gain independence. Humans are depicted as a threat to nature, and audience sympathy remains with Bambi and his forest friends. The scene in which the stealthy (and invisible) hunter kills Bambi's mother stands out as a lesson in pathos. We hear gunshots that shatter the forest calm and then, with the help of Bambi's father, experience the loss of a mother along with Bambi.

Bambi provides two messages about the natural world. It reinforces the early message about the destructive power of humans, but it also valorizes nature as a place of innocence promoting a cyclical worldview of the future. No species is threatened by another inside the pristine forest. Only outsiders (humans and their dogs) serve as a threat. If Bambi's mother's death is not enough, the next spring, after Bambi has matured, hunters return to the forest, setting up a campsite and building a large fire. The hunters destroy animals of multiple species with the crack of their guns, forcing the wild animals to seek shelter deeper in the forest. Man's destructive tendencies are heightened further, though, by their carelessness with their campfire. The fire escapes its ring and penetrates the forest, so the only escape for wildlife is an island even deeper in the forest.

Human exploitation and negligence of the natural world is contrasted with the idyllic life of wild forest creatures living in relation to seasons. Yet the film's distancing of the human world negates any cultural critique. The film ends sentimentally because of this cyclical worldview. After the death and destruction caused by the hunters, new life revives the forest haven. Humans, on the other hand, view the world linearly, seeking "progress" rather than a return.

Humans in *Mr. Bug Goes to Town*: Both Destroying and Preserving Nature

In *Mr. Bug Goes to Town* humans do not represent the only evil in a pristine wilderness but the more powerful inhabitants of a city they have created as a modern landscape built on technology and hard work. The shadowy art-deco humans of the street and the skyscraper are not deliberately harmful to insects, but they are "the human ones" about which Mrs. Ladybug says, "The way they're taking to tramping through the lowlands, it's getting so your life ain't worth a sunflower seed anymore. One never know who's gonna get it next." The humans tramp thoughtlessly, but they do not hunt animals on purpose or even knowingly destroy insects and their homes.

Yet the film highlights these humans as cold and threatening in comparison to Dick and Mary. Dick's music enraptures Hoppity, makes Dick less threatening to Bugville, and, when he uses the music proceeds to buy their penthouse cottage and garden, provides the bugs with a home. Mary's well-cared-for garden serves as a home for Bugville, and her willingness to help Bumbles out of her watering can and to open up her garden for the bug community sets her apart. Dick helps the bugs without realizing it. Mary helps them out of a love open to both human and nonhuman nature. Mary explicitly showcases the move toward interdependence between the human and natural world that the film articulates.

That interdependence also shows itself in the overlapping settings and artifacts in the human and insect worlds. Humans and bugs literally share space in the vacant lot, the gardens, and even the jazz club and "highlands" of Beetle's home. The bugs also share human artifacts, from houses made of matchboxes to beds constructed from ladies' compacts. Various discarded boxes and tins, laden with recognizable symbols, serve as houses and shops in Bugville. Although humans exploit the setting and seek to dominate it with the machinery of progress, they too live side by side with insects.

Mary and Dick take this interdependence further. Without the commercial success of Dick's song, neither the humans nor the bugs can prosper. Mary and Dick also literally house the residents of Bugville in their garden. But that garden becomes possible only because Hoppity frees Dick's royalty check from the crack where Beetle stowed it and delivers it to the proper mail carrier. The garden itself illustrates this message of interdependence since, unlike the pristine forest and meadow in *Bambi*, it is a constructed space clearly touched by humans on- and off-screen, where the bugs of Bugville can again prosper.

Conclusion

Bambi and *Mr. Bug Goes to Town*, then, rest on different and perhaps conflicting perspectives on nature that we assert stem from differing studio organizations. Disney and the Fleischer Brothers also had opposing ideological perspectives on modernism. The Disney studio controlled production "through control of the narrative" (Langer, "Institutional Power" 7). According to Mark Langer, "By using the script and the storyboard as a choke point, Disney could oversee production" (7). Ideas came from the animation department only after "a synopsis was prepared." At Fleischer Studios "there was not the same degree of centralized control. In contrast to Walt Disney, Max Fleischer's function was more remote from all but the major production decisions." And Max's brother Dave was also "no Disney." Fleischer Studios had no story department until 1932 and placed trust in its animators. According to Langer, the Fleischers also lacked the stable work force that the Disney studio had. The feature films *Gulliver's Travels* and *Mr. Bug Goes to Town* challenged this organizational structure. But the inadvertently less top-down structure at Fleischer Studios may also coincide with the message of interdependence highlighted in *Mr. Bug Goes to Town*, as well.

The ideology driving the two studios seems to have contributed to their differing visions of the modern and the natural worlds. According to Paul Wells, the Fleischer Studios' focus on the gag, rather than on orthodox story "as a narrative premise," was "essentially bizarre 'business' which accrues around the execution of movement itself." But the gag sets the Fleischers apart from the Disney studio's focus on maintaining stability rather than working toward interdependence (*Animation and America* 55). The Fleischer Brothers, then, embrace modernity rather than fighting against it through orthodox narrative (55). Wells sums up the ideologies of the Fleischers, Warner Brothers, and Disney Studios in relation to Americans' negotiation between aggression and goodwill: "The Fleischer Brothers' films, in effect, absorb the tension between aggression and goodwill in the inner directedness of the mise-en-scene, naturalizing the emotional flux within that tension in the aesthetic styling itself" (56). The Fleischer Brothers negotiate a resolution between the conflicting forces of aggression and goodwill, working toward interdependence rather than separation, just as *Mr. Bug Goes to Town* resolves conflict between humans and bugs in Bugville by absorbing tension between them in a penthouse garden where human and nonhuman nature can live interdependently.

Disney, on the other hand, perpetuates the tension by obscuring it and focusing almost entirely on the human-free world of the forest where, unless a spectral man appears, animals of all species live without fear in a paradise untouched by human hands. In this paradise even owls act like vegetarians. In Disney's natural world, interaction with humans ends only in death or suffering. The only real choice is a complete separation between the two worlds. Although *Bambi* provides a classic narrative with a hyperrealistic aesthetic that awes viewers, *Mr. Bug Goes to Town* embraces a more powerful environmental message that rests on both its aesthetic and the ideological grounding for its narrative. Scenes from *Mr. Bug Goes to Town* are as impressive as those in *Bambi*, but the urban setting and the multiple symbiotic relationships established between human and nonhuman nature most effectively establish the film as an example of filmic urban nature-writing worth watching.

These two final films of the first period of feature-length animation filmmaking set up a template still used in animation features today. *Mr. Bug Goes to Town* fore-shadows films from various studios that embrace inter-dependence between human and nonhuman nature and human and organismic approaches to ecology. See, for example, *Monsters, Inc.* (2001), *The Ant Bully* (2006), *Happy Feet* (2007), and WALL-E (2008). *Bambi*'s assertion that the human and nonhuman worlds must remain sepa-rate to maintain wild nature still resonates in films such as *The Jungle Book* (1967) and *Finding Nemo* (2003), with their sometimes preservationist perspectives on the natural world. These films demonstrate the power of ecology and the complexity of the questions raised by the environmen-tal movement, a movement discussed in animated features from *Mr. Bug Goes to Town* and *Bambi* to *Happy Feet* and beyond.

TWO

Animal Liberation in the 1940s and 1950s

What Disney Does for the Animal Rights Movement

Bambi is arguably a film that vilifies hunting and the human hunters who burn down the animals' forest, thus perhaps valorizing the rights of animals more forcefully than those of man. But the film also advocates for animal rights based on these animals' humanlike qualities, helping them build a community of family and friends in a protected forest free from human intervention. Despite the film's clear argument favoring at least some elements of nonhuman nature, such a position may conflict with tenets of the environmental movement.

This conflict between animal rights and environmentalism is also reflected in popular culture from the 1940s, when Aldo Leopold's *A Sand County Almanac* was first published. Walt Disney films from the 1940s and 1950s are no exception. According to Rebecca Raglon and Marian Scholtmeijer, "Advocates for nonhuman animals note the similarities between human and other animal spe-

cies and argue for rights for animals based on that close-
ness" (121), just as they do in *Bambi*. From Peter Singer's
groundbreaking 1975 work, *Animal Liberation*, to Norm
Phelps's 2007 overview, *The Longest Struggle: Animal
Advocacy from Pythagoras to Peta*, animal advocates base
their arguments on the close connection between humans
and nonhuman animals.

Disney films from 1937's *Snow White* through the
1950s advocate for animal liberation by personaliz-
ing criticism of human exploitation of the natural world
through humanity's connection to domesticated animals.
These films also promote animal welfare and the connection between human and nonhuman nature by highlighting the need to control human intervention and nurture
the natural world in order to strengthen human and nonhuman interdependence. For us, those Disney animated
features that valorize interdependence and an organismic
ecology embracing a biotic community come closest to the
mission of the modern environmental movement, whereas
films that promote personalized animal advocacy ignore
environmentalism.

Early Disney feature-animation films from 1937 through
the 1950s present varying attitudes that range from animal liberation and animal rights views to animal-welfare-
driven ethics. At times animals are aligned with humans
either through kindness, as in *Snow White* (1937) and *Cinderella* (1950), or benevolent ownership, as in *Lady and
the Tramp* (1955). But many of these Disney films separate
human and nonhuman nature to demonstrate blatantly animal liberation ideals. Whatever their stance in this debate,
Snow White, *Dumbo* (1941), *The Adventures of Ichabod
and Mister Toad* (1949), *Cinderella*, *Alice in Wonderland*
(1951), and *Lady and the Tramp* (1955) all demonstrate
that the tenets of the animal liberation movement were
well in place before the 1970s, when Peter Singer pub-

lished his groundbreaking work on the philosophy and ethics of animal rights.

Animal Rights versus Environmentalism

Animal rights and environmentalism are sometimes seen as resting on similar values and grounded in similar calls to action. "If we save the animal world, we save the environment" might be the call. According to Peter Singer, for example, "Animal Liberation is Human Liberation too" (vii). Singer also writes, "Human equality . . . requires us to extend equal consideration to animals too" (1) and to preserve their rights as we might other human rights, as in the civil rights or women's rights movements.

The animal rights movement, however, typically bases its arguments on principles of the human rights movement and nineteenth-century utilitarianism, which defined *good* as pleasure and *bad* as pain. Creatures capable of feeling pleasure and pain, in Singer's vision, have the same rights as humans because their "sentience" gives them inherent value. Other elements of nonhuman nature without such sentience do not share the same rights and are defined as "vegetables," which are living creatures with a consciousness somewhere between the oyster and shrimp.

The principles of organismic environmentalism, on the other hand, valorize biodiversity and interdependence and draw on Aldo Leopold's land ethic, which "enlarges the boundaries of . . . community to include soils, waters, plants, and animals, or collectively: the land" (204). Connecting animal rights and environmentalism, however, through what Mary Midgely calls "animal welfare" (qtd. in Callicott 252) can provide a space for interdependence between human and nonhuman nature. Animal rights principles, however, focus on individuals, a focus that may disrupt Aldo Leopold's concept of the "biotic community" (qtd. in Callicott 252), a principle that rests on the belief that humans are simply members of a community of living things who interact cooperatively and with equal ethical value. One species—humans or other "sentient" beings— is not constructed as a conqueror but as a group of "biotic citizens" (Leopold 223).

But, as Raglon and Scholtmeijer note, animal advocacy is not necessarily associated with the environmental movement. They write, "While environmentalism and advocacy share many concerns, they essentially have developed along separate lines." "Some of the differences informing the political and ethical debates between environmentalism and animal rights," they continue, "also emerge in the literary treatments of the two topics" (121). For us, media treatments of animal advocacy in animated features predating Peter Singer's work reveal these same separate lines of development. Although these animated films either explicitly or implicitly advocate for animals, they do not necessarily promote environmentalism, especially one based in organismic ecology, again either explicitly or implicitly. The films all, however, arise from Walt Disney's attraction to the pastoral milieu of his childhood home.

Disney and Animal Rights: Rural Romance "on the Farm and in the City"

Walt Disney's romance with the rural Midwest and its impact on his films have been well documented. According to Steven Watts, for example, when Disney returned to Marceline, Missouri, in 1956 to celebrate a swimming pool named in his honor, Disney remarked, "I feel so sorry for people who live in cities all their lives and . . . don't have a little home town. . . . I'm glad my dad picked out a little town where he could have a farm, because those years that we spent there have been memorable years" (3). Even though Disney only lived in Marceline for three and a half years, the town influenced Disney's ideology, according to his own admission. Disney's wife, Lillian, stated, "There was something about the farm that was very important to him. He worked hard but he enjoyed the work. He liked the animals and he liked being close to the soil. . . . He always said that apples never tasted so good as when they were picked off the trees on the farm" (qtd. in Watts 5). According to Watts, "Ward Kimball, a leading Disney animator and one of Walt's close friends, noted that his boss was 'very preoccupied with his own history' and set many of his pictures in 'the Gay nineties or the early 1900s—because that was when he was a kid'" (7).

Michael Barrier also notes Disney's nostalgia for rural life, asserting that "as idyllic as life on the farm had been for the boys, Walt especially, leaving it was correspondingly painful" (*The Animated Man* 17). Neal Gabler's *Walt Disney* highlights most dramatically the influence Disney's few years in Marceline had on his ideology and its manifestation in his work. Gabler asserts that the Marceline of Disney's memory "was a more rustic place that would become more rustic still in his memory. He idealized Marceline" (18). Disney stated he felt pity "for people who live in cities all their lives and . . . they don't have a little hometown. I do" (qtd. in Gabler 18). Gabler reiterates arguments various scholars have made about the effect Disney's years in Marceline had on attractions in Disneyland, as well as "early cartoons' preoccupation with farm life and animals, which Disney himself acknowledged."

Gabler takes these arguments further, asserting that, for Disney, "Marceline [was] a template for how life was supposed to be." According to Gabler, "Marceline would always be a touchstone of the things and values he held dear; everything from his fascination with trains and animals to his love of drawing to his insistence on community harked back to the years spent there." Gabler suggests these rural pastoral memories brought Disney the freedom he craved, noting that Disney himself said, "That's what it is—a feeling of freedom with the animals and characters that live out there. That is what you experience when you go to the country. You escape that everyday world—the strife and struggle. You get out where everything is free and beautiful."

That search for freedom in the pastoral manifests itself, however, not only in the setting of films such as *Lady and the Tramp*. We believe it also influences the animal rights focus of the films. Although Disney admits his early animal shorts were influenced by his years in Marceline, we believe later animal-centered films also felt this influence. In the best of these films, the move is toward interdependence, toward that "feeling of freedom with animals and characters that live out there" that Disney yearned for. For us *Snow White, Cinderella*, and *Lady and the Tramp* illustrate the interdependent freedom Disney describes while embracing a vision of animal welfare that connects more effectively with environmentalism than radical animal rights ideology.

Animal Rights versus Animal Welfare and the Environmental Movement

Robert H. Schmidt differentiates between animal rights and animal welfare as a step toward aligning animal treatment with the environmental movement. Schmidt explains that "the animal rights movement has as its underlying foundation the perception that animals have rights equal or similar to those of humans." This is the principle of equal consideration of interests (Singer 1980). In the view of the animal rights movement, "Biomedical, agricultural, and other uses of animals have no place in society unless the same treatment could ethically be given to humans" (Schmidt 459). From Schmidt's perspective, the animal welfare movement "is particularly concerned with reducing pain and suffering in animals" (459). Schmidt sees focusing the discussion on animal welfare rather than animal rights as a way to "follow . . . the direction of the rapidly increasing numbers of people concerned about environmental issues in general and animal utilization in particular" (460). Mary Midgley agrees and grounds the animal welfare ethic in a biosocial perspective that connects well with the land ethic Aldo Leopold outlines in *A Sand County Almanac* (Callicott 254). Animated films focusing on animal treatment, however, sometimes foreground animal rights rather than animal welfare, potentially discouraging alignment with environmentalism.

Although *Dumbo, Bambi,* The *Adventures of Ichabod and Mister Toad,* and *Alice in Wonderland* primarily focus on animal rights rather than animal welfare and, in the process, demonstrate that the animal rights and environmental movements may not always intersect, *Snow White, Cinderella,* and *Lady and the Tramp* illustrate how the movements can connect. These Disney films point to a unified animal-environmental ethical theory like that espoused by J. Baird Callicott. Such a theory combines an animal welfare ethic like that developed by Mary Midgley with an organismic approach to ecology and the environmental ethic of Aldo Leopold that this approach helped produce (Callicott 254).

Animal Rights in Early Disney Animated Features

Many Disney films from the 1930s through the 1950s foreground nonhuman nature and either espouse animal rights, sometimes at the expense of human nature, or assert a unified animal-environmental ethic that illustrates how the environmental movement can serve human and nonhuman nature most effectively. *Dumbo,* for example, foregrounds animal rights rather than environmentalism. According to David Whitley, the film is one of only two from the Walt Disney period that "manage[s] to resist the allure of wild nature" (7). In a circus setting that intertwines human with nonhuman animals, *Dumbo* highlights an animal rights–driven narrative that follows an ideological pattern similar to that of *Bambi*. Animals and humans live separate lives and, whenever humans connect with animals, animals suffer. The intensity of the violence associated with humans differs in the two films, however, and the burlesque representation of humans in *Dumbo* further validates the animal world, suggesting that animals are more human than their human exploiters.

Dumbo also adds conflicts within species as a source of suffering, but, once differences between animals are either erased or compensated for, that conflict is resolved. Humans, on the other hand, exploit, ridicule, and mistreat circus animals throughout the film. And, even though the film ends happily, Dumbo's success occurs without any reference to humans. Only selected cultural artifacts suggest the presence of human life. Articles in human newspapers announce Dumbo's exploits, and the circus train's best and most modern car transports Timothy Q. Mouse, Dumbo, and his mother; yet, any active human involvement in Dumbo's popularity once he can fly is completely erased. In *Dumbo*, animal rights take center stage, with animals gaining equal or even superior status in a narrative in which animal abuse is critiqued and resolved by animal behavior. As Bosley Crowther of the *New York Times* asserts, "The ringmaster and the clowns are the only suggestions of real people in the picture, and they are highly burlesqued. From first to last it is an animal story, and the animals are the miraculous Disney types" ("Walt Disney's Cartoon, 'Dumbo' . . . " 27).

Dumbo endorses this radical separation differently than does *Bambi*, which constructs humans as dangerous predators rather than laughable and easily suppressed enemies. This radical difference between the two films' worldviews may be, according to Mark Langer's assertion, that an East Coast animation style overpowers the traditional Disney West Coast style because Disney was absent during much of the production of the film. According to Langer, a West Coast style "presents a populist and positivist orientation" ("Regionalism in Disney Animation" 306). Langer asserts that "Disney films were invested with normative ideological meanings, endorsing middle-class values." The style "incorporated a nativist rural orientation" and remained "consistent with the codes of classical Hollywood cinema." According to Langer, "Disney's modernity lay in his ability to preserve the preindustrial conceptions of the artist by rendering invisible the tools and materials of the industrial process" (305).

The East Coast New York style, on the other hand, "emphasized artifice, nonlinear narrative, and 'rubbery' graphics." Unlike Disney's attempts to make tools of the process invisible, in the New York style "the artificiality of the characters and their drawn nature were emphasized through design, movement, and dialogue" (308). Unlike Disney's West Coast style, "New York animated films were far less likely to demonstrate moral homilies." They were also less likely to "use the fable convention of animal or child characters" (309) and included adult foibles such as cheating and, in the case of the "Pink Elephant" sequence, drunkenness. When Disney dropped the project and Dick Huemer and Joe Grant took over, the story was rewritten, and the "Pink Elephants" sequence was added. Langer asserts that this New York style intertwines with West Coast style segments throughout the film and that, although the film ends on a classic Disney note—"a celebration of the typical Disney restoration of family and prosperity" (318)—the New York style makes a mark on the film and demonstrates conflicts between the worldviews of the two coastal animation styles.

Animal Liberation in the 1940s and 1950s

The conflict between the two styles reinforces the conflicts between human and nonhuman nature in the film. The burlesqued humans are a product of the New York style and change the tone of the conflict between them and the circus animals, heightening the force of the animal world and its ultimate defeat of humans. Yet *Dumbo's* New York–style animation foregrounds conflicts within the animal world, which must be resolved for a more effective separation between human and nonhuman nature.

From the opening credits forward *Dumbo* constructs its circus setting as a world controlled by animals. The film's opening highlights this setting and animal focus. Credits appear in red on blue in Technicolor, with circus posters as background. Then the film reveals a view of a cloudy sky, the sound of thunder, and images of rain, snow, and sleet. A voiceover proclaims of the train, "ever faithful, ever true, nothing stops him, he'll get through," and the "Watch Out for Mr. Stork" song begins. Storks send baby animals down to Florida for bear, kangaroo, hippo, tiger, and giraffe mothers. An elephant in the circus waits for her baby, too, but it does not come before the animals all leave for the next performance.

Shadowy men enter the film here and, with the animals' help, load the circus train with animals, the first introduction to a human world. Mothers lead their babies, but Dumbo's mother boards the train looking sadly and wistfully at the sky. The train is anthropomorphized and seems to say "all aboard" with its whistle. Another stork flies over, stopping to rest on a cloud. The bag he carries almost falls through the cloud. He looks down on Florida as if looking from outer space and sees a train rolling through the state as if the state were a road map. Then the stork exclaims, "That must be it." Storks, elephants, and a train take precedence over humans in these scenes, highlighting their superiority.

When the stork delivers the elephant infant, the incident again shows us the film's focus on animals and their extrahuman characteristics, without human interaction that might lead to suffering. When the stork gets to the train, he yells for Mrs. Jumbo and meets other animals as he goes from train car to train car. The elephant trunks motion the stork toward them, and the stork reads a poem to introduce the baby, asks for a signature, and, saying, "This is still part of the service," sings "Happy Birthday" to Jumbo Jr. Mother Jumbo opens the bag to reveal a sweet blue-eyed baby elephant who sees his mother through a fog. "Adorable," the others say, in reactions like those of a new human mother's friends.

But then Jumbo Jr. sneezes and his large ears spring out, causing a conflict with the other elephants. The other elephants laugh, and the mother slaps one away. One elephant wearing a green hat says, "Jumbo, you mean Dumbo," and changes the infant elephant's name. But Dumbo's mother hugs him with her trunk, using his ears as a blanket in which to wrap him. The train is a silhouette against a red and pink sky. "I think I can," the engine says, as it climbs a hill. "I thought I could," it says, as it rolls down the other side after a successful ascent, perhaps foreshadowing Dumbo's trials.

Humans again appear when the train stops in an urban nighttime setting. It begins to rain, but the animals disembark, and they and faceless black workers set up the circus. They sing, "We work all day, we work all night . . ." while elephants and camels help raise tents, hauling up poles and braiding ropes. Using pulleys they put up a large tent. Here workers and animals seem to work together, but human workers appear as dark shadows, dehumanized by their laborious service.

Humans take on an exploitative role when the circus opens after a parade. White men sell tickets, and white boys with buckteeth tease Dumbo. A redheaded boy flutters his coat like Dumbo's ears, and Dumbo flutters his ears because he does not know he is being mocked. Dumbo's mother reacts to this ridicule and protects her son when a boy grabs him. She is locked in a caged wagon that reads, "Danger, Mad Elephant." Humans again are constructed as the source of suffering for animals as they take Mrs. Jumbo to a locked cell, but the other elephants, too, react negatively, gossiping about her and ostracizing Dumbo.

But the elephants do not represent the entire animal world. Timothy, a uniformed mouse with powerful human qualities, disdains their gossip and sticks up for Dumbo. The elephants say, "It's all the fault of that little F.R.E.A.K.," and pretend they do not see Dumbo when he walks in. Timothy scares them away and tells Dumbo that they are "giving him the cold shoulder." Timothy comforts Dumbo, suggesting he might get his mother "out of the clink."

Timothy and Dumbo form a friendship that illustrates animals' similarity to idealized humanity and, in the context of the film, their superiority to the boys who ridiculed Dumbo, the circus ringmaster and his men who cage Dumbo's mother, and even the other elephants who give Dumbo the cold shoulder. Ultimately, Timothy proposes a plan that eventually makes Dumbo the star of the circus. Dumbo's first attempts to raise a flag fail, so he is demoted to "clown." But Dumbo's eventual show-stopping triumph helps him overcome the torture he faces from the humans who seem to control his well-being.

Dumbo's failure leads the ringmaster and his men further to exploit and mistreat Dumbo. Dumbo is disgraced, and the film shows his embarrassment. The train plows through a rainstorm when the circus leaves. The other elephants suffer injuries and complain about Dumbo. One tells the others, "They've gone and made him a clown."

This is the last straw for the elephants. "The shame of it," they say. "From now on he is no longer an elephant."

As a clown, Dumbo is further humiliated. He is dressed as a baby in a fire-filled window of a burning house, jumps onto a trampoline, and falls through to a bucket of bubbles. The clowns cheer this exploitation, but later Timothy the mouse tries to cheer him up as he scrubs him with a toothbrush.

Dumbo realizes he has been humiliated but gains strength from Timothy and his mother, reactions that again highlight these characters' similarity to an idealized view of humanity. Dumbo cries until Timothy takes him to the prison wagon where Mrs. Jumbo is chained. When she sees Dumbo's trunk, she strokes and then hugs him with her trunk, turning it into a swing for him. In a montage sequence, other mothers hug their babies, highlighting, again, their similarity to humans before Dumbo and Timothy must leave, returning to find the clowns discussing Dumbo's success.

The clowns' drunken discussion and plan to increase the height of the "burning" house demonstrate their inferiority to the more humanlike Timothy. Dumbo and Timothy see the clowns' silhouettes clearly demonstrating their plan through the yellow-orange tent, but when the clowns rush to the ringmaster to propose this exhibition, one of the clowns' liquor bottles falls in a water bucket. Dumbo drinks water from the bucket to stop hiccups caused by his crying and turns pink and red. Now intoxicated, he shoots bubbles. Timothy exclaims, "What kind of water is this anyway?" and dives in, singing under the water and then on top until he, too, is drunk.

Dumbo and Timothy's drunken hallucination draws on the New York style, but it also further connects them to the human world in a psychedelic scene that begins with bouncing bubbles that turn into pink elephants that transform into a variety of shapes and movements. Pink elephants blow trumpets and begin to sing, "Look out, look out, pink elephants on parade." The elephants march over a bed and turn into camels, pyramids, snakes, snake charmers, ballet dancers and ice skaters, cars, sleds, and trains. "Technicolor pachyderms are really too much for me," Timothy says, but the pachyderms explode and form clouds above a tree, where crows wearing zoot suits look down on the elephant and mouse sleeping on a branch.

The crows embrace both Timothy and Dumbo and again point to an animal rights view in which animals are constructed as similar to humans. The crows help Timothy discover Dumbo's ability to fly—his source of success—when they wake them up in the top of a tree. Questions about how they got there lead to a revelation: One crow says, "Maybe you flew up," and they all agree, dancing and singing to "When I See an Elephant Fly."

Dumbo's successful flight provides the Disney-like ending of the film, but it also facilitates his further connection with the human world, in this case, a world of media. After some practice on a cliff, Dumbo does fly, casting his shadow on grassland below. Now with a magic feather from Timothy, he is ready to fly in the show with the clowns. At the moment when he must dive out of a very tall "burning" building, Dumbo flies, even after dropping the feather, in a wild loop-de-loop. Newspaper headlines declare his success, and the film ends with mother in a "star's" private train car with Dumbo flying in to hug her. The "When I See an Elephant Fly" song ends the film. The train's last car closes like an eye.

In these last scenes, humans play only peripheral roles. Animals, constructed as equal or superior to humans, build a safe world for themselves in a circus environment, perhaps in spite of the humans with whom they periodically interact. The conflict between animals has been resolved with Dumbo's success, but the conflict between humans and animals continues. The continuing conflict between West and East Coast styles parallels this conflict, with animals clearly gaining an upper hand over their comic human exploiters. Although Mark Langer asserts that the West Coast style ultimately dominated the film, the East Coast style's mark remains. In *Dumbo* one sees the irrevocable differences between the two coasts.

The Adventures of Ichabod and Mr. Toad, on the other hand, includes two distinctly different views, one of nonhuman and the other of human nature. The first narrative constructs nonhuman nature as ultimately good and kind in spite of villains thwarted by the heroes, but the second narrative constructs human nature as calculating and vindictive, with heroes demonstrating more weaknesses than strengths. This contrast is evident in the varying success of each. As a *New York Times* review asserts, "The human figures in these adventures are stilted awkward creatures. . . . But in 'Mr. Toad' [Disney] has limned a wondrously blithe bucko from Kenneth Grahame's *The Wind in the Willows*" (A.W. 18).

The first narrative, the story of Toad, draws on *The Wind in the Willows*, a classic children's book in which animal characters play distinctly human roles, highlighting Peter Singer's claim that "all animals are equal" (1). This part of the film anthropomorphizes animals so much that their actions support Singer's claim that "to avoid speciesism we must allow that beings who are similar in all relevant respects have a similar right to life" (19).

The second narrative retells *The Legend of Sleepy Hollow*, in which the very human Ichabod Crane "loses his head" (at least figuratively) over a beautiful daughter of a rich farmer. Juxtaposing the two narratives highlights the separation between human and nonhuman nature foregrounded in both *Bambi* and *Dumbo*, this time clearly at the expense of the less valorized human nature.

Toad, the hero in *The Wind in the Willows*, is represented as a lighthearted and carefree aristocrat with a taste for new, again human, technology, so much so that he attempts to buy a car in exchange for his manor house. Toad is accused of stealing the car. He is prosecuted and sent to prison but escapes to reclaim the deed to his home and, with the help of his friends Rat and Mole, to prove his innocence.

Toad and his friends are constructed as sympathetic humanlike, intelligent persons, but the weasels and their leader, Mr. Winky, represent more negative human qualities. When Toad escapes, the humane nature of his and his friends' characters emerge. When they all learn Mr. Winky, a bartender who double-crossed Toad, is the leader of the gang that has the deed to Toad Hall, they agree to help him. "To prove your innocence we've got to get that paper away from Winky," they say. They succeed. When Toad is exonerated, the narrator says Toad no longer craves human technology. By New Year's, however, he has purchased a biplane and flies it over Toad Hall! The likable Toad maintains his obsession with new technology, but he also shows how effectively he and his friends have been anthropomorphized as a way to draw on human sympathy. Even though Toad is depicted as a flawed character, none of his weaknesses harm others deliberately. The film constructs the weasels in a negative light, clearly foregrounding the positive humanlike qualities shared by all of these lovable animals.

In the story of Ichabod Crane, on the other hand, the narrative highlights the negative human qualities shared by all the human characters in conflict throughout the tale. Ichabod and Bron Bones compete for Katrina's hand in marriage. But Bron Bones wins Katrina by scaring Ichabod away, first by telling stories of a headless horseman and then, presumably, by disguising himself as the horseman literally to chase Ichabod away. In this retelling of *The Legend of Sleepy Hollow* animals play only a service role in the form of horses carrying the headless horseman and Ichabod. The human world is indeed separated from that of nature, even in the agricultural community in Sleepy Hollow. More important, the segment highlights a human world of sometimes violent duplicity with little chance for redemption, a stark contrast to the delightful animal world of *The Wind in the Willows*.

Alice in Wonderland demonstrates the need to separate the human world from the world of the imagination and, in so doing, argues for the separation of human and nonhuman nature. According to Deborah Ross, this bifurcation extends to the conflict between rational control and irrational imagination (54). In *Alice in Wonderland*, unlike *The Adventures of Ichabod and Toad*, the animal world is the treacherous and irrational world, and the human world is rational, peaceful, and calm. The film opens on the human world, a pastoral scene with shade trees and a lake with swans where Alice, "a rosy-cheeked, ruby-lipped darling right off Mr. Disney's drawing-board, a sister of Snow White, Cinderella, and all the fairy-tale princesses he has drawn" (Crowther, "Disney's Cartoon Adaptation" 12), throws a garland of flowers down from her tree limb onto her governess.

This secure space is disrupted when Alice and her kitten follow a talking rabbit into his rabbit hole, an animal world of imagination constructed as dangerous and frightening. On her journey, Alice encounters a beach where oysters are eaten by a carpenter, talking and singing flowers who deride her as a weed, an opium-smoking caterpillar who (as a butterfly) tells her about a magic mushroom, a Cheshire Cat, and the Mad Hatter and Door Mouse and their unbirthday party.

That sense of danger culminates in Alice's encounters in

two settings: a mystic forest and an evil queen's maze. In the mystical Tulgey Woods, Alice encounters walking eyeglasses, honky-horn ducks, frog drums and cymbals, umbrella dodo birds, digging shovel birds, cage-bird finches, and a pencil bird that shows her a path until a broom dog sweeps it away. "If I get home I shall write a book about this place," she says. As she cries, the moon transforms into the Cheshire Cat, causing Alice to exclaim that she must leave this dangerous world. "I'm through with rabbits. I want to go home," she says, and the cat opens a door in his tree and shows her the queen's maze, the last of the dangerous settings Alice must traverse. The maze is a shortcut, and she takes it to group of walking playing cards, who are painting roses. Alice is put on trial when the queen accuses her of lifting her skirt, but the animals, who earlier had confused Alice, help her escape. "Today is your unbirthday, too," they tell the queen and roll out an unbirthday party.

Alice must use elements of the dangerous world to escape it. She eats part of the mushroom she saved in her pocket and grows so tall she must leave the courtroom immediately. Alice fights back with new stature but grows small again. She calls the queen a fat tyrant, and the queen yells, "Off with her head." Alice runs through the maze with black-and-white cards chasing in an amazing effect. She passes each of the parts of her journey in Wonderland: the circle of birds on the shore, the tea party, the caterpillar, and the doorknob.

In clear opposition to the novel from which the film was adapted and a reinforcement of the bifurcation between rational human and imaginative nonhuman worlds, Alice is saved, according to Ross, "not by facing [the cards] down with dawning maturity and confidence, like the 'real' Alice, but by waking up" (57). She sees herself asleep through the keyhole, drifts into consciousness, and wakes up, reciting the caterpillar's crocodile poem. The governess tells her to come along. "It's time for tea," she says. Alice goes willingly, glad to escape the danger of the animal world where walruses eat oysters presented as babies in bonnets. No matter how imaginatively constructed this alternative world, Alice seeks the safe human world in which she lives.

All three of these films foreground the need to separate human and nonhuman nature. Although only *Alice in Wonderland* paints a negative picture of an animal world filled with terror and danger, none of these films provides a space in which environmentalism and animal welfare can connect.

Disney Animated Features and Animal Welfare: A Move toward Environmentalism

Other Disney films of the period, however, demonstrate that, as J. Baird Callicott asserts, "Animal welfare ethicists and environmental ethicists have overlapping concerns" (249). Callicott draws on Mary Midgley's argument that "since we and the animals who belong to our mixed human-animal community are coevolved social beings participating in a single society, we and they share certain feelings that attend upon and enable sociability—sympathy, compassion, trust, love, and so on." According to Callicott:

> Mary Midgley's suggested animal welfare ethic and Aldo Leopold's seminal environmental ethic thus share a common, fundamentally Humean understanding of ethics as grounded in altruistic feelings. And they share a common ethical bridge between the human and nonhuman domains in the concept of community—Midgley's "mixed community" and Leopold's "biotic community." [By] [c]ombining these two conceptions of a metahuman moral community we have the basis of a unified animal-environmental ethical theory. (252)

This unified animal-environmental ethical theory acknowledges preferences for specific examples of human or nonhuman nature but places more value on community, working from a holistic perspective that rests on the notion that the mixed and biotic community matters. Films that illustrate an animal welfare ethic like Midgley's provide a way to connect animal liberation and environmentalism and thus work toward interdependence between human and nonhuman nature instead of the valorization of the individual no matter how it disrupts the biotic community.

Although David Whitley argues that "wild aspects of animal identity are subsumed within the realm of the domestic" (35) in *Snow White*, *Cinderella*, and *Sleeping Beauty*, we assert that *Snow White*, *Cinderella*, and, later, *Lady and the Tramp*, provide a space in which human and nonhuman nature gain interdependence through Snow White's and Cinderella's relationships with the animal world. In spite of evil stepmothers in both films and evil stepsisters in *Cinderella*, humans gain equal footing with animals because Snow White and Cinderella protect the birds, mice, and other animals around them. For example, Cinderella clothes, protects, and feeds the domesticated animals around her, establishing them as humanlike, but the move transcends an animal rights view because animals serve her, as well. Within the magic animated world of *Cinderella*, a biotic community thrives.

In *Snow White and the Seven Dwarfs*, too, Snow White interacts with the animal world, but this time the animals are wild woodland creatures, domesticated only by her beauty and song. Snow White's escape to the forest highlights her connection with the natural world, a world safe from the evil intentions of the queen, a wicked and jealous stepmother, who orders her woodsman to kill Snow White so she can again be deemed the most beautiful of all. When the woodsman recoils from his mission and brings back the heart of a pig instead, the queen attempts to kill Snow White with a poison apple, but her plan is thwarted by true love's first kiss. In *Snow White*, unlike *Alice in Wonderland*, the forest is safe and secure, and the human world means danger. Snow White's connection with the animal world reinforces her connection with nonhuman nature, a biotic community she nurtures.

After Snow White enters the forest, the animal world serves at least three purposes: their incongruent presence entertains audiences; their worship of Snow White validates her worth; and their humanlike roles as Snow White's domestic helpers and musical chorus further connect them with the human world. According to Roger Ebert, animals are integrated into the film with powerful technical skills that capture audience members' attention:

> The film's earliest audiences may not have known the technical reasons for the film's impact, but in the early scene where Snow White runs through the forest, they were thrilled by the way the branches reached out to snatch at her, and how the sinister eyes in the darkness were revealed to belong to friendly woodland animals. The trees didn't just sit there within the frame. ("Snow White and the Seven Dwarfs")

Animals also help Snow White find a home with the seven dwarfs. With enthusiasm animals help her clean it. According to Ebert, "Snow White doesn't simply climb up the stairs at the dwarves' house—she's accompanied by a tumult of animals. And they don't simply follow her in one-dimensional movement. The chipmunks hurry so fast they seem to climb over each other's backs, but the turtle takes it one laborious step at a time, and provides a punch line when he tumbles back down again" ("Snow White and the Seven Dwarfs"). Ultimately, according to Ebert, animals also serve as "a chorus that feels like the kids in the audience do." As soon as she enters the forest, Snow White's connection with a nonhuman world is clear.

Cinderella, too, interacts closely with the natural world. As the daughter again of a wicked stepmother, Cinderella's outsider role suggests that she has rejected human-centered culture in favor of a more interdependent relationship with nonhuman nature. When her father dies, the stepsisters (Anastasia and Drizella) abuse Cinderella with their mother's approval and help. According to the narrator,

> Once upon a time in a faraway land there was a tiny kingdom, peaceful, prosperous, and rich in romance and tradition. Here in a stately chateau there lived a widowed gentleman and his little daughter, Cinderella. Although he was a kind and devoted father who gave his beloved child every luxury and comfort, still he felt she needed a mother's care. And so he married again, choosing for his second wife a woman of good family with two daughters just Cinderella's age, by name, Anastasia and Drizella. It was upon the untimely death of this good man, however, that the stepmother's true nature was revealed. Cold, cruel, and bitterly jealous of Cinderella's charm and beauty, she was grimly determined to forward the interests of her own two awkward daughters. Thus as time went by, the chateau fell into disrepair, for the family fortunes were squandered on the vain and selfish stepsisters while Cinderella was abused, humiliated, and finally forced to become a servant in her own house. And yet through it all Cinderella remained ever gentle and kind, for with each dawn she found new hope that someday her dreams of happiness would come true.

Cinderella maintains her good temperament in spite of this treatment because she accommodates nature, and nature accommodates her. She can talk to the birds that wake her up. She sings "A Dream Is a Wish Your Heart

Makes" as she awakens, and other birds come to listen and respond with a whistle now and then. Mice come out of bed to listen, wearing shirts, hats, and dresses. Birds fill a sponge with water and shower her. They prepare her clothes and dress her in a frock, shoes, and apron. When they tie back her hair and tell her there is a new mouse in the house—a visitor in a trap—her connection with them becomes clearer. She serves them, too. She gets a mouse shirt out of a drawer to take to him and frees him, naming him Octavius or Gus for short, and tells the others not to forget to warn him about the cat. Cinderella interacts on a human level with all the animals in the house and yard. She puts Bruno the dog outside when Lucifer tricks him into barking. Cinderella feeds the cat milk and then feeds the chickens corn while the mice steal some food and frighten her stepsisters.

Lucifer the cat, the stepsisters, and their mother are the only negative characters in the film. Since they represent both the animal and human worlds, neither world is completely denigrated. In fact, Disney added a sequence to the filmic adaptation of the Perrault fairy tale: "a conflict between Cinderella's pets/allies, the mice, and the stepmother's pet, the cat" which, according to Naomi Wood, "metaphorically recapitulates the cat-and-mouse struggle between Cinderella and her stepmother and accentuates the life-and-death competition that motivates their actions" (26). The sequence also emphasizes Cinderella's connection with the natural world.

When Cinderella overhears the decree that all eligible maidens must attend a ball for the prince, her relationship with the animal world again assists her. She is an eligible maid, and the stepmother says she can go if she finishes all of her work and prepares herself. The mice and birds hear the proclamation and help her fix up a gown from her mother, again connecting her with the animal world. They sing, "We can do it," as they sew. Jaq and Gus, two integral parts of the Cinderella romance plot, acquire cloth and beads from the floor where Lucifer sits in a comic scene, which ends with Lucifer getting caught in a shirtsleeve. According to Wood, "Jaq, the planner, is the picture of self-containment. Always thinking, he is instrumental in developing and carrying out schemes on behalf of Cinderella. Gus is his opposite: foolishly confident about his ability to deal with Lucifer, always one beat behind everyone else, and continually jeopardizing his own and others' safety by his inability to control himself" (40). The other mice also exhibit such human qualities, singing as they refurbish the gown. According to Bosley Crowther's *New York Times* review, "It is when they are joined with Cinderella in advancing her undismayed career—singing and busy about business—that the picture has real and flowing joy" ("The Screen: Six Newcomers Mark Holiday" 33).

When Cinderella's stepmother tricks her daughters into tearing their discarded items from the gown, leaving her in tatters, Cinderella's attendance at the ball seems hopeless until both her animal friends and a supernatural fairy godmother intervene. The godmother sings "Bibbidi Bobbidi Boo" as she animates nature, transforming a pumpkin into a carriage, mice into four white horses, Gus, the horse, into a coachman, and the dog into a footman. Cinderella is transformed, as well, and is now dressed in a white gown and glass slippers. The prince falls in love with her. The familiar story of the glass slipper ensures Cinderella's happiness, but, in a final act of interdependence, she takes her animals with her to the castle, sealing the interconnected view of animal welfare and environmentalism with festive birds and mice waving farewell as the film ends.

Lady and the Tramp with domesticated dogs also connects human and nonhuman nature. Although dogs are "imprisoned" by dogcatchers and a visiting aunt, ultimately they are on equal ground with their human owners in a relationship like that described by Midgley's and Hume's ethical theories. According to Bosley Crowther's *New York Times* review, "The various types of canines that are burlesqued in human terms are amusing—if you like canines endowed with the mannerisms of human beings" ("Disney's 'Lady and the Tramp'" 17). Although Crowther asserts that "Mr. Disney's affection for dogs is more sugary than his appreciation of mice and ducks," their representation highlights an interconnection between animal welfare and environmentalism similar to that in *Cinderella*.

From its opening forward dogs are at the center of the film. The film opens with a dedication to dogs that shows us how loved and appreciated dogs can be in a small town at Christmas. The focus is on one house and family, with a puppy in a laundry basket in the spotlight. We do not see the humans' faces, only the pup, Lady. Lady's space is opulent, and she is valued as a member of the family. When Lady cries because she is locked in the laundry room, father knocks on the floor from their bedroom and then on the door, telling her to go back to bed. But Lady keeps trying to open the door to the laundry room, even though it is blocked with a chair, and succeeds. Lady climbs upstairs to the bedroom where we hear snoring. Lady howls and Jim, the father, wakes up and lets Lady on the bed.

When Lady is an adult, the interdependent relationship between herself and Jim and Darling continues; she still sleeps in her owners' bed and gets Jim his slippers. She catches the newspaper and takes it in the house. Jim and Darling feed her doughnuts and coffee and give her a license on a collar at six months.

Lady shares her equal footing in the human world with other dogs, as well: with a Scottie dog named Jock and a hound dog named Trusty, who dreams of tracking animals through a swamp. With a collar, Lady is now full grown, since the collar represents a "badge of faith and respectability." She runs to "Jim Dear" when he whistles and holds a treat on her nose while up on hind legs. She is happy on the carpet between her two human companions.

Tramp, on the other hand, is a carefree bachelor mutt living in a barrel at a train station, but he also shares an interconnected relationship with humans, even though he lives on the street, begging meals from a chef at Tony's Restaurant. But Tramp also helps keep dogs free from exploitation. When a dog-pound wagon goes by and the driver posts a sign about unlicensed dogs being confiscated, he sets two dogs in the wagon free and distracts the dogcatcher by leading him away from the other dogs and to "snob hill" where he overhears Lady's complaints about her owners: "Jim Dear and Darling are acting so" strange she says, so she feels less like a family member.

We see the scenes of Lady's mistreatment in flashback: Jim tells Lady to get down instead of giving her the usual treat. He calls her "that dog." Darling knits in a rocking chair and says "no" when Lady brings her the leash to walk her. Darling will not play ball and gets angry when Lady picks up yarn. After hearing about these changes, Trusty and Jock tell her about the coming present—a baby.

Tramp walks by while they explain, and he tells her about some of the bad consequences of a new baby. It seems that the biotic relationship will be shattered. When a baby moves in, a dog moves out. Then we see a montage of scenes that prove he is right—baby shower, birth, Lady forgotten and ignored, predictions that seem real when her owners leave her with Aunt Sarah and her two conniving Siamese cats.

Aunt Sarah blames Lady for her cats' misbehavior and punishes her, seemingly negating the biotic community established earlier in the film. When Sarah decides to muzzle Lady, she runs away, escaping feral dogs with Tramp's help. She is free until a dogcatcher captures her. The aunt further breaks up the biotic community Jim and Darling seemed to build with Lady when the aunt takes Lady home from the pound and chains her to a doghouse in the backyard. Jock and Trusty want to help her by marrying her. They have comfortable homes where she would be welcome. Tramp comes in with a bone, and they turn their backs on him, blaming him for Lady's plight. Lady is upset about the dog pound, but a storm comes in. A rat in the woodpile heads toward the baby. By thwarting the rat, Lady and Tramp prove their dedication to humans and again gain access to their world, in spite of the aunt's vile treatment of them.

The return of Lady's owners reignites the biotic relationship between humans and at least domesticated animals in the film. When Darling and Jim come home, they see the dogcatcher taking Tramp away and think Tramp attacked their baby. But Lady shows them the now-dead rat. Jim sees it, and the other dogs save Tramp from the dogcatcher, leaving Trusty with a broken leg. Lady and Tramp have four puppies by the next Christmas with the baby looking on. And Jock and Trusty come to Lady's house for breakfast. Trusty tells stories to Lady and Tramp's pups and the story ends, with the human and animal worlds interconnected, at least in this domestic realm.

Conclusion

Snow White and the Seven Dwarfs, *Cinderella*, and *Lady and the Tramp* highlight a holistic environmental ethic that, as Callicott suggests, "provides for various coexisting, cooperating, and competing ethics—each corresponding to our nested overlapping community entanglements" (259). Disney films from the 1940s and 1950s that grapple with animal treatment may range from those advocating

Dumbo: Dumbo flies.

animal rights, sometimes at the expense of other species, to those that rest on a biosocial moral paradigm that provides a space for interdependence in service to the community. But they all demonstrate that the animal rights/ animal welfare debate was well under way before Singer's animal liberation movement gained force.

These Disney films lay the groundwork for a later film with a more explicitly forceful animal rights message such as that found in *The Secret of* NIMH (1982). The latter film is the first feature from Don Bluth after he left Disney Studios to join an independent animation team, a connection that aligns the film further with the earlier Disney animated features. According to Aljean Harmetz of the *New York Times*, *The Secret of* NIMH "is an attempt to return to the rich, fully detailed animation that is known as 'classic' Disney animation" (C17), a goal that, according to Roger Ebert, Don Bluth and his team successfully executed. Ebert asserts regarding the film: "They have succeeded in reproducing the marvelous detail and depth of the Disney classics. This is a good-looking, interesting movie that creates a little rodent world right under the noses of the indifferent local humans" ("The Secret of NIMH").

Ebert also likes the film's premise. In a seemingly direct reaction to earlier Disney features and Singer's text, the film argues vehemently against animal testing and experimentation and, according to Ebert, asks the question: "What if a group of laboratory animals were injected with an experimental drug that made them as intelligent as humans?" ("The Secret of NIMH"). As Nicodemus, the rat narrator, reveals, scientists from NIMH, the National Institute of Mental Health, captured and performed dangerous experiments on mice and rats that ultimately increased their intelligence. Nicodemus explains the plight of the rat community to Mrs. Brisby, a mouse who comes to the rats for help, telling her that her husband, Jonathan, "made possible the rats' escape from the terrible . . . NIMH."

Mrs. Brisby helps them outsmart human farmers and NIMH, ensuring a move to Thorn Valley away from the bulldozers meant to destroy them. In *The Secret of NIMH* the rights of animals overshadow those of humans, not only because human characters serve only minor roles in the film but also because humans mistreat animals both in the laboratories of NIMH and on the farm. *The Secret of NIMH*, then, explicitly argues against mistreatment of animals both in laboratories and in "the field," while demonstrating that animals deserve rights because they so resemble us. Together these films also paved the way for environmentally conscious animal-welfare films such as *Bee Movie*. For us they also highlight that the roots of both the environmental and animal rights movements were well in place before either Singer's animal liberation movement or the contemporary environmental movement.

Gay Purr-ee: Mewsette and Jaune-tom on a Paris carriage ride.

THREE

The UPA and the Environment

A Modernist Look at Urban Nature

At the same time the Disney Studios were producing animal rights-driven animated features, a new animation studio was born, United Productions of America (UPA). This studio drew its stance on ecology from its technology-driven modernist perspective that is reflected in both the narrative and aesthetic content of its animated films. UPA grew out of the 1941 strike at Walt Disney Studios that enticed three ex-Disney artists, Stephen Bosustow, Zack Schwartz, and Dave Hilberman, to leave Disney and challenge its antiunion culture. Since the UPA studio also grew during the World War II era, they first produced industrial films for the then liberal policies of the federal government.

As the Industrial Films and Poster Service, for example, their company name before UPA, they produced an election film for Franklin Delano Roosevelt entitled *Hell-Bent for Election* (1944) and a human-rights film about race relations, *Brotherhood of Man* (1946). Both of these films not only demonstrated their support for Roosevelt's governmental programs but also illustrated the studio's own leftist politics and, at least to a certain extent, its modernist aesthetic. *Hell-Bent for Election* immerses a pro-FDR political message in a Chuck Jones–directed cartoon "with the same self-conscious use of both modern design and film techniques (matched dissolves, odd angles . . .)" (Barrier, *Hollywood Cartoons* 511). The backgrounds in *Hell-Bent for Election*, described as "very designed and abstract," anticipate the later work of UPA, the "stylization of movement, of what Hilberman called 'a different kind of animation that came out of the stylized characters'" (514).

John Hubley's design of *Brotherhood of Man*, according to Barrier, pays homage to the work of Saul Steinberg, a magazine cartoonist. Barrier asserts that "Hubley's design is not just flat and simple . . . but has in addition a sharp edge with no real precedent in Hollywood animation" (514). Barrier continues, "What shaped *Brotherhood of Man*, even more than it shaped the earlier films— and what gave United Film so unusual a tenor compared with other cartoon studios—was a belief that modern design had a political, not to say moral, dimension" (515).

Wells asserts that this aesthetic and political philosophy of UPA lined up with his interpretation of Gene Youngblood's concept of "expanded cinema" (*Animation and America* 60). Expanded cinema serves as a "re-interpretation of 'modernity' as a consequence of the counterculture's engagement with new technological imperatives, and the implicit re-formulation of the avant garde." UPA saw animation as "capable of embracing the ambiguous and contradictory through its symbolic vocabulary, becom[ing] the literal depictions of the artist's perceptions as they have transmuted into metaphysical entities" (63).

UPA embraced a philosophy that advocated making the presence of the animator transparent and foregrounded stylized representations of figures and setting within a modern technologically driven sociocultural context manifested in the abstract. From an ecocritical perspective, this modernist view of culture highlights and then blurs boundaries between human culture and the natural world. Unlike Disney and, to a certain extent, like Rankin/Bass, UPA advocates an interdependent relationship between the human world of technology and the natural world, typically in an urban mythological or historical setting. But unlike Rankin/Bass, UPA's aesthetic contributes to a modernist view of culture driven by a Bauhaus-like vision of balance rather than existential doom.

Although Michael Barrier, in his seminal *Hollywood Cartoons*, suggests that UPA failed to reach its potential as a modernist aesthetic-driven studio, he elucidates the grounding for the studio's style. According to Barrier, UPA animators led by Bill Hurtz "became very excited by *Language of Vision*, a book by Gyorgy Kepes 'on design, really, as taught at the Bauhaus . . . a book of revelation'" according to Hurtz (qtd. in Barrier 515). Barrier explains, "Kepes presented modern art as not just different from earlier art—specifically, the art of the Renaissance—but superior to it" (516). Kepes asserted that "visual language . . . must absorb the dynamic idioms of the visual imagery to mobilize the creative imagination for positive social action, and direct it toward positive social goals" (14). The artists at UPA embraced this philosophy of the activism driven by an abstract image refined to its most elementary structure. For Kepes, art should serve society as "a positive popular art, an art reaching everybody and understood by everyone" (221). UPA saw animation as the popular art that could best serve society's needs.

Although it grounds earlier political cartoons such as *Hell-Bent for Election* and *Brotherhood of Man*, this philosophy is most evident in shorter animated works such as *Gerald McBoing Boing* (1951) and *Rooty Toot Toot*

(1952). We assert, however, that it continues to resonate in two of the animated feature films produced by UPA, *1001 Arabian Nights* (1959) and *Gay Purr-ee* (1962), a film that highlights urban nature through both its narrative and aesthetic, foregrounding the interconnections between nature and a culture driven and constructed by technology. *1001 Arabian Nights* builds on the modernist narrative of *Gerald McBoing Boing* in which human nature becomes subsumed by technology, even within the fantasy world of the *Arabian Nights*. *Gay Purr-ee* takes a more blatant human and organismic approach to ecology as it heightens the modernist aesthetic of *Rooty Toot Toot* in a narrative valorizing pastoral nature over corrupt urban technology.

Created by children's-book author Dr. Seuss (Theodore Seuss Geisel) and the writer for *Rocky and Bullwinkle*, Bill Scott, *Gerald McBoing Boing* centers on Gerald, a boy who can only speak in sound effects. Instead of inhibiting his success, however, Gerald's "defect" becomes an asset when a radio station hires him as its sound-effects department. This premise embraces an environmental message that takes an ambivalent stance toward technology. Although Gerald does find his sound-effect voice beneficial when a mysterious corporate officer stops him at the railroad tracks and hires him to work for the radio station, he is shunned by friends and family and nearly runs away from home to escape their scorn. In *Gerald McBoing Boing*, technology becomes a tool only when it subsumes the language that would make Gerald human and connect him with both the human and natural worlds.

Still, the film's clever premise and innovative aesthetic valorize goals of modernity found in Kepes's *Language of Vision*. The film won the Academy Award for the best animated short-subject film in 1951. Don Markstein asserts that "what made [the cartoon] stand out from the UPA crowd . . . is that it was simply an animated version of a children's record written by Dr. Seuss. Seuss's and Scott's script, which consisted almost entirely of voice-overs and sound effects, was unusual even for that gifted rhymester, in that it not only used polysyllabic sound effects to fill out lines, but even pulled off a few rhymes with them" ("Gerald McBoing Boing"). But the aesthetics driving this script heighten the modernist edge in the film, an edge that led to multiple versions of the cartoon. Sequels to *Gerald McBoing Boing* and a brief animated series in 1956–57 cemented the character, so much so that Cookie Jar Entertainment included him in its *Tickle U* anthology on Cartoon Network in 2005.

The aesthetics of *Gerald McBoing Boing* foreground the immersion in a modernist perspective and hark back to UPA's mid-1940s Bauhaus-like philosophy behind *Brotherhood of Man*. According to Barrier, Robert "Bobe" Cannon, the film's director, and William Hurtz, the film's designer, "clothed their story of childhood distress in harmonious colors, shapes, and movements—so that the film is soothing and even therapeutic in its total effect" (*Hollywood Cartoons* 525). *Gerald* echoed the ideas that had shaped UPA's films in the middle forties, the ideas that Gyorgy Kepes had advanced in *Language of Vision*. Cannon and Hurtz avoided the violence of Warner Brothers and the conservative aesthetic of Disney to produce "inventive stylization of movement in *Gerald McBoing Boing*; it shows up, for instance, in the way a doctor's slightly gawky legs accent his rigid verticality" (Barrier, *Hollywood Cartoons* 525).

The goal for Cannon and Hurtz was to, as Hurtz put it, "boil it down" (qtd. in *Hollywood Cartoons* 525). Hurtz explains, "What can we get rid of? We frequently talked about that, Bobe and I, saying, 'Let's be sure we don't get too much of so and so.' . . . We decided to dispense with all walls and floors and ground levels and skies and horizon lines" (qtd. in *Hollywood Cartoons* 525–26). Such a minimalist and stylized, almost abstract, animation aesthetic illustrates this modernist edge and foregrounds the notion of a dynamic landscape or space. UPA emphasized this minimalist aesthetic rather than narrative and conveyed its political stance in the same way abstract modern art communicates its message—through visual symbol and metaphor.

The same thematic and aesthetic philosophy underpinning *Gerald McBoing Boing* guides *1001 Arabian Nights*. *Gerald McBoing Boing* has clear connections to Mr. Magoo, the protagonist of *1001 Arabian Nights*. In *1001 Arabian Nights* technology plays a vital role in building not only the stylized aesthetic, but also in driving a narrative in which Magoo's bumbling character assists his hapless son only because technology intercedes. The sophisticated design and color of the film augments a narrative in which the technology of a genie in his bottle, a flying carpet, and a magic flame supersede bumbling and incompetent human and nonhuman nature. Yet technology does not serve as a tool for destruction in *1001 Arabian Nights*. Instead, it serves to preserve and protect humans and their natural world and illustrates the interconnected interdependence between culture and the nature of humanity. The supernatural, however, most powerfully facilitates this "technology," so its connection to the modern world is diluted.

Gay Purr-ee, on the other hand, highlights a pastoral nature that contrasts with the ugliness of urban space and depicted, if briefly, in *Rooty Toot Toot*. *Rooty Toot Toot* is arguably one of the best cartoons to come out of UPA. It tells the story of Frankie and Johnny through song and from the perspective of two lawyers, a bartender, and Nellie Bly, Frankie's rival for Johnny's love—all in a Technicolor, stylized courtroom setting complete with judge and jury. Although the lawyer prosecuting Frankie for Johnny's murder, the bartender, and Nellie Bly all tell their tale within the confines of the bar in which Johnny is shot, Frankie's defense lawyer paints a pastoral image of Frankie's home that highlights her innocence and her connection to nature and that connects *Rooty Toot Toot* with *Gay Purr-ee*. *Rooty Toot Toot*'s narrative and thematic grounding point to the innocence of pastoral nature as superior to a corrupt urban space riddled by the rooty-toot-toot of weapons. But it also demonstrates its stance toward technology through its uniquely modern and abstract design and animation aesthetic. According to Barrier, "The design element is stronger in *Rooty Toot Toot* than in any of [John] Hubley's earlier UPA cartoons, resting in part on a very free and inventive use of color. . . . Like John McGrew in Chuck Jones's *Fox Pop* ten years earlier, Hubley changes his color scheme to correspond to changes in mood," so that design works hand in hand with UPA's stylized animation rooted in the work of Norman McLaren, a filmmaker specializing in abstract film (*Hollywood Cartoons* 530).

Although Klein asserts that *Gay Purr-ee* is "too labored" and "too coy" (*Seven Minutes* 336) and *Newsweek* claims that "there seems to be an effort to reach a hitherto undiscovered audience—the fey four-year-old of recherché taste" in its review (qtd. in Maltin, *Of Mice and Magic* 336), *Gay Purr-ee* continues stylistic and thematic patterns found in *Rooty Toot Toot*, especially in developing its Technicolor pastoral and urban settings. The feature's modernist aesthetic highlights a dynamic landscape that valorizes both urban and rural nature. But the film's narrative, as in *Rooty Toot Toot*, validates the pastoral as a space where the natural world can thrive.

From its opening *Gay Purr-ee* highlights high art, with images by Paul Cézanne during the credits and backgrounds influenced by various modern artists. We see the Eiffel Tower, and a voice says, "This is Paris, but not all love stories start there." The scene jumps to the country, a farm in Provence, where an idealized pastoral setting becomes the scene of innocence maintained later in the urban setting of Paris. With impressionistic paintings as background, a hot sun-drenched natural world emerges with homages to Van Gogh's painting *Sunflowers*, reinforcing the pastoral innocence of the setting. Mewsette (Judy Garland), a beautiful female cat, is sunning herself, and a song describes a tomcat's love for her. The singer, Jaune-tom (Robert Goulet), and his kitten friend Robespierre (Red Buttons) approach Mewsette because Jaune-tom admires Mewsette, even with a butterfly on her head. But when he offers her a mouse, she exclaims, "You're a clumsy country clod," establishing the film's urban/rural binary.

Mewsette resists rural innocence and yearns for life off the farm in the Paris of the film's opening. In a dream facilitated by her owner's sister, Mewsette enjoys Paris in neon and Technicolor. A flower grows on top of the Eiffel Tower in the dream, but the tower becomes a Ferris wheel, fireworks, a fountain, and fire under the Arc de Triomphe. Mewsette wakes from the dream in a window overlooking bright fields painted in an Impressionistic style that suggests pastoral values. But she sees city life as the ideal. Even though the fields outside her window are more beautiful and true, Mewsette leaves for Paris with her owner's sister.

Although Jaune-tom embraces the pastoral, he loves Mewsette and follows her to Paris along railroad tracks. A train drives through green painted landscapes to highlight the contrast between rural and urban, pastoral and technological. Mewsette is on board and comes out of a basket to sing about roses and violets. A tracking shot of a landscape covered in bright flowers leads to interior shots of birds in a cage above Mewsette in the car, again highlighting the conflict between free pastoral nature and the prison of technology and the city. Roses and violets bloom outside the train. Then the landscape looks more and more urban and industrial, as the shot continues to track the train and the landscape it crosses. The city Mewsette enters is depicted as corrupt and technology-driven, not only in relation to the contrasting settings, but also because of the contrasting figures of Jaune-tom, a representative of the pastoral, and Meowrice (Paul Frees), a con man who nearly sells Mewsette to the highest bidder once he and Mademoiselle Henriette Rubens-Chatte (Hermione Gingold) transform her into the belle of Paris. While Mewsette shows Henriette how little she knows about the subterfuge a "lady" uses to beguile a man, music and setting exaggerate the corrupt milieu of Paris and again heighten the value of the pastoral. On a rooftop, Meowrice sings, "Time is on the side of the scoundrel." Black cats that look like hooded assassins or the Siamese cats from *Lady and the Tramp* join him and agree to keep an eye on Mewsette. "Evil is the root of all money. Money trees that is," he says. Then another song, "The Money Cat Can," features silhouetted cats as a chorus in front of a red-and-black background. They dance and sing on the roof with a full moon lighting them. "The money cat knows that the money tree grows," Meowrice sings on a throne of a large chimney that makes his black coat and yellow-and-blue eyes glow, emphasizing his corruption.

Even though Meowrice nearly stops Jaune-tom and Robespierre by getting them drunk and selling them to a ship captain bound for Alaska, Jaune-tom and Robespierre return to Paris to save Mewsette before she can be mailed to Pittsburgh. Since they were able to strike it rich, they can go back to Paris in style and bring the beauty of nature to the city, so Jaune-tom sings Mewsette's song while his ship sails through a rainbow.

A strange scene reveals Meowrice's plan to send Mewsette into a forced marriage with someone from Pittsburgh. To demonstrate Mewsette's beauty, Meowrice is having her portrait painted and tells her future husband about

Gay Purr-ee: Paris connects with the pastoral.

the plan in a letter that introduces viewers to artists and their styles. Illustrations accompany information about Mr. Monet—the father of Impressionist shimmering light, Toulouse-Lautrec, Degas, Seurat, Cézanne, Picasso, Van Gogh, Gauguin, among others.

All hope seems lost. The pastoral is subsumed by urban technology until Jaune-tom comes back in a carriage. He and his kitten colleague go to Henriette's to find Mewsette. The henchmen know he is coming. Mewsette is locked inside a basket, but she writes Jaune-tom a note before she goes off to the train. Once they find the note, Robespierre and Jaune-tom chase after the train. Jaune-tom imagines Meowrice is a mouse so he can better catch him. After a fight, Jaune-tom and the kitten exchange Mewsette for Meowrice in the basket bound for Pittsburgh. Now Jaune-tom has money and takes Mewsette on buggy rides in Paris, but flowers burst out as if they are in Provence. Instead of the city subsuming the country, the pastoral supersedes urban corrupt technology because Jaune-tom and Mewsette are together and in love. Meowrice has been defeated.

Conclusion

In *1001 Arabian Nights* and *Gay Purr-ee*, the modernist aesthetic of *Gerald McBoing Boing* and *Rooty Toot Toot* is somewhat muted by the loss of talent and vision that followed changes in UPA's personnel, including John Hubley, Herb Klynn, and Jules Engel. But their influence continued in both of these feature films that draw on a modernist aesthetic in which a dynamic setting inspires spiritual and philosophical enlightenment, representing both urban and rural nature. The films again recall Kepes's assertions about humanity's need "to search for a temporary equilibrium in his conflicts with nature and in his relations with other men" (14). The move then is toward order, an equitable interdependent relationship among humans, culture, technology, and the natural world.

Although *1001 Arabian Nights* illustrates the power of technology as a necessary tool to maintain the ideals of nature, it also demonstrates the interconnectedness and interdependence of technological culture and human and nonhuman nature. *Gay Purr-ee*, on the other hand, first highlights the superiority of the pastoral ideal in relation to a corrupt urban and technologically driven Paris space. But by connecting the pastoral, represented by Jaune-tom, with an uncorrupted urban representative, Mewsette, the feature again demonstrates the power of interconnections. Both films hark back to Kepes's *Language of Vision* in that, as S. I. Hayakawa explains in his preface to the book, "To cease looking at things atomistically in visual experience and to see relatedness means, among other things, to lose in our social experience, as Mr. Kepes argues, the deluded self-importance of absolute 'individualism' in favor of social relatedness and interdependence" (10). When nature and culture maintain an interdependent relationship, they both can prosper, the films suggest, in a move toward both human and organismic approaches to ecology.

The Incredible Mr. Limpet: Limpet the fish plans attacks against Nazi subs.

FOUR

Animation and Live Action

A Demonstration of Interdependence?

Live action has combined with animation from nearly the beginning of film history. Winsor McCay's *Gertie the Dinosaur*, which he wrote, directed, and produced in 1914, is an apt example. In this twelve-minute silent film Gertie, an animated dinosaur, interacts with a live-action world, somewhat like Disney's *Pete's Dragon* (1977) did years later. The animation allows a whimsical plot point to take shape, so that McCay can interact with an animated character that just happens to be a prehistoric now-extinct herbivore named Gertie. At the end of the film, McCay takes a ride on Gertie's back to show she does not fear him, an effect made possible because of animation. McCay's hand-drawn animation allowed him to transcend the rules of live action. Including himself in the film heightened the effect of the whimsy on display. This lure of animation continues today. A 2003 *New York Times* column by David Carr explains, "Because animation is less rule-bound than live action, writers can use the kind of shtick that would seem preposterous on film. . . . In a medium in which a character can end up smoking a stick of dynamite, people expect something surprising with each advancing frame." When combined with live action, animation offers a contrast to the rules of live action that stuns as it entertains. It also sometimes offers up opportunities for ecocritical readings that highlight either a valorization of nonhuman nature or a critique of humans' exploitation of the natural world.

Winsor McCay's early animated figures added a new dimension to live-action theater and film. McCay incorporated his first animated cartoons, *Little Nemo* (1911) and *The Story of a Mosquito* (1912), into his vaudeville act, but audiences "suspected that the movement was some sort of trick produced with wires and figures" (Goldman), so he created Gertie the dinosaur, a long-extinct herbivore, to offset their skepticism. Inserting himself into the animated short reinforced the film's authenticity. McCay interacts with Gertie, asking her to perform small acts such as raising right and left feet, and when, at the end of the film, McCay's tiny figure "rides" off screen on Gertie's back, he successfully uses a mixture of live action and animation to demonstrate Gertie's authenticity as an animated character.

After viewing McCay's work, other studios combined animation with live action during the silent era, as well. Max Fleischer, for example, created his "Out of the Inkwell" cartoons that first featured Koko the clown, a figure modeled on his brother Dave's clown role. Max Fleischer's rotoscope technique helped him create fluid animation for Koko that interacted with live-action figures and settings. In *The Tantalizing Fly* (1919), a cartoonist draws Koko, but a fly interferes with the drawing. The fly then becomes a source of conflict for both Koko and the cartoonist. Koko eventually fights the fly off with the cartoonist's pen.

This fluid interaction between live action and animation ends only after the cartoonist retrieves both Koko and the fly in his inkwell.

Disney also began his animation history with films that combined live action and animation. His Alice comedy series, which began with *Alice's Wonderland* (1923), highlighted the entertainment value of animation introduced in Alice's dream sequences. In *Alice's Wonderland*, Alice after visiting a cartoonist's studio dreams of riding (as a live-action figure) an elephant in an animated animal parade and fighting a fierce battle with animated lions. In *Alice Gets in Dutch* (1924), Alice falls asleep while being punished for popping an ink-filled balloon in a one-room schoolhouse. Her animated dream, again with Alice as a live-action figure, responds to her teacher's punishment and reputation as an "old hen." Both the Fleischer "Out of the Inkwell" cartoons and the Disney Alice comedies illustrated genuine interaction between the animated and live-action worlds.

Although McCay included himself as a character in *Gertie the Dinosaur* to combat critics' claims that he mechanized live-action characters such as mosquitoes in his cartoons, most sound-era live-action films include animation to add sparkling comedy or stunning effects. The early Fleischer and Disney films, in a marked aesthetic sign of interdependence between the live-action and animated worlds, are examples. *Anchors Aweigh* (1945) and *Two Guys from Texas* (1948), for example, include animated sequences that add entertainment value. In *Anchors Aweigh*, Joseph Brady (Gene Kelly) dances with Jerry from the Tom and Jerry animated series, heightening the impact of Kelly's choreography and dance talents. According to Pam Grady's "Reel.com" review, "This sequence was a groundbreaking achievement for the MGM animation department, who had to trace each live-action frame onto animation paper before drawing the mouse and then marrying the two images with an optical printer." Grady calls the sequence "a spectacular, gymnastic duet with man and mouse dancing, jumping, and tumbling together in intricate harmony." Ultimately, the sequence also highlighted Kelly's innovative dance steps, challenging him to move beyond previous live-action partners.

In *Two Guys from Texas*, a Warner Brothers film, an animated sequence reinforces both story and theme. One of the protagonists, Danny Foster (Jack Carson), relates a dream to someone he thinks is a psychoanalyst, Dr. Straeger (Fred Clark). The dream narrative is illustrated through an animation sequence and serves to reinforce character types and themes in the film. Foster sees the doctor to address his fear of animals, and his dream offers a cure for his phobia. In the dream, Foster looks like an animated version of himself, but he herds sheep in spite of his phobia and loses them to a "wolf," equated with his handsome singing partner, Steve Carroll (Dennis Morgan), in the doctor's interpretation. The doctor suggests that the sheep represent the women Carroll has stolen from Foster. Bugs Bunny enters the animated dreamscape to offer advice the doctor reinforces. To overcome his phobia, the dream reveals that Foster must outwit Carroll and steal a woman away from him, the doctor explains. The animated sequence not only moves the plot forward; it also foregrounds the theme of the film and offers a cure for a phobia, so Morgan can find romance of his own.

Some films, however, intertwine animation and live action to demonstrate conflicts as well as connections between human and nonhuman nature, as in *King Kong* (1933) and *Song of the South* (1946). In *Dangerous When Wet* (1953), for example, Katie Higgins (Esther Williams) swims with Tom and Jerry in a dream sequence that reveals her own romantic conflict between Andre

Lanet (Fernando Lamas) and her own natural inclination to swim, even across the English Channel. In a cartoon dream sequence, Lanet becomes an animated octopus who holds Higgins tight with tentacles, even when she swims away with Tom and Jerry's assistance. When Higgins awakens, she is pulling herself out of bed, connecting animation with live action through a filmic bridge. Ultimately, Higgins swims the English Channel, but with Lanet's support rather than his resistance, perhaps connecting Higgins's "nature" with the culture of romance.

Four films from different decades in which live action and animation are interconnected move beyond entertainment and illustrate not only the interdependence of two aesthetic forms but of the worlds of nature and culture. *The Girl Next Door* (1953), *The Incredible Mr. Limpet* (1962), *Who Framed Roger Rabbit* (1988), and *Enchanted* (2007) all intertwine live action with animation, but they also illustrate blatant environmental messages about the need for interconnected relationships between human and nonhuman nature.

The Girl Next Door uses two animated sequences from UPA to highlight both the bifurcation between nature and culture and, in the second sequence, their alliance through a Noah's Ark scene that also illuminates human generational differences. *The Incredible Mr. Limpet* valorizes the natural while also demonstrating our dependence on its representative, Mr. Limpet, when he is transformed into an animated fish. In *Who Framed Roger Rabbit*, animated animal characters work together with live-action humans to counter a toxic-waste scheme, in a blatant environmental critique that draws on human approaches to ecology. And in *Enchanted*, an animated princess (Amy Adams) is thrown into a live-action world where she establishes an interdependent, perhaps organismic, relationship with urban nature while assimilating into a live-action world.

The Girl Next Door, a Twentieth Century Fox musical, integrates animation into two key scenes that foreground a comic artist's son and demonstrate the bifurcation of nature and culture. The two main characters, Jeannie Laird (June Haver), a musical star, and Bill Carter (Dan Dailey), the cartoonist, fall in love after Jeannie moves from chorus girl to star, takes a world tour, and moves back to the United States to the house next door to the cartoonist and his son, Joe (Billy Gray). Jeannie's home is built with intriguing modernist architecture and furniture and highlights her connection with culture. Bill's rustic house looks like part of the great outdoors. Bill and his son even cook most of their meals in the backyard.

When Jeannie moves in, she attracts Bill both as a woman and a representative of culture. Joe, on the other hand, loses some of his father's attention and catches him in a lie about nature in his comic strip. Bill draws comics about himself and his son and, according to Bill, "tells the truth" in his strip. But instead of taking a trip to the North Woods with his son, as he promises his editor, he stays behind to woo Jeannie. Yet he still writes about fishing with his son in the woods in his comic strip even though he is not there to "tell the truth."

This conflict between Bill's relationship with Jeannie and his comic-strip lie also sets up a binary between culture (Bill's love for Jeannie, a musical star) and nature (his natural relationship with his son and their yearly journey into the North Woods). Joe's animated dream sequence illustrates and clarifies the bifurcation and its implications. After he realizes his father has lied in his comic strip, a despairing Joe goes into a dreamscape in which the first UPA animation sequence comes up. In the sequence the background and foreground are in bright blues and greens to highlight a connection with nature. Bill and Joe drive into the woods and pass chopped trees on their way toward a fish-laden lake. Low-Life the raccoon and the family dog catch fish together, and Bill sets up camp, blows up a raft, and takes them out on the lake. Bill and Joe wear bright red shirts that contrast with the blue water and blue and pink fish. In the dream, the raccoon catches twenty-nine fish.

As the animated dream sequence progresses, however, the world of culture intervenes. Jeannie, representing a world outside this natural setting, appears, dressed like a wicked witch and riding a broom. She seems to "reel" Bill in. Jeannie the witch even dives in the water and takes Joe's fish off his hook and puts it on Bill's. She then pops the inflated raft. Bill and Joe fly back to shore as the raft deflates. When Bill sees the witch, he seems pleased to see her, since she is Jeannie. Joe, on the other hand, thinks she has ruined their fun, but Bill and Jeannie kiss and go to a party at Jeannie's, leaving the natural world behind. Joe is upset as Jeannie takes them away on her broom, and the sequence ends.

The story continues this binary between culture and nature until Joe realizes his place in the natural order. After a neighbor girl, Kitty (Mary Jane Saunders), talks with Joe, he sends a letter to Bill's boss telling him Bill lied, but Joe has second thoughts about sending the letter and tries to retrieve it from a mailbox. A police officer witnesses him tampering with the mailbox and takes him down to the police station. His father and Joe fight over Joe's behavior, and Bill also has a dream about Jeannie. But Bill's dream is not animated and includes a song-and-dance number that demonstrates his passion for Jeannie.

After Joe and the little girl, Kitty, become best friends, however, Joe realizes that he should let Bill and Jeannie have their romance. Then he can spend more time with Kitty, as well. Joe puts together a story in cartoons to explain his feelings. After Bill understands Joe's change of heart and retrieves Jeannie, the second animation sequence begins. Joe had drawn the story of Noah's Ark, and the animation sequence alludes to it, showing a series of paired animals entering the ship. Three human pairs enter the ark from the end of the line of animals, demonstrating their interconnected relationship: Bill and Jeannie, Joe and Kitty, and Jeannie's friend, Rosie (Cara Williams), and Jeannie's manager, Henry Fields (Hayden Rorke).

These three human pairs enter two by two and prove Kitty's claim that "children are not the important thing." They are "extra" until they grow up, so only adult pairs of animals enter the ark. She and Joe are the only children lining up to enter. The sequence also connects the human and nonhuman worlds of nature through the pairs of people and animals entering the ark, illustrating explicitly the interdependent relationship between the worlds of culture and nature. Here an organismic approach to ecology is also explicitly illustrated by the biotic community established on the ark.

The Incredible Mr. Limpet reinforces this interdependence. In the film an animated fish, Henry Limpet (Don Knotts), helps the U.S. Navy destroy Nazi U-boats during World War II. Limpet, however, becomes a fish when he falls in the Coney Island Bay because he values fish and their lifestyle more than the human life he leads with his wife, Bessie (Carole Cook), and best friend and rival, George Stickel (Jack Weston). The film, then, both valorizes "peaceful" aquatic life and reinforces the need for an interdependent relationship between human and nonhuman nature.

As an adaptation of a Theodore Pratt novel of the same name, *The Incredible Mr. Limpet*—"One of the strangest films ever made that didn't involve David Lynch" (Null)—opens with a Navy message of approval. The film is framed by a scene in the film's present that demonstrates

Henry Limpet's continuing value as a connection between human and nonhuman nature. Navy sailors march to an office that says "Top Secret." Something was locked in a file back in 1945, and it was hoped they would not need to open it.

The reason behind the top-secret designation is revealed when the Navy officers open a file that begins in September 1941. "That's when it first started," the officer, Admiral P. P. Spewter (Larry Keating), explains, "I never knew him before." The film flashes back to 1941, when a still-human Henry is working as a bookkeeper in Brooklyn at the Atlantic and Gulf Line shipping office. His eyesight prevents him from joining the Navy, but his connection with water and fish is clear. He has a fishbowl on his desk and fish in the water cooler to take home in a jar with holes in the lid because, Henry exclaims, "Fish are so bright and cheerful. So beautiful." He even has a popular guide-to-science window blind at home that describes different eras, including the Devonian era. "Our ancestors were fish," Henry says. He even sees fish as the salvation for this violent planet: "Hope in the war of Europe comes from thinking of fish turning into men, so they might turn out even better."

Limpet wishes he were a fish, but his wife, Bessie, and friend and rival for his wife's love, George, want him to give up on fish, to get rid of his fish tank, and to go to Coney Island instead of a lecture on the mating habits of shellfish. Yet on their way to Coney Island, Limpet's service to the Navy as a source of an interconnected relationship between human and nonhuman nature is foreshadowed: a newspaper headline on the train reads, "Nazi Subs Infest Waters." When they arrive, Limpet sits on the boardwalk and talks to the fish below, explaining that he has read the *Theory of Reverse Evolution* by Radcliff and hopes he can devolve just as Radcliff explained it: "More than anything I wish I could be one of you right now. I wish, I wish, I was a fish," he says and jumps in.

Now the underwater scene is animated. Before our eyes, Limpet changes into an animated fish with glasses, connecting live action and animation as well as human and nonhuman nature. He fits this aquatic role more than he ever fit in as a human. Bessie keeps saying, "He doesn't know how to swim." But he does, even swimming up to George, who just sees a fish. "Bessie. What's going to happen to poor Bessie, George?" Limpet asks, but George does not hear him. "I saw a fish wearing his glasses," George tells Bessie and takes Bessie home.

The animation from here on effectively ties Limpet's character to the sea and human characters to cities and ships. The film fluidly integrates animation in the primarily live-action film with the help of animators from Disney. The animation director was Bill Tytla, who created the "Night on Bald Mountain" sequence for *Fantasia*. Warner Brothers director Robert McKimson assisted with direction. The Web site *Animated Views* writes that Art Babbit, who developed Disney's Goofy character and who brought *Fantasia*'s Chinese mushrooms to life, was an uncredited animator. Other Disney artists contributed to the animation sequences (Simon).

The film moves beyond bifurcating animation and live action, however, and demonstrates contrasts between human and nonhuman nature when Limpet literally swims away from the human world. As a way to highlight his difference from humans as an animated fish, the further Limpet swims, the more assimilated he becomes. Even colors become more brilliant. It takes him awhile to determine his place in this new world. He tries to address a school of fish, but they swim away. Clam shells close when he passes them. Then Limpet sees the food chain in action as one fish after another eats a smaller fish. He hides from a shark in a cave, to which a hermit crab tells him to scram. Now Limpet is connected with the natural world through a crab he calls Crusty (Paul Frees). Limpet discovers that he has a powerful voice as a fish, and his roar further connects Limpet both with Crusty and with the human world he left behind. Limpet opens his mouth and roars, scaring off the shark. When an octopus grabs Crusty, Limpet saves him with another trumpeting roar. Crusty joins him, calling him Flat Bush. They see a freighter "killed" by a torpedo, and Limpet finds a way to connect with the human world. When Limpet swims in, he sees Red Cross trucks, weapons, ammunition, tanks, and a ship's log. The freighter was carrying important cargo for the Allies: "There must be some way to stop Nazi subs. If only I could help," Limpet says. He sees himself in the captain's cabin mirror, making his first explicit move toward interdependence. At the same time, however, he enjoys this life in the sea and wants another fish like him to share it with. He finds his potential mate Ladyfish (Elizabeth MacRae) when he saves her from a fishing boat. After Limpet scares off a barracuda with his roar, they swim together with a love song in the background. Their pink-and-blue tails intertwine as they swim in circles around blue-and-white opaque waters and sea plants. Red-and-blue, pink-and-blue neon effects shine around them until Limpet remembers he is still married to Bessie. Ladyfish swims to the nesting grounds without him, despite his roars.

Limpet's roars eventually bring her back, and these roars also establish a way for him to stop the Nazi submarine attacks. A Nazi sub hears his roar. Believing it to be a message, officers send a reply in Morse code.

When the Pearl Harbor attack leads the United States to war, Limpet swims back to Brooklyn to find George Stickel and to offer his help with the war effort, establishing an interconnected relationship between human and nonhuman nature. While Crusty looks after Ladyfish in a sunken ship, Limpet enters a battle in which he sees a U.S. Navy ship attacking a Nazi submarine with depth charges. These depth charges destroy people and submarines, but they primarily kill marine life. Limpet exclaims, "They are missing the U-boat," and tries to speak to the ship's crew. But they fire on him until he calls into their underwater listening device, telling them they missed the sub and explaining where to go and how to set their charges. When they follow his instructions, they hit the sub. Now they will listen to him, so he tells them to bring George Stickel from the USS *Starbright*, and George will gladly help them.

Now Limpet can serve the military as a fish in ways he could not as a human. His animated presence demonstrates the interdependent relationship between human and nonhuman nature. The commander, P. P. Spewter, helps establish that relationship when he confers with the rear admiral (Charles Meredith) to enlist the "voice" of Henry Limpet. He calls in George Stickel, since Henry will only talk to him. "He's a secret weapon," the commander explains of Limpet. The commander tells him about the voice from the sea that summoned him. When George hears the voice, he recognizes it as Limpet and eventually helps the commander. Limpet's roar or "thrumb" becomes an effective secret weapon against the Nazis. By scouting U-boats and thrumbing to highlight their location, Limpet tells the Navy when to drop charges and destroy the subs. A montage sequence of hits shows the extent of Limpet's help and the strength of the interdependent relationship Limpet has established with George and the rest of the U.S. Navy.

Despite the Nazis' discovering how Limpet uses his thrumb to destroy their U-boats, Limpet's service to the Navy—and his interdependent relationship with human nature—culminates in a successful mission that facilitates the invasion of Europe. When Limpet loses his glasses, Ladyfish and Trusty join forces with Limpet to cement that interdependence. With Trusty's help, Limpit's thrumb successfully thwarts the Nazis and provides a safe passage for the convoy. When Limpet thrumbs, the Navy hears him, but so do the Nazis, who send off torpedoes set to follow him. Limpet keeps thrumbing, so the missiles continue after him, following him where they came from, blowing up the Nazis' own U-boats. "Just let them knock themselves out," he says, and boats are knocked out one by one. The explosions are spectacular and then the U-boats sink. An exhausted Limpet swims up to explain to George. George puts him back down into water, and they agree to meet at Coney Island when the war is over. Then the viewer sees a montage of headlines: "Secret Weapon Defeats Nazis" and "Victory." Limpet makes his connection with the natural world more explicit by taking Ladyfish as his spawning partner (with Bessie's permission).

Limpet's interaction with Ladyfish connects him with animated nature and helps separate him from his human past. When Limpet tells Ladyfish he was once human, she says: "I don't care how terrible your past was, Limpet. I'll help you forget."

"You and I could be the beginning of a new and better world," Limpet says. He tells Bessie and George, "Maybe all along I was meant to be a fish. Maybe nature just corrected her error." They say goodbye.

Years later the interconnected relationship Limpet established seems to continue when he brings human intellect to the animal world. In the final frame the commander and George are gray-haired. George asks, "Is he really teaching porpoises?" The answer seems to be yes, because after advancing Limpet to the rank of commodore in reserve, they hear his thrumb. As Limpet explained it, "Nature just corrected her error."

In *The Incredible Mr. Limpet*, Limpet helps make a better world by reversing evolution, a valorization of the more peaceful life of fish. But that reversal allows him to move human and nonhuman nature closer toward an effective interdependent relationship in which Limpit's thrumb can help win a war and his knowledge can educate porpoises to serve the Navy. These are possibilities only imaginable in animated portions of a fictional film, but they are illustrations of an effective way to bridge the gap between human culture and the natural world, a bridge that may draw on organismic approaches to ecology.

Only a few more-recent films that combine animation and live action demonstrate this interdependence. Disney films *Mary Poppins* (1964), *Bedknobs and Broomsticks* (1971), and *Pete's Dragon* (1977) integrate animation into primarily live-action films to provide the comic surprise of *Gertie the Dinosaur*. Disney's *Tron* (1982) and Ralph Bakshi films such as *Fritz the Cat* (1972), *Heavy Traffic* (1972), *Coonskin* (1975), *American Pop* (1981), and *Cool World* (1992) intertwine animation with live action, but foreground an urban or technology-centered setting seemingly empty of nonhuman nature.

Who Framed Roger Rabbit (1988) connects human and nonhuman nature in an urban setting because animated figures from "Toontown" are anthropomorphized animals. But the film makes a more explicit statement about humans' treatment of the environment that draws on both human and organismic approaches to ecology by foregrounding and critiquing two destructive practices: (1) toxic-chemical use and disposal and (2) overdevelopment of the landscape. The villain, Judge Doom (Christopher Lloyd), first creates a toxic chemical mixture of turpentine, acetone, and benzene called Dip that will destroy all the "toons" and clear Toontown for a destructive construction project, a superhighway around which Doom plans to build hotels, restaurants, gas stations, and strip malls. When combined with Doom's elimination of urban mass-transit systems, such destruction and overdevelopment blatantly attacks the natural world.

The film begins as a detective story in which Eddie Valiant (Bob Hoskins), who hates "toons" because he thinks they killed his brother, finds Roger Rabbit (Charles Fleischer) innocent of murdering Marvin Acme (Stubby Kaye). During the investigation, however, Valiant discovers Judge Doom's plot to destroy Toontown and to build his concrete highway and suburb, literally paving over nature as its representatives are melted down with toxic waste.

The film's opening shows us the foundation for Roger Rabbit's position as a suspect as it establishes the bifurcation between the animated "nature" of anthropomorphized animals and live-action "culture" of humans. Although Roger Rabbit is "alive" in Hollywood and co-exists with humans as a coequal, he also inhabits Toontown, an irrational space aligned with the natural world. The film first reveals this irrational world through what looks like a short film with Roger Rabbit and Baby Herman (Lou Hirsch). Roger babysits Baby Herman and suffers multiple injuries while trying to stop Baby from climbing after a cookie. Seen from the top cupboard, the floor of the kitchen is a black-and-white checkerboard, so detailed and well-drawn that it attracts the eye. Although Baby Herman is unscathed, Roger is despondent and cannot see stars as he should when a refrigerator falls on him; birds fly around his head instead.

In the live-action world Roger coinhabits, Eddie, the live-action private detective, consults with the studio head, Maroon (Alan Tilvern), about Roger's predicament. Roger

Rabbit is unhappy because Jessica (Kathleen Turner), his wife, may be with another man, so Eddie agrees to spy on her. When Eddie climbs on the back of a Red Car Trolley and exclaims, "Who needs a car in Los Angeles? We've got the best public transportation in the country," his claim foreshadows the real mystery: Doom's planned ecological disaster. Cloverleaf Enterprises sits at the stop where Eddie gets off the trolley, and as Eddie discovers from a laid-off friend, Cloverleaf bought the Red Car Trolley so that Doom could systematically destroy the Hollywood landscape after eliminating Toontown and destroying the animated figures that inhabit it. By eliminating Toontown, Doom also destroys nature, at least symbolically, since the irrational animated world is associated with the natural, especially in contrast with the rational live-action world of Hollywood.

The bifurcation between the "rational" live-action and "irrational" animated worlds is amplified by Eddie's investigation. Eddie has separated himself from the irrational animated world since his brother's death but now must confront the irrational confusion of the animated world to find Jessica. If this happens, Roger's depression will be lifted and his acting will improve. Glimpses of Toontown highlight its irrational confusion: Eddie enters a Toontown speakeasy only after stating an animation-friendly password, "Walt sent me." In the speakeasy, when Marvin Acme, who creates gags for Toontown, spills ink on Eddie, the ink disappears. A cartoon penguin even serves Eddie a drink with real rocks instead of ice.

Eddie's spying in Toontown also has irrational results. He discovers Acme in Jessica's dressing room and takes pictures of him playing patty-cake with her, pictures that throw Roger Rabbit into hysterics. Roger drinks whiskey, a potent drug for a toon, and explodes like a siren. He jumps out a window, presumably running to Jessica and

Acme. When Eddie discovers Acme has been killed by a dropped safe, then, Roger Rabbit is suspected in an investigation that provides a first glimpse of Doom, the officer in charge of the murder investigation. Doom has no respect for Eddie because he is a drunk and immediately blames Roger for the murder. Toontown is under Doom's jurisdiction. He intends to make toons respect the law, he says, revealing one of his ways to destroy nature. He has found a method of killing toons with a mixture of turpentine, acetone, and benzene.

Eddie becomes Doom's unlikely opponent, however, when Roger's guilt is called into question, first by his acting partner, Baby, and then by Acme's obituary picture. Since the will is seen sticking out of Acme's pocket, the picture validates Baby's claim that Acme had drafted a last will and testament that promised to leave Toontown to the toons. Eddie is further convinced of Roger's innocence when he finds Roger waiting for him. Roger claims he broke into his own home and wrote a love letter for Jessica but took it with him when the police arrived. When Doom's Toon Patrol arrives, Eddie agrees to help Roger and hides him in wash water. Eddie now works for a toon despite his animosity toward them and begins to close the gap between the human and toon worlds.

Because Eddie now doubts Roger's guilt, he agrees to investigate Acme's murder, first discovering through an interview with Jessica that Cloverleaf, which now owns the Red Trolley, also wants to own Toontown. Another motive for Acme's murder has been revealed, since his last will and testament has disappeared. Eddie teams up with Roger to solve the case, blurring boundaries between the rational and irrational, between culture and nature, and ultimately saving Toontown and the natural world. When a newsreel in their movie-theater hideout highlights a real-estate deal between Maroon Studios and Cloverleaf Enterprises, connections between Doom, Maroon Studios, and Acme's murder become clearer. Eddie interrogates Maroon and discovers that Cloverleaf Enterprises would not buy the studio until Acme sold his property. When Acme refused, he was killed. Before he can reveal more details, Maroon is shot, and Eddie escapes into Toontown.

It is in Toontown, the representative setting for the natural world, that Doom's destructive plan is revealed and thwarted. Eddie reenters Toontown after loading a toon gun in the tunnel between worlds. Toontown, as a natural world, is both more irrational and less corrupted than the Hollywood Eddie leaves behind. In Toontown the cartoon characters sing about being happy as Eddie rolls in. But the world defies logic. Eddie crashes into a piano. He sees what he thinks is Jessica in a window and climbs up in a toon elevator operated by a toon dog, Droopy. The woman is not Jessica but a Tex Avery–like female who chases Eddie into a bathroom without a floor. Eddie falls and, after a couple of gags with Bugs Bunny and Tweety Bird, lands in the woman's arms. She chases him, but he crashes her into the wall by moving the road.

When Eddie and Jessica confront Doom, they discover the scope of his plan. After an unsuccessful car chase, Doom exclaims, "In the next fifteen minutes, Toontown will be legally mine." Doom captures Eddie and Jessica. After Eddie and Jessica's toon car tells Roger where Doom has taken them, Roger learns more about Doom's plans for environmental destruction. He climbs through a bedroom window and overhears Doom's plan to annihilate and reconstruct Toontown and its "natural" setting. According to Doom, he is the sole stockholder for Cloverleaf Industries and has enough liquid death, his chemical mixture called Dip, to erase Toontown from the face of the earth and bring in a freeway. Doom killed Acme and Maroon for the freeway and all it offered—fast food, gas stations, motels, and billboards. "My God, it will be beautiful," he exclaims. Doom explains how his freeway plan through Toontown will be possible:

> That's right, my dear. Enough to Dip Toontown off the face of the earth. A vehicle of my own design. Five thousand gallons of heated Dip pumped at enormous velocity through a pressurized water cannon. Toontown will be erased in a matter of minutes. . . . Who's got time to wonder what happened to some ridiculous talking mice when you're driving by at seventy-five miles an hour?

Doom has also found a way to eliminate Los Angeles' existing public transportation system to force people into cars. Doom tells Jessica and Eddie:

> Several months ago, I had the good providence to stumble upon this plan of the City Council's. A construction plan of epic proportions. They're calling it a freeway! Lanes of shimmering cement running from here to Pasadena. Smooth, safe, fast. Traffic jams will be a thing of the past. I see a place where people get on and off the freeway. On and off. Off and on. All day, all night. Soon, where Toontown once stood will be a string of gas stations, inexpensive motels, restaurants that serve rapidly prepared food, tire salons, automobile dealerships, and wonderful, wonderful billboards reaching as far as the eye can see. Oh, they'll drive. They'll have to. You see, I bought the Red Car so I could dismantle it.

Roger wants to stop such a catastrophic end to his more natural world and attacks Doom. But Doom's thugs drop a ton of bricks on Roger and tie him up with Jessica, so Doom can torture them with his benzene spray. Because the poison spray destroys toons not humans, Eddie must save them, fending off multiple attacks from Doom.

Now that both environmentally destructive plans have been revealed, Eddie takes action. Once Doom discloses that he, too, is a toon, Eddie exclaims, "That lame-brain freeway idea could only come from a toon," to throw Doom off guard. Doom may represent live-action figures' own overdevelopment of suburban sprawl, but Doom, the only humanoid among animated animals, is the toon that killed his brother and now has a rotating saw for an arm! Eddie is on the ground but sees a shooting hammer and uses it to open up the poison sprayer on Doom. Doom melts like the Wicked Witch in *The Wizard of Oz*. The spraying machine moves closer to Roger and Jessica, but Eddie shoves them out of the way. The machine rolls harmlessly into Toontown and is destroyed. Eddie cleans and drains the floor, so they are all safe. Eddie, who hated all toons, has saved Toontown.

Since Toontown represents a more irrational natural world, Disney's *Flowers and Trees*, an animated Disney short valorizing nature, is on view outside the warehouse. Doom and his plan have been destroyed, and the case has been solved. Acme's will even reappears on the back of Roger's love letter in disappearing and reappearing ink.

Roger and Eddie connect the two worlds. Their parallels demonstrate that animated and live-action worlds can coexist peacefully. Roger reunites with Jessica, who exclaims, "C'mon Roger, let's go home. . . . I'll bake you a carrot cake." Eddie and his girlfriend Dolores reunite, as well, when a cab brings her and the live-action police to him. Roger zaps Eddie with a handshake gag, and Eddie pretends to be mad but kisses Roger. The "Smile" song and Porky Pig end the film with animated nature and live-action culture again at peace.

Although the interconnections between these two worlds only metaphorically parallel the biotic community valorized by organismic ecology, the environmental critique on display draws on both human and organismic approaches to ecology. It draws on human approaches that seek to eradicate pollutants like toxic Dip and organismic approaches that attempt to limit overdevelopment like those that Judge Doom plans. In this live-action, animated feature, then, blatant representations of the modern environmental movement are on display.

Enchanted, on the other hand, maintains a separation between the live-action and animated sequences. The majority of the film responds to the series of animated fairytale features that have been part of Disney fare since 1937's *Snow White*. In *Enchanted*, as in *Snow White*, *Sleeping Beauty*, and *Cinderella*, the female protagonist, Giselle (Amy Adams), maintains an interdependent relationship with nonhuman nature. In the animated space of the film's opening, forest animals from bluebirds to rabbits and an owl follow the pattern of the earlier Disney films and help prepare her for marriage by constructing a figure of a prince (James Marsden). Giselle encounters the prince in the forest. After she and the prince are engaged, animals coif her hair and assist with her dress on the way to the wedding.

In the live-action world Giselle enters when pushed into a well, she establishes a similar interdependent relationship with nonhuman nature. But she is now in an urban setting and summons pigeons, rats, and cockroaches instead of woodland creatures when she hums her working song. The animals help her clean her new friend's (Patrick Dempsey) apartment in a scene that comically points out the ridiculous nature of this conceit. When mice and bunnies become rats and cockroaches, they no longer meet the "cute" standard of Disney films, but they serve a similar ludicrous role—serving a princess-in-waiting by cleaning her house and sewing her clothes. Yet in *Enchanted*, nature and culture, nonhuman and human nature, meet

Who Framed Roger Rabbit: Roger Rabbit confronts housing development.

head-on. In fantasy the film demonstrates the effectiveness of interdependent relationships and perhaps demonstrates, at least metaphorically, the pull toward a biotic organismic community.

Combining live action with animation provides an effective way to emphasize the nature/culture binary, but it also, in these four films, highlights ways this binary breaks down when the two "worlds" collide, demonstrating the interdependent, interconnected relationships between human and nonhuman nature. *Who Framed Roger Rabbit* takes this connection further by critiquing humans' destruction of the natural world, either through toxic chemicals meant to kill toons or overdevelopment meant to pave over a natural (if animated) landscape and to serve a consumer culture driven by unhindered greed. Although later films combine live action with animation—see, for example, *Waking Life* (2001), *A Scanner Darkly* (2006), and *Avatar* (2009)—*The Girl Next Door, The Incredible Mr. Limpet, Who Framed Roger Rabbit,* and *Enchanted* demonstrate most effectively how such a mix may also illustrate the necessary alliance between the worlds of nature and culture and the ongoing influence of human and organismic approaches to ecology.

Mad Monster Party?: Frankenstein's destructive invention explodes.

FIVE

Rankin/Bass Studios, Nature, and the Supernatural

Where Technology Serves and Destroys

Unlike other studios discussed here, Rankin Bass—a pairing of Arthur Rankin Jr.'s artistic ability and Jules Bass's more business-conscious and practical understanding—produced stop-action animated shorts and features in which technological savvy was used to interrogate a variety of technological advances. In these films, technology is constructed as either a dream maker or a machine that disrupts a mythic natural garden. Although the studio is most well-known for producing a series of holiday iconic television specials, especially during the 1950s and 1960s, it also created at least four feature-length critiques of modernity, three in the 1960s and the last, their only hand-drawn feature, in 1982. These four animated features draw on the combined, perhaps contrasting, strengths of Arthur Rankin and Jules Bass. As Rankin explains, "Our intention was to combine his advertising know-how with my television and artistic know-how" (qtd. in Goldschmidt and Sykora).

This pairing of opposites seems to coincide with the two conflicting themes prevalent in the few feature films produced by the partners. Two of the four Rankin/Bass animated features released by the studio—*Willy McBean and His Magic Machine* (1965) and *Mad Monster Party?* (1967)—demonstrate the force of technology but also illustrate ways it can be integrated effectively into the world of human and nonhuman nature when used for constructive rather than destructive purposes. *The Daydreamer* (1966) and *The Last Unicorn* (1982), on the other hand, argue against disrupting the garden (a literal Garden of Eden in *The Daydreamer*) with knowledge and technology that overwhelm faith. Together, however, these four films all assert the need to guard against misuse of technology, science, and an epistemology that valorizes humans over nature. *Mad Monster Party?* most effectively advocates interdependence, however, since it offers hope that, when used effectively, artifacts of modern culture can serve both human and nonhuman nature.

Willy McBean and *Mad Monster Party?* rely on Rankin/Bass's "animagic" stop-motion process. These productions, as well as many of their animated productions, were animated in Japan. Throughout the 1960s, the animagic productions were headed by Japanese stop-motion animator Tadahito Mochinaga. Many of Rankin/Bass's traditional works were also animated in Japan, by the studio Top Craft, which was formed in 1972 as an offshoot of the legendary studio Toei Animation. Some of the Top Craft staffers, including the studio's founder Toru Hara (who was credited in some of Rankin/Bass's specials), would go on to join Studio Ghibli and work on Hayao Miyazaki's feature films, including *Nausicaa of the Valley of the Wind* (1984) and *My Neighbor Totoro* (1988).

Tadahito Mochinaga, however, created the puppet figures and settings that served Rankin/Bass so well in their early animagic features and holiday television specials.

Although based in science fiction rather than fact, *Willy McBean and His Magic Machine* uses animagic to illustrate the dangers of placing a technological wonder such as a time machine into the wrong hands, those of a mad scientist who wants to write himself literally into history. With this time machine, Professor Von Rotten attempts to integrate himself into key moments in Western history: replacing Wild Bill in a Tombstone, Arizona, gunfight, discovering America instead of Christopher Columbus, pulling King Arthur's sword from the stone, building the pyramids, and discovering fire for cave dwellers. With help from the professor's monkey, Pablo, however, Willy builds his own time machine and stops all of the professor's attempts. Ultimately, he successfully controls technology in *Willy McBean*, so that history can be preserved and the balance between nature and culture can be maintained.

Mad Monster Party? on the other hand, takes this critique further and anticipates and reacts to technological advances (the potential of nuclear weapons destroying humankind), illustrating one way to adapt to a changing landscape: destroy the monsters of humanity so that a "kinder" technology can prevail. In *Mad Monster Party?* technology is interrogated as both a dream maker and a machine that disrupts the garden. This stop action animagic film focuses on a mad scientist, Dr. Frankenstein, who has created the means to destroy matter. He declares, "Ha ha ha. Quoth the raven, 'Nevermore.' I've done it. Created the means to destroy matter. They must all know. Know that I, Baron von Frankenstein, master of the secret of creation, have now mastered the secret of destruction." He invites his monster colleagues to celebrate his discovery.

With this premise in place, monsters from Dracula to the Invisible Man fight for Frankenstein's formula. Frankenstein is retiring while "he's on top" and turning over all of his secrets to his nephew, Felix, a young pharmacist. After Frankenstein saves his nephew by destroying himself, the other monsters, and his island, Felix floats off with Frankenstein's assistant and his newfound love, Francesca. But the film ends with a twist. Francesca is "just a machine with hundreds of parts that will eventually wear out." And by the film's end, Felix also seems more like a machine than a human. The film, then, replaces the violent destruction of "monsters" like us with (apparently) peaceful android technology.

The years following the end of World War II produced great prosperity in the United States along with anxieties over the capabilities of science and technology to perfect methods of destroying the planet. While much of the world slowly recovered from the massive loss of life and property, the major Cold War powers continued to develop and test atomic and hydrogen bombs and the means to deliver them by land, air, and sea. Nuclear testing most powerfully highlighted humans' ability to destroy the world.

Atmospheric nuclear testing persisted in the United States and the USSR until the 1960s and continued in China until the 1980s. At the same time, the means to deliver unstoppable nuclear weapons also led to the space race, manned orbits around the Earth, and to John F. Kennedy's promise that a man would land on the moon by the end of the 1960s. The disturbing above-ground testing of radioactive weapons finally led to the Limited Test Ban Treaty of 1963, but advanced societies brandished the hair-trigger warnings of instant and total annihilation. These destructive repercussions contrast with technological advances such as Dr. Christiaan Barnard's successful 3 December 1967 heart transplant in South Africa. Such conflicts reinforce Dr. Frankenstein's boast in *Mad Monster Party?* He could now create and destroy life, the two contradictory repercussions of technological advancement explored in *Mad Monster Party?*

Technology and its oppositional uses become transparent in *Mad Monster Party?* not only because the film illustrates how technological creations can either destroy or revive the world. As Goldschmidt and Sykora explain, the film production in *Mad Monster Party?* also integrates filmic technology with the Rankin/Bass animagic stop-motion puppet technique and puppets whose strings are sometimes in view, according to Walter Chaw of *Film Freak Central.* Howard Thompson of the *New York Times* explains, "In this peppery and contagiously droll little color package, a collection of animated puppets scamper across some clever miniature sets, exchanging sass and barbs and occasionally warbling some sprightly tunes. The rubbery-faced puppets themselves are modeled after the best-known movie 'monsters.'"

Walter Chaw calls *Mad Monster Party?* "a sort of Jay Ward Lite stop-motion revue featuring the vocal talents of Boris Karloff (shudder) and Phyllis Diller (shudder) as well as Allen Swift doing his best Jimmy Stewart, Peter Lorre, and Bela Lugosi." For Chaw, the animation aesthetics and technology make up for a thin plotline. With help from *Mad* magazine's Harvey Kurtzman, the film spoofed monster movies with a series of comic scenes and characters. Kurtzman not only helped found *Mad* and created some of its most memorable characters, including Alfred E. Neuman (the comic face on every cover of *Mad*). He also influenced the ideological direction of the magazine, an adult comic book that drew on and critiqued contemporary issues, just as his antiwar comic strip *Hey There!* did from 1946 to 1950. According to Don Markstein's *Toonpedia*, *Mad* began by "poking fun" at other comic books and then poked fun at American icons, so much so that "local governments banned it, a man selling a copy to a policeman was arrested for selling what the cop called 'disgusting' literature, and even the FBI investigated it—more than once!" Such censorship in the 1950s is explored extensively in David Hajdu's *Ten Cent Plague: The Great Comic-Book Scare and How It Changed America*.

Markstein explains that Kurtzman served as the magazine's top cartoonist from 1952–56 before leaving to illustrate other adult avant-garde magazines such as *Trump* (for *Playboy*) and *Humbug*. His *Help!* lasted from 1960–65 with twenty-six issues in all. It was at *Help!* that Kurtzman became the first editor to publish the work of R. Crumb (*Fritz the Cat*), Gilbert Shelton (*Wonder Warthog*), and Jay Lynch (*Nard 'n' Pat*). He continued drawing Little Annie Fanny cartoons for *Playboy* until 1988.

Kurtzman was foremost a cartoonist. His first cartoon was published in *Tip Top Comics* when he was fifteen. After graduating from the High School of Music and Art, he began working for comic-book creator Lou Ferstadt and continued cartooning until his death in 1993. According to *Film Freak Central*, "*Mad Monster Party* is a mod-phile's dream—all hipster chic set to the nostalgic rhythms of Rankin & Bass' perverse sensibilities." The review also argues that the film influenced Tim Burton and Henry Selick's *The Nightmare before Christmas*, "proving Burton's contention that stop-motion displays the touch of true anima with each movement manipulated by a human hand."

The opening shots of *Mad Monster Party?* reinforce this connection with *The Nightmare before Christmas*, since they highlight skeletons and raven puppets in a dark forest outside a mad scientist's castle. As an ingeniously constructed animated puppet figure, the mad scientist tests the contents of his new formula by giving a drop to a bird. The bird flies over to a tree, lands, and explodes. While opening credits roll, Dr. Frankenstein sends party invitations to Frankenstein, Dracula, Werewolf, Mummy, Dr. Jekyll and Mr. Hyde, the Hunchback of Notre Dame, and the Invisible Man. He plans to unveil his new invention at a "Mad Monster Party."

His nephew, Felix, a pharmacist who looks more like a professor than a monster, receives one of the invitations. Felix's character contrasts with the rest of the party guests, not only because he is a bumbling assistant who drops more bottles than he fills, but also because he projects an honest innocence that allows his boss, Mr. Kronkite (a play on Krankheit, the German word for illness), to continue employing him despite his clumsiness.

Differences between the monsters and Felix's naive and clumsy intellectualism are immediately revealed. The Monster's Mate (Phyllis Diller) sings a song, "You're Different," to her husband, Frankenstein, while, in Dr. Frankenstein's laboratory, a Venus flytrap eats a watering can. Francesca, Dr. Frankenstein's secretary, seems surprised when the doctor receives word that Felix Flankin is coming to the party and tells Frankenstein, "We also received a very strange reply from someone who says he's arriving on the 13th. Someone named Felix Flankin."

Dr. Frankenstein exclaims, "He's coming? That is good news. What else does he write?"

Felix's letter reveals the naive bent of his character: "Looking forward to meeting all those fun people at your resort," Francesca jokes. "Resort? Fun people? He doesn't mean Dracula and the Werewolf surely," Francesca continues before finishing the letter. "Can't hardly wait to dip into the pool in the front of your resort and lie on your beautiful beach." Francesca asks him about Felix, saying, "Doctor, does he know about the crocodiles in the lagoon and the quicksand on the beach? Who or what is this Flankin?"

Dr. Frankenstein's reply points to the film's negative representation of humans: "Oh, don't be alarmed. Felix Flankin is a mere human." Dr. Frankenstein tells his secretary that his nephew Felix's mother was the white sheep in the family, so he plans to bequeath his island and secret formulas to him. At the party, he will present him as his successor.

Felix's difference from the monsters is amplified on board the ship leading to the island. Since he has lost his glasses, Felix does not fear the Werewolf or the Invisible Man. When he meets Dr. Jekyll, he sees him turn himself into Mr. Hyde and believes he is telling him to play hide-and-seek. In a scene right out of *Mad*, Mr. Hyde keeps pointing and saying, "Hyde. Hyde." But Felix only replies, "Hide? You want me to hide? Well if you want to play games, you must be feeling better. Certainly don't look it. OK, I'll hide and you try and find me."

The monsters object to Dr. Frankenstein's plan to leave Felix his formulas primarily because he is human and, in their minds, inferior, so Dracula seems ready to follow Francesca's plan and kill Felix for the formula. Dracula asks her, "What kind of a monster is he? A ghoul? A demon? A spook, or . . . ?" And Francesca answers, "A human." Dracula reinforces the film's negative representation of humans. "They're the worst kind," he declares. With Francesca's help, Dracula attempts and fails to kill Felix three times.

As if to heighten the bifurcation between human and machine, Dracula, Frankenstein, and Frankenstein's wife double-cross Francesca, but she falls into a secret passage and sends a note by bat across the sea to bring King Kong to destroy them. Felix fishes in the moat to think about the doctor's offer and decides to turn it down, saying, "Felix Flankin, head of the World Wide Organization of Monsters. I can't do it. I just can't do it. I could never face that board of directors." But Francesca, while trying to escape, falls into the moat. By chance, Felix saves her life. She falls in love with him, and, in a blurring of boundaries, she agrees to escape the island with him.

Ultimately, Francesca and Felix do escape and, with help from Doctor Frankenstein, thwart the monsters. When it is clear that Felix and Francesca have escaped, the doctor blows up the island and with it himself, the monsters, and the ape. The doctor says, "You wanted my vial, you'd kill my nephew for it? Now you shall see that Baron von Frankenstein is not one to cross. True you won't see it for too long a time, but for one second, oh boy."

Now it seems that humans have not only overcome the supernatural monsters that would attack them but also ensured that technology, even that which destroys, remains in their hands. Felix asks Francesca to marry him, telling her, "My place isn't much. Two small rooms, a furnished medicine cabinet, but we'll be married. And soon there will be the sound of little Flankins running around."

But Francesca starts to cry, "Oh, Felix."

And Felix asks her, "What? What have I said? We'll get a bigger place. I'll give up sneezing. What is it?" She demurs, saying, "I'm just a machine with hundreds of parts that will eventually wear out."

But in a surprising twist, Felix reveals that he, too, is a machine. He tells her, "Well, Francesca, none of us are perfect [click] are perfect [click] are perfect [click] are perfect [click]," and the film ends. This repeated phrase highlights for Francesca their common origin—technological innovation. Felix, the so-called mere human, shows us that he is a technological "other," so different that this last scene pays homage to *Some Like It Hot* (1959) in which Jack Lemmon's character (Jerry "Daphne"), dressed as a woman, floats off in a boat with another man, Osgood Fielding III (Joe E. Brown), who loves Daphne in spite of her gender and, like Felix, exclaims "nobody's perfect."

In *Mad Monster Party?* creatures constructed by humans (Francesca and Felix) prove more humane than their creators, and technology housed in Felix and Francesca offers the world a second chance. Felix comments on this rebirth by remarking, while watching The Isle of Evil being obliterated, "I know it's wrong, but I have a tremendous urge to sing Auld Lang Syne." Felix and Francesca will marry and, if technology permits, hear "the sound of little Flankins running around."

Arthur Rankin Jr. and Jules Bass's *Mad Monster Party?* negotiates a solution to the binary set up by technological advancement. If technology can be either good or evil in human hands, with little control over the outcome, why not try another tactic?—place the world in the hands of technology itself. When humanity proves so destructive it destroys itself, it may be better if technology takes its place, rejuvenating a once-human world and its cultures and bringing peace to a war-driven civilization.

In *The Daydreamer* and *The Last Unicorn*, however, any machine in the garden disrupts its peace. These Rankin/Bass features—the first a mixture of live action and animagic, the second traditional celluloid-drawn animation—illustrate the danger of technological advancement and the knowledge on which it builds. Technology in these two features proves too destructive to facilitate, even in hands that are more "peaceful." Leo Marx's *Machine in the Garden* describes America as a lush, unexplored "garden" that is in a tumultuous relationship with the "machine," or social and technological advancements throughout American history. The machine overwhelms the garden and attempts to cultivate raw resources for consumption. Marx's thesis, therefore, is that the machine alters the landscape in order to make it fit current measures of productivity. Both *Daydreamer* and *The Last Unicorn* reinforce this premise.

Leo Marx bases his argument on two different definitions of the pastoral, "one that is popular and sentimental, the other imaginative and complex." The first, a sentimental type, is "an expression less of thought than of feeling." According to Marx, "An obvious example is the current 'flight from the city'" (5). In literature, however, Marx asserts, the pastoral becomes imaginative and complex, as when Washington Irving describes Sleepy Hollow as a peaceful space where humans and nature can interconnect, "a state of being in which there is no tension either within the self or between the self and the environment" (13) until the peace, Irving writes, is broken by "the whistle of the locomotive—the long shriek, harsh, above all harshness, for the space of a mile cannot mollify it into harmony" (qtd. in Marx 13). Marx sees this as a revelation of sorts that illustrates his more complex vision of the pastoral. As Marx explains, "What began as a conventional tribute to the pleasures of withdrawal from the world—a simple pleasure fantasy—is transformed by the interruption of the machine into a far more complex state of mind" (15).

Scott MacDonald's *The Garden in the Machine* illustrates how such a vision of the pastoral translates into American film. In his study, MacDonald is "fascinated by a considerable number of modern American Independent films that, by both accident and design, have invigorated traditions of thought and image-making generally thought to characterize the nineteenth century" (2). He reinforces "the importance of landscape in American cultural history," noting that "landscape was a dominant issue in American painting and writing throughout the nineteenth century and . . . has remained crucial throughout this century, as the nineteenth-century fascination with 'wilderness' and 'nature' increasingly gave way, first, to a focus on cityscape and city life and, more recently, to a fascination with the forms of human signification that, in our postmodernist period, are the inevitable overlay of both countryside and city" (3).

But our "earlier fascinations do not simply disappear" (3). According to MacDonald, at least some independent filmmakers "share an interest in landscape with nineteenth-century artists and writers" because, especially in the 1960s and 1970s, "a broad and penetrating cultural critique was essential" for filmmakers, and "was often directed at the commercialism of Hollywood" (4). MacDonald explores Larry Gottheim's *Fog Line* (1970) to illustrate how such a critique might hark back to nineteenth-century visions of landscape. According to MacDonald, the film demonstrates "the intersection of natural process and human technology" (10), a theme found in paintings such as Thomas Cole's *The Oxbow* (1836). In the context of *Fog Line*, however, "history had transformed the American scene from a garden housing a potentially dangerous machine into a continental machine in which vestiges of that garden, or really metaphors for it, are safely contained within grids of roads, fields, and power lines" (11–12).

The same effect is explored in *Daydreamer* and *The Last Unicorn*. Whereas *Mad Monster Party?* and, to a certain extent, *Willie McBean* valorize "the machine," as long as it is in the right hands, *Daydreamer* and *The Last Unicorn* emphasize the disruptive force of a machine, even a subjective one like unfettered humans empowered by supernatural elements—a Sandman in *Daydreamer*, and a curse in *The Last Unicorn*. As in Larry Gottheim's *Fog Line*, "all that remains of an earlier concept of untouched wilderness and of the ideal, pastoral 'middle state' is an illusion" (12). Although in *Fog Line* the machine "functions entirely within those technological systems developed to exploit it," in *Daydreamer* and *The Last Unicorn* it functions entirely within the world of fairy tale and fantasy.

Illustrating this fairy-tale world, the narrator begins *Daydreamer* as a Sandman in blue clouds (Cyril Ritchard) looking down on "one small friend" in a pristine pastoral landscape. The friend, Chris (Paul O'Keefe), is the son of an unsuccessful shoemaker (Jack Gilford) who will not sell his wedding ring, gives his son the larger bowl of food, and talks about the Garden of Paradise while they work on Chris's studies. The garden entices Chris, because if he finds it he will never have to study again. The blue figure—the Sandman—comes to him. The mice who make shoes watch as Chris asks the Sandman to show him the Garden of Paradise, and the Sandman puts him to sleep. In this supernatural world, the Sandman takes Chris through a series of trials to determine whether he is worthy to see the garden.

When Chris wakes up for his first trial, he is an animated (stop-action) figure floating in a boat in an animated world. The river where he floats becomes wide and dangerous with tall waves that look like shining colored cellophane in a storm. When he falls out of the boat and into the sea, a little mermaid (Hayley Mills) saves him and takes him to her family's castle under the ocean. Neptune (Burl Ives), her father, says the boy has drowned. He only has an immortal soul, so the little mermaid wants to help save his body. When she learns about the sea witch (Tallulah Bankhead) from her sisters, she visits her and agrees to live as an outcast if the boy does not love her after taking a potion that revives him.

With unselfish devotion, she sacrifices herself for Chris, but he reveals to her sisters that he is going to the Garden of Paradise and cannot stay. Instead of feeling bitterness, the mermaid sacrifices herself again and shows him the way to Paradise. She hopes to go with him, but he says she will be in the way. She cries when he leaves, but Chris wakes up in his boat and selfishly continues his quest for knowledge, unwilling to share it with the little mermaid who must now live as an exile from her family.

When Chris awakens for his next trial, he is again an animated figure. This time he is lying beside a road when two men in suits walk by. They are Zilch (Terry-Thomas) and Zenith (Victor Borge). They say they will take him to the Garden of Paradise if he finishes a job for them. Chris agrees and carries fabrics to a castle, where a king admires himself in a mirror, singing, "He looks simply wonderful in bourbon/sable/satin." But the king is unsatisfied with every piece.

The familiar story of the emperor's new clothes ensues. But in this version, Chris sees the subterfuge the tailors are weaving and does nothing. The tailors claim they are from France and extort money for cloth, gold, and silver thread while Chris builds their loom. As in the fairy tale, they only pretend to weave cloth and sew new clothes for the king. Instead, they tell the king they have made him clothing that only those who are not fools can see, so almost everyone claims they can see the cloth, including Chris. The king even joins a parade wearing invisible clothing, "naked as a newborn to tell a wise man from a fool." None but a child will admit he is nude. The townspeople chase Chris and the tailors off.

Chris has again failed his trial, thinking of himself instead of others. But when he is chained as a poacher, Thumbelina (Patty Duke) helps Chris, again demonstrating how to sacrifice unselfishly for another. Chris eats a seed and shrinks to the size of a thumb, so he can get away. They are welcomed into a rat's home where the rat (Boris Karloff) offers them cheese tea. After they go to bed in bunk beds, Chris hears the rat talking to a mole (Sessue Hayakawa) and is given a chance to help Thumbelina. The mole plans to buy Thumbelina for his bride, and the rat plans to take Chris as his slave. The next day the rat sends them to get "medicine" from the mole, so the mole will give them gold to purchase Thumbelina. Thumbelina again acts with unselfish empathy, but Chris thinks only of himself. They pass a dead bird on the way, and Thumbelina wraps it in her coat. She goes back and gives it a blanket that night. She even plans to take Chris to her paradise, but he does not want to stay small and refuses, leaving her behind to meet her fate, again selfishly destroying nature as he seeks "paradise."

After this self-centered act, Chris floats away and sings, "Real Lucky Guy," falling asleep in the walnut boat safe from outside threats. When he awakens, he asks the Sandman why he cannot find paradise. The Sandman says it is because he has deserted his friends, highlighting the need for interconnected relationships. When Chris promises, "I'll never let my own ambitions hurt others," a flower near them grows, and Chris is in the Garden of Paradise. It is bright orange and pink with birds and seeds and a flowering tree of knowledge. He must resist the temptation to eat the flower of knowledge but still wants to stay, so the Sandman agrees, telling him that the garden will disappear from Earth. He will be lost forever in the land of nothingness if he leaves. Chris's every wish will be revealed instantly if he stays. But a devil tempts him, and he eats one of the flowers. The tree turns into a gnarled root, the garden disappears. The devil pushes him into a crack in the earth, but Chris wakes up with a duckling on his chest. He is chained. His father is being pulled toward them. The father pays the game warden with Chris's mother's ring, and they go home, where the father is still a lousy shoemaker and motivates his son to do his lessons. Chris is saved, then, only when he accepts help and recognizes the interconnected relationship between nature and culture. *The Daydreamer* demonstrates that disrupting the garden destroys both human and nonhuman nature. The garden of nonhuman nature must be preserved for the survival of all.

The Last Unicorn, a fully animated film, also highlights the need to separate nature from culture in order to preserve it. According to Janet Maslin, "With a screen play by Peter S. Beagle based on the novel, the movie takes the shape of a whimsical, picaresque adventure, preoccupied with the differences between myth and reality." This myth and reality also correspond with the film's exploration of problems of nature in opposition to culture.

The film's opening highlights this binary. In a pristine landscape, birds sing in a blue forest with a flute accompanying them, an opening that Ken Hanke describes as "terrific multiplane camerawork of a forest done up in the colors of a Maxfield Parrish painting." The camera pans past a waterfall and then draws back, panning around to a well-lit stream. A dog and hunters come out of the woods. A unicorn's shadow appears. The hunters have bows and arrows and speak about the landscape as they ride on horseback: "Why is it always spring here?" they wonder.

When one of the hunters sees the unicorn (Mia Farrow) he warns her, "Stay in your forest and keep your trees green, for you are the last"; however, the unicorn disagrees. She declares, "We did not vanish." Asking herself, "Am I truly the last?" she begins a quest for more of her kind beyond the pristine garden in which she lives.

To heighten this pristine garden scene, a butterfly (Robert Klein) lands on the unicorn's horn and sings "everything from pop standards to poetry by Yeats," according to Hanke. The butterfly song turns into a medley, and the butterfly seems not to know the unicorn's name. She asks him if he has seen others like her, but words work like analogies to the butterfly, who sings songs that connect to the questions the unicorn asks. Disappointed, the unicorn declares, "All butterflies know are songs and poetry and anything else they hear." The unicorn wanders on. "I must find someone who has seen others like me," she says. Then the butterfly calls her name and tells her to listen to his tale about how a "red bull followed close behind and covered their footprints." With horns of a wild ox, he pushed the unicorns to the ends of the earth, the butterfly explains. The unicorn must leave the forest to find out if others exist and if they need her help. She looks at the other animals but leaves, noting, "I must go quickly and come back as soon as I can." She runs through flowers, an autumn wood, and then a winter forest, showing how much time has passed and perhaps highlighting the death of her natural world.

As if to emphasize this view of nature as subordinate to culture, the scene shifts to a farmer who tries to catch the unicorn with his belt. He says she will be the prettiest white mare, since her horn is not visible to him. She bats away the belt and runs, telling herself, "I had forgotten man cannot see unicorns, so other unicorns may exist without anyone knowing it."

The unicorn's pristine landscape has all but disappeared as she travels farther beyond her forest, even sleeping beside a roadway, a disruption of her world. Here a witch, Mommy Fortuna (Angela Lansbury), captures her for her midnight carnival. Schmendrick (Alan Arkin), a magician riding with the unicorn, tries to protect her. The witch puts a sleep spell on the unicorn, and a troll cages her. Captured and paralyzed, the unicorn grows weaker, a parallel to the receding natural environment around her.

The menagerie itself is unnatural, a series of caged creatures disguised by the witch. Only the Harpy—a mythological creature that is part woman, part bird—is real. With the wizard's help, however, the unicorn escapes. The unicorn frees all the beasts, even the Harpy. The Harpy flies away but does not kill the unicorn. She kills the witch instead and eats her. The unicorn takes the magician with her. She tells her companions, "You must never run from anything immortal," while admitting she cannot make the magician's magic real. Now an interdependent relationship between nature, represented by the unicorn, and culture, represented by the magician, has formed.

Illustrating this relationship, the magician and unicorn

The Last Unicorn: The last unicorn in her pristine wood.

work together to thwart a band of outlaws led by Captain Cully (Keenan Wynn). As they walk, one of the bandits, Molly (Tammy Grimes), joins them because she recognizes the unicorn and yearns for the pristine nature the unicorn represents. "Where have you been?" she asks, explaining that she has been looking for a unicorn all her life. She also directs them to King Haggard's (Christopher Lee) castle, where the red bull lives. They travel through a dying forest to get to the castle. With the innocent nature of the unicorns gone, the environment suffers.

Although the red bull attempts to capture the unicorn, Schmendrick the magician intervenes, again demonstrating their interconnection. The magician can only capture her in a human form in which, according to Molly, she will go mad. Ultimately, however, the unicorn, the magician, and Molly save the other unicorns from Haggard and, in the process, save nature, the natural garden they represent.

Once Molly and Schmendrick enter the red bull's lair through the clock mentioned in a riddle, the unicorn herds the red bull to the sea. The other unicorns come out on waves and run to shore. King Haggard watches, and his castle starts to fall apart. The king and his castle fall into the sea as the unicorn runs toward freedom. The unicorn stays and comforts Molly and uses her horn to help Haggard's adopted son, Prince Lir (Jeff Bridges), who had fallen in love with her human body.

After the unicorn runs away, the prince, magician, and Molly find themselves in a lush green world. The prince rides away, but the magician asks Molly to go with him, and the unicorn comes to him. "You are a true wizard now," she tells him. "Has it made you happy?" she asks. The unicorn is afraid to go home because she now feels regret. She tells the magician not to be sad since unicorns are in the world again. Her own words comfort her: "I will try to go home," she says. The world turns green wherever she runs, returning to its pristine state where human and nonhuman nature can thrive side by side.

Conclusion

In *The Last Unicorn*, as in *Daydreamer*, the world of nature conflicts with the destructive technology-driven world of culture, even in the films' fantasy settings. Yet in a move that harks back to Leo Marx, as in *Mad Monster Party?* interdependent relationships between humans and the natural world preserve the garden. The last unicorn must pair up with a wizard to free other unicorns and preserve the natural world they sustain. Chris, the daydreamer, learns that the garden he seeks can only exist if nonhuman nature is preserved. These four films from Rankin/Bass Studios demonstrate the power of human-driven or supernatural technology as a force that destroys when placed in most humans' hands. Only those willing to view the relationship between nature and culture as interdependent will save and maintain a "garden" that ultimately preserves us all, a garden preserved, perhaps, by a land ethic rooted in organismic approaches to ecology.

The Fox and the Hound: Hound dog Copper saves his
fox friend, Tod.

SIX

Disney in the 1960s and 1970s

Blurring Boundaries between Human and Nonhuman Nature

Whereas studios such as UPA and Rankin/Bass embraced modernism thematically or aesthetically or both, Disney Studios stayed in conflict with modernism, even while engaging the technology of the modern age. Steven Watts described Walt Disney as "a sentimental modernist" (87). Although Disney experimented with the forms and techniques of modernist art, "[h]is true aesthetic heart . . . continued to beat to an internal rhythm of nineteenth-century sentimental realism," a realism Watts equates with the Victorian age. According to Watts, "Modernism emerged in direct opposition to the principles and sensibilities of nineteenth-century Victorianism," seeking to reconcile dichotomies perpetuated by Victorianism: "human and animal, civilized and savage, reason and emotion, intellect and instinct, conscious and unconscious." Disney both embraced and resisted this modernist move, blurring boundaries based on the separation of reality and fantasy in his aesthetic while valorizing Victorian binaries that perpetuated a bourgeois status quo. Disney counters a sometimes modernist aesthetic with "flourishes of sentiment and naturalism" (92) in many of his films, highlighting an orthodox domesticity that conflicts with modernist ideals.

Peter Pan (1953) illustrates such orthodox domesticity in relation to fantasy and hyperrealist aesthetics. In the film two boys and their older sister enter the fantastical realm of Peter Pan but return home to a domestic space in which Wendy must acknowledge her need to leave the playroom of her childhood and embrace her feminine role as a mother figure who must separate from fantasy and imagine only in dreams. An overhead shot of London opens the film, showing the bourgeois household to which Wendy must return, a Victorian house in which Wendy and her brothers still believe in the fantasy of Peter Pan. Because of their continuing belief in fantasy, Peter Pan appears and takes them to Neverland. John and Michael play pirates because they believe Peter Pan is a real person. Wendy, the eldest, not only believes, but she is also, according to the narrator, the authority on Peter Pan.

Their mother, Mrs. Darling, believes in the spirit of childhood. But their father, Mr. Darling, is too practical for dreams; he represents the extreme sublimation of fantasy. Because he is harried, he stumbles several times while searching for cuff links. He laments a shirt bib ruined by one of his son's drawings. After these mishaps, their father's annoyance transfers to Wendy, the eldest. She must stop acting like a child and believing in fantasy, he seems to say, telling her this is her last night in the nursery. It is time for her to grow up, he explains. In this harried state, the father even banishes the dog, Nana, outside, because he stumbles over her on the way out the door.

Wendy, on the other hand, represents the fantasy realm she must leave behind when she grows up. She tells her brothers stories of Peter Pan and his shadow. And because Peter Pan and Tinkerbell overhear, they appear and search for and find Peter's shadow, and Wendy sews it back on. Fantasy and reality have merged for the children. Only Wendy's urge to kiss Peter Pan and Tinkerbell's attempts to stop her foreshadow Wendy's movement into an adulthood devoid of tangible fantasy. Because of their childhood innocence, however, the children learn to fly with the "We Can Fly" song, and Peter takes Michael, John, and Wendy back to Neverland. In Neverland they all experience a series of adventures with Captain Hook, Tinkerbell, the Lost Boys, "Indians," and mermaids. In this fantasy world, however, Wendy grows jealous of an Indian maiden who shows interest in Peter, and she moves closer to an adulthood in which fantasies exist only in dreams.

Back at the hideout, Wendy takes on another adult role when she reminds the boys of their mothers, tells them stories, and tries to protect them from Captain Hook. Because of Tinkerbell's jealousy, Hook captures Wendy and the boys and takes them to his ship. Ultimately, Tinkerbell feels remorse and escapes the ship to save Peter Pan from Hook's bomb. Peter comes back and defeats the pirates with the children's help. Wendy and her brothers' fantasy must end here, however, so their parents will not worry. Peter Pan flies Wendy and her brothers home in the pirate ship, before their parents return from their party. As Peter leaves, Wendy watches the ship out the window. The parents look out and see it floating across the moon. They remember their own childhoods, and the song "You Can Fly" ends the film. But the domestic sphere has been perpetuated. Fantastical elements are allowed only in memories and dreams. Wendy has returned for her last night in the nursery before adulthood requires separating fantasy from reality, at least according to Victorian mores.

This adherence to "orthodoxy" continued in most of

the Disney films from the 1960s forward. But in several films both before and after Walt Disney's death, Disney blurs boundaries between "human and animal, civilized and savage, reason and emotion, intellect and instinct, conscious and unconscious" (Watts 87). Because of such blurring, the binary between human and nonhuman nature breaks down. Borders become more permeable while still adhering to the ideas of sentimental populism Watts describes. According to Watts, Disney "carried into adulthood an ideology—like his aesthetics, it was instinctive and emotional rather than systematic and articulate—that glorified ordinary Americans, blended democratic sympathies and cultural conservatism, and flowered from the roots in his rural, Midwestern background" (96).

In *Sleeping Beauty* (1959), for example, the Russian ballet is transformed into a fairy-tale story like *Snow White* and *Cinderella* in which domestic bliss is achieved with the help of woodland creatures such as birds and rabbits. Aurora, the princess in *Sleeping Beauty,* and nature are one in a rural cottage and meadows where she hides from an evil curse. As Aurora sings, an owl dons a prince's cape to dance with her, and birds hold up the sleeves as they join in. All the animals support her in the meadow. And of the three fairies that save her, each represents a natural element. Here nature and the supernatural are one, with Maleficent, the evil fairy who cast the spell to place Aurora into an eternal sleep, turning a forest into a briar patch that looks as mean as she is. She even turns into a dragon to fight Prince Philip and to keep him from kissing and awakening Aurora. The two sides of nature reside in the two extremes of supernatural, but the "good" side wins. Domestic bliss is restored. In *Sleeping Beauty* domesticity is a force as natural as the creatures that help Aurora attain her dream of marriage to a prince and a happily-ever-after ending.

The same domestic bliss is attained and perpetuated in *One Hundred and One Dalmatians* (1961), but this time the nuclear family, living in the Victorian era, includes a pair of Dalmatians and their pups. Cruella De Vil serves as the source of environmental destruction in *One Hundred and One Dalmatians*. She traipses everywhere in fur and finds Dalmatians' coats so appealing that she wants to collect them to make a coat of her own. In fact, she buys or steals ninety-nine Dalmatians, including fifteen puppies from the mate (Perdita) of the film's narrator. Pongo the narrator serves his "pet" human Roger so well that he finds him a mate, Anita, and in turn finds Perdita. Cruella's henchmen steal their pups, however, when Roger refuses to sell them, and they hide them in a country house with the other eighty-four pups, waiting for them to age, so their spots will appear.

Roger and Anita fail in their attempts to find the pups, so the two adult Dalmatians, Pongo and Perdita, work together with other country animals in an underground intelligence-gathering structure like that in Fritz Lang's *M* (1931). They find the pups in the abandoned De Vil country house and rescue them. During their escape, the dogs demonstrate their intelligence repeatedly: walking along a stream to avoid footprints, wiping a road clean of tracks with a tree branch, and covering themselves in soot to hide their spots. Pongo and Perdita get the dogs home by Christmastime. "Cruella De Vil" is playing on the radio, a sign of prosperity to come. Roger and Anita can now keep all ninety-nine pups and save them from the clutches of Cruella.

Cruella shows us that in this filmic context fur coats are a product of murder and intrigue and desired only by evil witchlike humans willing to kill puppies in cold blood. In a beautiful hand-drawn film, environmental messages are blatant. Animals have rights that overrule a human's desire for fur. In fact, animals outwit even the benevolent humans in the film, proving their superiority even to Roger and Anita, not masters but pets of Pongo and Perdita. Yet their efforts are motivated by a desire to build and maintain a domestic space that embraces traditional values and orthodoxy, not modernist ideals.

Other Disney films from this period follow a similar pattern in which characters move through trials, usually with the involvement of nonhuman nature, but ultimately achieve an orthodox domestic bliss. Consider, for example, *The Sword in the Stone* (1963), *Mary Poppins* (1964), *The Jungle Book* (1967), *Bedknobs and Broomsticks* (1971), *Robin Hood* (1973), *Pete's Dragon* (1977), and *The Many Adventures of Winnie the Pooh* (1977). In these films, as in most later Disney films, including *The Little Mermaid* (1989) and *Lilo and Stitch* (2002), nature serves to perpetuate the status quo, to help characters escape uncontrolled "wild" nature, and to enter a "garden" in which both nonhuman and human nature are controlled by the rules of domesticity. As David Whitley explains in *The Idea of Nature in Disney Animation*, "The cultural work of the films of the Disney era tends towards making wild nature safe . . . as it is made to perform in harmony with domestic rituals" (14).

Although this loss of "wild" nature seems bittersweet in *Mary Poppins*, *The Jungle Book*, *Pete's Dragon*, and *Winnie the Pooh*, it is also constructed as necessary and desired in order to "grow up" and become a responsible adult who can succeed in this domesticated culture. In *Winnie the Pooh*, for example, the last film chapter highlights Christopher Robin's goodbye to the animals of the wood. "All stories have an ending, you know," he says. But Christopher Robin is going away to school and asks Pooh to come see him when he has nothing to do. Pooh agrees, proud to be asked to visit a grown-up boy. In order to "grow up," Christopher Robin must leave wild nature behind.

Lee Artz takes Watts's premise regarding Disney's domestic orthodoxy further, asserting that "Disney successfully reflects, clarifies, and popularises existing dominant cultural values and meanings. . . . Indeed, the communication of specific dominant themes such as individual happiness, family values, and the triumph of good over evil, is remarkably consistent across cultures." According to Artz, "In the process of being entertained, we are held hostage to a highly individualistic, consumerist perspective that leads us to understand these films in terms of social privilege and individual escapism." Although most of the Disney animated features, before and after Walt Disney controlled the studio, do perpetuate these values and "dismiss . . . solidarity, democracy and concern for community needs and interests" (Artz), at least a few films subvert these values and the dominant ideology on which they rest.

Although products of a post-"classic" Disney period in which the studio struggled to recover from the loss of its founder, three Disney films from 1970, 1977, and 1982, at least to a certain extent, call this domestic orthodoxy into question and valorize an "irrational" uncontrollable nonhuman nature as a space for both adventure and creativity. *The Aristocats* (1970), *The Rescuers* (1977), and *The Fox and the Hound* (1982) not only demonstrate the need for an interdependent relationship between human and nonhuman nature. In a nod toward organismic approaches to ecology, they also suggest that domesticated culture need not subsume irrational nature for both to thrive.

As a reverse of *Gay Purr-ee*, *The Aristocats* takes a city cat and her kittens and places them in the country, taking them from a domestic Victorian space to the wild. Ultimately, wild nature meets and changes even the domesticated Victorian household the cats seek to retain. The cats are pampered pets of Madame, a rich English woman in Paris, who opens the film in her carriage riding through Paris in 1910. Duchess, the mother cat, and her three kittens are welcome members of the family in Madame's mansion.

Edgar, Madame's butler, however, resents his role as servant to cats. When he overhears Madame talking with the lawyer about leaving all she owns to her cats, he realizes he must preserve his own domestic bliss. According to her last will and testament, Edgar will inherit only after the cats are gone. To speed up his inheritance of the mansion and its treasures, Edgar makes a plan to get rid of Duchess and her kittens.

This thin plot reinforces Eric Henderson's claim that *The Aristocats* "is one of the slightest of [its] director['s] contributions to the Disney animated feature canon." According to Henderson, the film borrows "liberally from Reitherman's own *101 Dalmatians* (and, to a lesser extent, *The Jungle Book*.)" Henderson asserts that the film "merges visual vitality with bestial fidelity. Both are ultimately retrograde in their innovations, but come to some sort of redemption as their family values are offset by the Disney equivalent of brash, jazzy sensibilities." In *Of Mice and Magic*, Leonard Maltin criticizes the film for relying too heavily on Phil Harris's voice to replicate *The Jungle Book*'s Baloo the Bear. To Maltin *The Aristocats'* Thomas O'Malley Cat is "essentially the same character, dictated by the same voice personality" (76).

When compared with *One Hundred and One Dalmatians*, the movie does not stack up: "Whereas the earlier film's downright innovative (for Disney) slapdash sensibilities seemed entirely of-the-moment in 1961, and its jaggedly slashed lines of animation seemed to have been summoned from the blood-drenched pelts of Cruella itself," applying those same techniques to *The Aristocats*, a film from 1970, does not make sense, Henderson claims. Yet Henderson also sees the film as "among the studio's least suffocatingly ornate and ideologically risible" and as a Disney feature that "doesn't push the dramatic conflict any further than it's worth, and the low stakes are themselves a shot of fresh air in comparison to the last decades of Disney output."

Attitudes toward domesticity and orthodoxy parallel this ambiguity regarding *The Aristocats* filmic excellence: The aristocratic cats first perpetuate Disney orthodoxy. They are ideal domesticated pets reinforcing the safety of a controlled domestic space. The kittens (Toulouse, Berlioz, and Marie) relax in the music room, preparing to practice. Toulouse paints while Berlioz plays piano and Marie sings. But Edgar changes his pampering routine after learning of his employer's plans and makes them some special milk for dinner—warm milk with sleeping pills, which they all willingly drink because domestication has made them less cautious.

Edgar takes them to a natural world for which they seem unprepared, driving them off to the country in a basket he tosses in a motorcycle sidecar. To reinforce the lack of domesticity in this rural setting, two hound dogs chase him and nearly steal his motorcycle. When Edgar ends up near a stream and a mill, the basket flies toward the stream and the sidecar rolls toward a haystack. Edgar does escape, but in this wild country he loses his hat, umbrella, and sidecar to the hounds and the rough terrain.

The contrast between domestic space and irrational nature is amplified after the cats awaken and find themselves outside in wild nature, away from their comfortable home. Tom O'Malley, a wild cat, saves them from a variety of dangers on their journey home. They are experiencing a wild adventure but seek a return to the domestic space they left behind.

In the domestic space, Madame misses her pets, but Edgar is overjoyed and mistakenly reveals to the horse that he left his hat and umbrella in the country. The horse and mouse wish to protect the cats and try to stop Edgar from returning. Nonhuman nature will join forces to reunite the Aristocats with their Madame.

In wild nature, the Aristocats and their guide, Tom O'Malley, also join forces to journey home to their Parisian palace, overcoming obstacles such as railroad tracks, rivers, and geese. O'Malley even introduces Duchess and her kittens to wild nature in an urban space: Scat Cat and his band playing modern jazz in O'Malley's hideout.

Ultimately O'Malley and his wild urban friends successfully usurp Edgar's place in the household. After a long fight, Edgar ends up in a trunk bound for Timbuktu. The cats are safe and happy, and O'Malley has joined Madame's pampered pet family. But in a turn toward wild nature, Madame opens her home to the alley cats of Paris. Ultimately Scat Cat and his band play downstairs, and another neon psychedelic scene with dancing cats and humans (Madame and her lawyer) show us that irrational modernity may appropriate the domestic bliss of a Victorian household, at least in the world of *The Aristocats*.

In *The Rescuers*, on the other hand, domestic orthodoxy is attained and maintained on one level while a valorized wild nature is sustained on another. Mice assigned as rescuers save a human child and return her to a happy domestic space, just like Little Orphan Annie of the Broadway hit of the same year, *Annie* (1977). But the anthropomorphized mice highlight the adventure that wild irrational nature may provide.

Although Vincent Canby in his *New York Times* review suggests that *The Rescuers* "doesn't belong in the same category as the great cartoon features from *Snow White* to *Fantasia*," he claims "it's a reminder of a kind of slickly cheerful, animated entertainment that has become all but extinct" ("Disney's 'Rescuers' Cheerful Animation"). Leonard Maltin calls the film "the best cartoon feature to come from the studio since *101 Dalmatians* more than fifteen years before. It has what so many other animated films have lacked—heart" (77). That slickly cheerful entertainment with heart seems to align with the orthodoxy typically associated with Disney and attained and maintained in one level of *The Rescuers*.

The film's opening foregrounds the "orthodox" level of this narrative, showing a young girl's dilemma and valorizing her need to return to domestic security. On a deserted steamboat in a thunderstorm, a door opens showing a little girl who walks out of the red-lit cabin to the edge of the boat, where she drops a bottle into the water. The sky is red where the sun is setting. During the opening credits passing images show the bottle's journey across a sea. The bottle holds a note. We can see "help" written either on the bottle or on the note inside. Then a song begins with a female voice singing "I'm lost at sea without a friend" and "rescue me," reinforcing the little girl's dangerous situation.

When the bottle lands on a dock where mice find it, the second level of the narrative begins—wild untamed nature not only offers danger but adventure and should also be embraced. The scene shifts to the United Nations in New York; world ambassadors walk in front and into the building. They are clearly rotoscoped in order to separate the human forms from those of hand-drawn animals. Inside the United Nations, a briefcase opens. A mouse comes out. Then other briefcases open, and other mice from around the world walk to their own meeting for the Rescue Aid Society. Mice from all continents sit at UN-like desks made of matchboxes. They are the R.E.S.C.U.E. Aid Society and "never fail to do what's right." Bianca (Eva Gabor), the adventurous representative of wild nature, however, arrives late.

Bianca's entrance highlights the contrast between her wild untamed nature and the domesticated world the little girl, Penny, represents. When Penny's request for help from the Morningside Orphanage is read, Bianca is the first to volunteer and, in spite of every other mouse volunteering to accompany her, asks Bernard the janitor (Bob Newhart) to go with her.

Bianca and her reluctant partner, Bernard, begin their adventurous mission to save Penny, enhancing both wild nature for themselves and domestic orthodoxy for Penny. When they learn that Medusa has kidnapped Penny from the orphanage and imprisoned her in Devil's Bayou, where a huge diamond is buried, they follow the trail by flying Albatross Air.

Although Bianca is constructed from the beginning as wild and irrational, Bernard must experience adventure to appreciate it and seems anxious as the albatross "airplane" flies them to Devil's Bayou. While they travel, Bernard reads an atlas describing Devil's Bayou and again is concerned because it is uncharted and hazardous. Bianca, on the other hand, falls asleep on his shoulder, waking up when the albatross arrives at the bayou, where Penny is imprisoned in a steamboat. When they see both Penny and Medusa from the air, the scene amplifies the conflicts Bianca and Bernard must overcome to free Penny and provide her with domestic comfort.

Because Medusa is universally hated on the bayou, Bianca and Bernard have the support of surrounding wildlife to rescue Penny. She is small enough to climb down a black hole to a cave where pirates have hidden jewels, including a huge diamond called the "Devil's Eye." Medusa must have this diamond, even though Penny has already brought Medusa other jewels from the cave. Medusa plans to lower Penny into the hole when the ocean tides are low and wait until she gets the diamond. Penny, on the other hand, thinks that she will go back to the orphanage if she finds the diamond. Then she can be adopted and find the home she seeks.

To force Penny down the hole the next morning, Medusa takes her teddy bear. Penny must find the diamond or lose Teddy forever, so she goes down in the hole in a bucket. The Rescuers go down with her but hear an explosion of surf and see where the ocean comes into the cave. Together they find the Devil's Eye diamond, but to escape once Medusa pulls them up in the bucket, they must jump to land from the bucket and outrun Medusa and her henchmen.

The climax highlights the wild adventures Bianca and Bernard enjoy while helping Penny. They seem to embrace a wild and irrational nature that opposes the domesticity Penny seeks. Eventually they rescue Penny, her Teddy, and the diamond. They leave Medusa to the mercies of her hungry crocodiles.

At the story's close, based on television shots of Penny and her new adopted parents, Penny has found a family. Domesticity is maintained for Penny. Reinforcing their own alignment with nature and the irrational nature it provides, however, Bianca and Bernard take the next case they are offered and fly off on the albatross for another wild adventure. Even though Penny has found domestic bliss, Bianca and Bernard maintain connections to a wild and untamed nature in their drive for adventure.

The Fox and the Hound takes this valorization of wild nature further, even suggesting the limitations of domestic orthodoxy without, as in *Bambi*, condemning it as a vicious enemy to the natural world. A hunting scene that opens the film suggests the need for a clear bifurcation between humans and nature, but the interactions between a fox cub and both a human and a domesticated hunting dog call that binary into question. Although contemporary and more recent reviews of the film seem ambivalent about the film's valorization of nurture over nature and its revisionings of domesticated and wild nature, we see the film as complicating *Bambi*'s message that wild nature and domesticated culture of humans must remain separate in order to survive.

Vincent Canby of *The New York Times* argues, for example, that *The Fox and the Hound* "breaks no ground whatsoever. This is a pretty, relentlessly cheery, old-fashioned sort of Disney cartoon feature, chock full of bouncy songs of an upbeatness that is stickier than Krazy-Glue and played by animals more anthropomorphic than the humans that occasionally appear" ("Old Style Disney"). Yet Canby also asserts that "it is the sweetly realized point of *The Fox and the Hound* . . . that Tod, a fun-loving, orphaned fox, and Copper, a hound dog that grows up to take his job seriously, somehow manage to preserve a friendship that began when each was a pup, innocent of the roles society would impose on them."

Roger Ebert agrees that *The Fox and the Hound* "looks like a traditional production from Walt Disney animators" ("The Fox and the Hound"). Yet according to Ebert, "For all of its familiar qualities, this movie marks something of a departure for the Disney studio. . . . It's not just cute animals and frightening adventures and a happy ending; it's also a rather thoughtful meditation on how society determines our behavior." The mixed feelings Ebert asserts are reinforced by a later reading by Leonard Maltin. According to Maltin, *The Fox and the Hound* is a "pleasant but extremely low-key film that relies far too much on formula cuteness, formula comic relief, even formula characterizations . . . a synthesis of old ideas that had been worked before, and that smacked of executive-level 'What would Walt have done?' fears" (*The Disney Films* 275).

But the good news, according to Maltin, was that *The Fox and the Hound* demonstrated that new leadership, like twenty-seven-year-old Tom Wilhite, were in control of the studio and were "interested in genuine, not cosmetic, change." In *The Fox and the Hound*, this change "showed that the Disney crew was still without peer in its ability to bring appealing animal characters to life. A full-blooded fight scene between a dog and a bear, animated by Glen Keane, drew particular praise as an animation tour-de-force." Bringing life to two best friends (Tod the fox and Copper the hound) reared to be enemies amplifies the environmental message on display, a message that breaks down the split between nature and culture.

Reviews of the twenty-fifth-anniversary DVD edition of the film concur with Maltin's determination that *The Fox and the Hound* was a mixed bag. Although he notes the film's flaws, Dan Callahan of *Slant* suggests that the film is perhaps Disney's "only animated feature that gently questions the status quo." According to Callahan, "The film openly dramatizes what's wrong with the world and the toll that time and circumstances exact on the deepest of our youthful feelings. Its star-crossed friends are forced to fight. They stand up for each other through fierce personal bravery, and they are eventually kept apart." According to David Whitley, "*The Fox and the Hound* represents the forest areas surrounding the rural homesteads of its setting in ways that bear some superficial resemblance to *Bambi* . . . , [but] the film shows much more affinity with the narratives of domesticated animals that had become Disney's mainstay in the intervening years" (80).

Bill Chambers of *Film Freak Central* asserts that "Copper and Todd are archetypal opposites, and the movie's oneiric cant goes a long way towards offsetting the perversity of insisting on the primacy of nurture over nature in a natural setting." Chambers also suggests that "these creatures are humanized as opposed to romanticized—one might say that the movie honors their essential 'animalness' by segregating them into two groups: predator and prey." Yet Chambers highlights the nurture over nature argument: "So methodically does the picture lay out its thesis on the perils of indoctrination that Tod is nonplussed when a mother hen goes berserk over him frolicking with her chicks. Obviously Tod's mother dies before she could teach him the pecking order, so to speak."

A hyperrealistic vision of nature like that highlighted in *Bambi* opens *The Fox and the Hound*. A foggy forest with birds and frogs contrasts with a distant drum and a barking dog before music begins. The conflict between human and nonhuman nature is established. The dog gets louder and the camera blurs before revealing a fox and cub running from dogs. The cub is in its mother's mouth. As the music gets more frantic, the camera tracks the fox running and jumping off rocks and under a fence. An owl comes out of a hole. The fox leaves her cub beside a fence post to save it, and gunshots explode. The mother fox is hit.

But domesticated human and nonhuman nature save the fox's cub and connect domesticity and wild nature. An owl, Big Mama, swoops down to help the cub. The cub rubs against her. "You need some caring for," she says and leaves to find help from a woodpecker and finch. But the finch and woodpecker have a better idea. While the woodpecker pecks on a widow's door, the other animals take her laundry off the clothesline so the widow, "Granny," will find the fox cub covered by her underwear. "Bless my soul. It's a baby fox," she exclaims. A connection between wild and domestic nature is broached.

The binary between wild and domesticated nature,

however, is also reinforced in the same scene. As the widow rescues the fox pup, a hunter who lives next door brings a hunting-dog pup to Chief, the elder hound dog, so he can teach him his hunting strategies.

The fox (Tod) has an idyllic early life on the widow's farm that in some ways demonstrates how instincts must be nurtured. Instead of attacking other animals as prey, he sees them as playmates, ultimately even befriending a hunting dog trained to kill him. He plays with a cow's tail while the widow milks her, investigates a few chicks until the mother hen chases him, knocking over the milk. When a butterfly flutters toward the hound dogs, Tod follows, and Copper the hunting-dog pup goes out to smell, beginning his and Tod's friendship and an unlikely connection between domesticated and wild nature.

Amos, the hunter, works to destroy the bond between Copper and Tod, demanding that the natural order of predator and prey be preserved. When Tod and Copper continue to interact and attempt to overcome the restrictions Amos puts in place to keep Copper close to home, Amos finally tries to shoot Tod. Granny must stop his wild firing after he starts to destroy her milk barrels with stray buckshot. Tod is now forced to stay inside Granny's home for protection.

While Amos takes Chief and Copper on a hunting trip meant to teach Copper how to hunt, Big Mama tries to enlighten Tod about their hunting mission. In spite of Tod's belief that he and Copper will always be friends, after a season of hunting Copper has changed. Because Copper has learned his hunting lessons so well he proudly sits in the front seat when they go home in spring, taking Chief's place as the best hunting dog.

When the hunter and hounds come back, Chief is jealous. Tod still thinks Copper is his friend. Tod tells Big Mama he will be careful and goes to see Copper after dark. Copper, though, says he cannot be Tod's friend: "I'm a hunting dog," Copper explains. When Chief is hit by a train and knocked into the water below because he tried to catch and kill Tod, Copper vows revenge for Chief's injuries: "If it's the last thing I do, I'll get you for this," he tells Tod.

Now that Tod is blamed for Chief's injuries, he must return to wild nature to protect the natural order, Amos explains. The widow takes him to a nature preserve, but Tod is unprepared for even this protected wild nature. A storm brews, and he hides under a tree. Squirrels and birds run for cover, but Tod cannot find a safe haven and runs into a badger's house. The badger runs him off, but a porcupine invites him in. Tod seems safe in the preserve, but still Amos wants revenge. Since Chief's leg was broken, Amos shows Copper a trap that will destroy Tod.

Now wild nature rather than the domesticated widow must protect Tod. Hoping to help Tod, Big Mama finds a female fox, Vixey, and advises her to partner with Tod. After a few missteps, Vixey shows him the forest—a Disney view with a sparkling waterfall under a full moon.

But the hunter comes to the preserve and defies "no hunting" signs, foregrounding the need to separate humans from wild nature. The hunter puts down traps near the water and Tod's den, but Vixey senses something is wrong even though leaves cover the traps. She tells Tod to be careful when he enters a clearing near the stream and nearly walks into the traps. The traps snap, and Copper chases him and Vixey into the burrow. They seem to be trapped in the burrow, with Copper on one end and the hunter on the other, but when Tod bites Copper's foot, and the hunter lights a fire at the other end to smoke them out, Tod and Vixey jump through the fire and run away. The hunter shoots after them, and Copper chases them to the top of the waterfall where Tod and Vixey climb a tree.

But when a bear appears, and the hunter fires and misses, Tod and Copper's friendship overcomes their conflict. The bear knocks the hunter down onto one of his traps. Copper tries to fight off the bear because Amos cannot reach his gun. It looks as if wild nature has successfully countered domestic predators, but Tod sees and hears Copper when he is thrown by the bear and runs back to help, attacking the bear and chasing him away from Copper. The bear knocks Tod onto a tree branch and climbs after him. With another swat, they both fall over the falls into the lake below. It is quiet there, but Tod crawls out unscathed. Copper sees him, and the hunter nearly shoots. But Copper stands in front of him and cries, so the hunter lets Tod go.

The boundaries between domestic and wild nature are blurred here as Tod and Copper interconnect and form an interdependent relationship that saves them both. Copper and Tod may live in separate spaces, but they share an alliance. The next year the caterpillar has turned into a butterfly, demonstrating how any creature can change, including the violent and angry hunter. Because a fox named Tod saved him and his hunting dog, Copper, Amos rejects his former hatred of wild nature and builds an alliance with the widow, the bridge between domestic and wild nature. Copper sleeps and dreams of Tod while Tod and Vixey watch the house from their hill, separated in their nature preserve without the overwhelming fear of human nature reinforced in *Bambi*.

Disney in the 1990s and Beyond:
Maintaining the Nature/Culture Binary

Although Disney films such as *The Fox and the Hound* from the early 1980s highlight the need to control human intervention and nurture the natural world in order to strengthen their interdependence, animated Disney features from the late 1980s and 1990s typically show us the power of nature and the supernatural over the human world. This move harks back to a more traditional vision of nature that rests on a powerful representation of nature and culture as binary oppositions. With the exception of *Pocahontas* (1995), these films sustain the conflict between humans and the natural world without critiquing the destructive force of humans' exploitation of the natural world or encouraging interdependent relationships between the human and natural worlds.

The Little Mermaid, Beauty and the Beast (1992), *Aladdin* (1992), *Mulan* (1998), *Tarzan* (1999), *Dinosaur* (2000), *Atlantis: The Lost Empire* (2001), and *Lilo and Stitch* (2002) all highlight and maintain the opposition between nature and culture. By asserting the power of nature and/or the supernatural, these features minimize the costs of human exploitation and, in fact, suggest that, because they lack supernatural (or natural) force, humans bear no threat toward nature. Only *Pocahontas* illustrates the possible destructive force humans may wield against nature, but it too perpetuates the opposition between humanity and the natural world when John Smith leaves Pocahontas, her people, and, perhaps, wild untamed nature behind. Although *Captain Planet* had a television presence in the 1990s, and Ted Turner further promoted the show's environmental themes with the creation of an advocacy group, in films from the period Disney perpetuates the nature/culture binary begun with *Snow White* and cemented with *Bambi*. Disney's perspectives from the 1990s merely maintain the binary while accommodating contemporary audiences.

Disney animated features from the 1990s also succeeded at the box office, but they promote an ideology that perpetuates a racist and sexist status quo and maintains the nature/culture binary. While perpetuating antifeminist gender roles, *The Little Mermaid* from its opening forward bifurcates land from sea and humans from nature. The addition of Ursula, a sea witch, demonstrates the power of the supernatural over both settings. But, in spite of Ariel's and her father's sacrifices, nature is valorized over both human culture and the supernatural when natural attraction between Ariel and Prince Eric entices him to kiss Ariel and to fight for her and her father's souls.

Although David Whitley suggests that "*The Little Mermaid* could be read as playing out a longing for some form of resolution to the nature-culture divide," we see that divide maintained and reversed, with nature providing the superior pole in the binary. Ariel loans Ursula her voice in exchange for legs so she can woo the prince, earn his love, and regain her voice. Ultimately Ariel fails because Ursula intervenes with her magic, but once Ariel's sea friends free Ariel's voice and break Ursula's spell, the prince fights and kills Ursula and returns sea and land to their original dichotomy. Although the supernatural witch has been destroyed, it is nature—the natural affection Prince Eric feels for Ariel—that saves them all. Ariel does marry the prince, but the marriage is based on irrational wild nature instead of the logic of human culture. Nature and culture remain divided, this time with nature gaining an edge and stereotypical gender roles safely in place.

The same bifurcations are maintained in *Beauty and the Beast*. The only difference here are the settings—a country town and a castle surrounded by a wilderness where artifacts are controlled by a supernatural spell. Again the supernatural prevails until natural attraction breaks a spell, and the spell is again broken by a kiss. Here, however, the beast reverts to his better nature, a domesticated culture-based ideology, when love overcomes his selfishness. The binary between nature and culture is strengthened. Belle's submission to stereotypically feminine gender roles is less evident, since the beast is somewhat feminized as he is domesticated.

In *Aladdin* the supernatural force of a genie and his magic carpet prevail, bringing Aladdin and Princess Jasmine together in spite of Jafar's and Iago's attempts to control them and steal the princess's fortune. Here, as in *Beauty and the Beast* and *The Little Mermaid*, the natural attraction between a young man (this time the peasant) and his true love (a princess) demonstrates the powerful force of nature, but it is the supernatural power of a genie and his magic carpet that ensures their success. In *Aladdin*, the supernatural proves more powerful than the human world of Jafar and Iago, strong enough for a princess to marry a boy from the gutter, and, perhaps, overt enough to disguise the racism toward Arabs and stereotypical gender roles on display in the film.

Although the film perpetuates racism, *Pocahontas*, on the other hand, is a blatantly environmental film that contrasts British invaders with Native Americans who nurture the earth. John Smith works for Ratcliffe, a British imperialist, but immediately befriends Pocahontas, who chooses not to marry Kocoum, a brave Native American warrior, after talking to Grandmother Willow. John Smith's friend, Thomas, kills Kocoum by accident to protect Smith. A war seems inevitable, but Smith speaks with Pocahontas's father. Pocahontas falls on Smith's body before they can kill him, telling them to choose life instead of death. Ratcliffe goes away in chains when his men decide to live in peace and take Smith home for medical help. In this version of the tale Pocahontas stays behind. The ship turns into an illustration for a book as the film ends.

The songs point out the environmental message of the film. In one, Pocahontas sings, "You can own the earth and still / All you'll own is earth until / You can paint with all the colors of the wind." The song suggests that it is as impossible to own the earth as it is to paint with the wind, a message that argues against exploiting the natural world. In a song at the film's climax, Native Americans sing in chorus, "You think I'm an ignorant 'savage' and you've been so many places; I guess it must be so, but still I cannot see if the savage one is me." The song occurs as the film shows the brutality of the British imperialist Ratcliffe and his need to own and control Native Americans and their natural home.

But the film fails to resolve the conflict between nature—as represented by Pocahontas, her people, and their world—and culture, as represented by Ratcliffe and the British soldiers sent to support his mission. In fact, the gap between the binary oppositions widens when Ratcliffe's ship leaves with John Smith and his men aboard while Pocahontas watches from the shore. In *Pocahontas*, nature and culture clash so powerfully that they must remain separate, even though nature is idealized in the pristine state in which it is presented. This innocent nature proves so strong that it chases humans representing "culture" away.

Bifurcations between nature and culture and naturalized racial and gender roles are also maintained in *The Lion King* (1994), *The Jungle Book* (1994), and *Dinosaurs*, in which what David Ingram calls the "food chain" (24) and Wells "the circle of life" (*The Animated Bestiary* 200) maintain nature's rules in species-specific ways. *The Hunchback of Notre Dame* (1996), *Hercules* (1997), *Mulan*, *Tarzan*, *Atlantis*, and *Lilo and Stitch* also maintain gender and racial binaries as natural essentials. They do this with a nod to contemporary views that, in the end, are seen as problematic and better replaced with more traditional beliefs that maintain a variety of hierarchies. The films ultimately promote the orthodox Disney ideology of innocence based in conservative values that, as Henry Gi-

The Little Mermaid: Ariel yearns for her human prince.

roux explains, "turn children into consumers" (94). According to Giroux, "The conservative values that Disney films promote assume such force because of the context in which they are situated and because they resonate so powerfully with dominant perceptions and meanings" (97).

Giroux outlines some of the lessons children learn from Disney: "In both *The Little Mermaid* and *The Lion King*, the female characters are constructed within narrowly defined gender roles. All of the female characters in these films are ultimately subordinate to males and define their power and desire almost exclusively in terms of dominant male narratives" (98–99). The more complicated gender roles in *Beauty and the Beast*, *Pocahontas*, and *Mulan* all resolve in favor of subordination, as well. Such subordination is "defined by men" (100), according to Giroux, suggesting that "social problems such as the history of racism, the genocide of Native Americans, the prevalence of sexism, and the crisis of democracy are simply willed through the laws of nature" (107).

Conclusion

In *The Aristocats*, *The Rescuers*, and *The Fox and the Hound*, the domestic orthodoxy of earlier Disney animated films is reinvigorated by wild nature, even in the urban space of *The Aristocats*. Domesticity is modernized in *The Aristocats* when literally wild jazz scat cats are welcomed into Madame's household. Both domesticity and wild nature are valorized in *The Rescuers*, with neither pole of the binary constructed as superior to the other. Penny returns to an adopted domesticated nuclear family after her rescue, while Bianca and Bernard choose the wild road of adventurous nature as they volunteer for another dangerous rescue mission. In *The Fox and the Hound*, however, the ideology of orthodox domesticity changes when wild and domestic nature are bridged through unlikely friendships that connect hunter and hunted. Although the domestic is maintained in all three of these films, in *The Fox and the Hound* it becomes transformed to accommodate the natural world in a move toward interconnection such as that found in Aldo Leopold's biotic community.

The Land before Time: Dinosaur children reach the Great Valley.

SEVEN

Dinosaurs Return

Evolution Outplays Disney's Binaries

During the period when Disney was releasing blockbusters such as *The Little Mermaid* (1989), Don Bluth, an experienced Disney and independent animator, joined Steven Spielberg and George Lucas to direct *The Land before Time* (1988), an animated feature that complicates the nature/culture binary and draws on both organismic and chaotic approaches to ecology. Five years later, Spielberg directed *Jurassic Park* (1993), a feature film that takes the message of *The Land before Time* further while combining live action and animation driven by Lucas's Industrial Light and Magic technology. Despite Disney's resurgence in the 1990s, for us *The Land before Time* and *Jurassic Park* provide richer ecocritical readings than later films and offer an alternative to the Disney orthodoxy. *The Land before Time* and *Jurassic Park* are based in Spielberg and Lucas's Amblin Entertainment philosophy that, from the beginning, emphasized evolutionary narratives, environmental ethics, and a need for interdependent relationships between culture and nature.

Amblin Entertainment not only embraced an alternative message. Because Spielberg and Lucas served as Amblin's driving force, the studio gained prominence in the industry almost from its inception. Disney reigned supreme in the world of animated features from 1937 until the 1980s. Disney's animated features after the classic era lost luster, however, until Michael Eisner signed on as CEO in 1984 and hired Jeffrey Katzenberg to lead the motion-picture division. Katzenberg created some of the most critically acclaimed animated films and box-office successes Disney had seen since its golden years, *The Little Mermaid*, *Beauty and the Beast* (1991), *Aladdin* (1992), and *The Lion King* (1994). Katzenberg was also responsible for connecting Disney with both Miramax Films and Pixar Studios.

Katzenberg brought back Disney's dominance in the animated-film industry, but he also demonstrated that animated features could, once again, reach wide audiences. By the 1980s, commercially successful animation was no longer just an American province, and Disney was no longer only interested in animation. Katzenberg's success with animated features convinced other studios to distribute individual animated features. With Katzenberg's success other studios were willing to provide support for independent studios exploring different visions through animated features. Multiple family markets, from DVD and cable to larger international audiences, not only resulted in the success of films such as Disney's *The Little Mermaid* but encouraged successful filmmakers such as Spielberg and Lucas to move deeper into the world of the animated feature, building on Spielberg's work with *An American Tail* (1986) and *Who Framed Roger Rabbit* (1988).

Lucas's and Spielberg's earlier live-action fantasies from the 1970s and '80s had begun the split from adult filmmaking to films and games geared primarily for a young or family audience, connecting with 1930s' serial movies more than the adult films of the period. Nigel Morris offers three characteristics of Spielberg's films that illustrate this move: "extensive pastiche and quotations from other films, including Hollywood classics, European art cinema, and his own oeuvre" (6); a "distinctive lighting code"; and "a recurring narrative structure centered on a family splitting which leads eventually either to reunion or a spiritual substitute" (7). Philip Taylor asserts of Spielberg films that "younger audiences revel in the reinforcement of their childhood fantasies, while adults are reminded of how they once saw that world, and are taken back there" (37), a suggestion that producers' goal of reaching a broad audience succeeded.

According to Taylor, Spielberg "became a movie mogul with the establishment of Amblin Entertainment in 1984" (7). When Don Bluth left Disney and Spielberg and Lucas formed Amblin, the animator and filmmakers made a critical movement toward fantasy and a family and children's audience. And with the clout they produced from the success of films such as *Jaws* (1975), *Star Wars* (1977), *Close Encounters of the Third Kind* (1977), and *E.T.: The Extra-Terrestrial* (1982), Lucas and Spielberg were able to take on some of the same trappings as Disney. According to Nigel Morris, "Steven Spielberg offers a promise analogous to stardom and genre. This is arguably unprecedented except by Disney and Hitchcock" (4). Spielberg's box-office power translated to success in the world of animated films.

Disney demonstrated that there was money to be made with animated films, and Lucas and Spielberg reinforced their own economic strength with the success of *Star Wars* and *Raiders of the Lost Ark* (1981). Universal Pictures, therefore, was willing to provide the financing Lucas and Spielberg needed to dive into animated filmmaking. Lucas and Spielberg, then, were able to overtake the Disney franchise, first through their live-action films and then through animation that continued when Spielberg formed Dream-Works. Frank Sanello calls them "the McDonald's of the box office," especially in response to the deal Lucas and Spielberg made with Universal: "The studio would get no distribution fee, typically 30 percent of the film's gross, and it would not be allowed to charge overhead, another 20 percent" (91). Although the studio would eventually receive 50 percent after the first million earned, "just in the case the movie flopped and there were no profits to divvy up, Lucas would get up front a $4 million producer's fee, and Spielberg $1.5 million for his directorial services" (92).

Interdependence in *The Land before Time*

Although *The Land before Time* and *Jurassic Park* also promote blatant consumerism for children and adults and maintain some sexist and racist ideals, as do Disney films of the period, they also provide an alternative vision of the natural world. The films do not depict a hierarchy of laws or a pristine innocent world for which we yearn, as in animated features from Disney, but they show the natural world as a dangerous place where only communal values can ensure survival. According to Paul Wells, *The Land before Time* follows a narrative pattern that mediates between nature and narrative.

Wells notes that Littlefoot, the young dinosaur hero in *The Land before Time*, overcomes his weaknesses in strength and expression (124) and "reaches his natural home in the Great Valley when reunited with his own kind" (125), seemingly cementing the narrative structure in which "community is normally restored, and the main character in completing the journey is advanced spiritually and practically" (*The Animated Bestiary* 124).

But the resolution to this cinematic animal narrative is complicated in two ways. The Great Valley is constructed as a temporary haven for the last of Littlefoot's kind based in an evolutionary narrative, and Littlefoot, a brontosaurus or "long neck," maintains relationships with animals outside his species. Several reviewers note that the film focuses on evolution without stating it explicitly. Hal Hinson asserts in his *Washington Post* review, for example, that "death and separation are the themes of *The Land before Time*, and unlike *Bambi*, in which we had to deal with the death of the mother on our own, the filmmakers here have attempted to address these issues in an instructional manner." According to Hinson, "The heaviest share of this burden falls to a creature named Rooter, who tells Littlefoot about the great cycle of life, at the end of which the grieving youngster will be reunited with his mother."

The Land before Time, then, draws on organismic approaches to ecology and follows what Joseph Meeker calls a comic evolutionary narrative. According to Meeker, humans typically embrace a tragic evolutionary narrative that counters the stable and well-developed climax communities of plants and animals, which are "extremely diverse and complicated" (162). But this position comes at a price and may cost humanity its existence, Meeker asserts: "We demand that one species, our own, achieve unchallenged dominance where hundreds of species lived in complex equilibrium before our arrival" (164). This attitude may not only lead to the destruction of other species but of humanity itself. Meeker believes humanity has "a growing need to learn from the more stable comic heroes of nature, the animals" and to adapt to a biotic or climax community such as that described by organismic ecologists, including Aldo Leopold.

The evolutionary narratives of *The Land before Time* and *Jurassic Park* explore what might happen if humanity did learn from these more stable comic heroes, since, according to Meeker, "Evolution itself is a gigantic comic drama, not the bloody tragic spectacle imagined by the sentimental humanists of early Darwinism" (164). Meeker asserts:

Nature is not "red in tooth and claw" as the nineteenth-century English poet Alfred, Lord Tennyson characterized it, for evolution does not proceed through battles fought among animals to see who is fit enough to survive and who is not. Rather, the evolutionary process is one of adaptation and accommodation, with the various species exploring opportunistically their environments in search of a means to maintain their existence. Like comedy, evolution is a matter of muddling through. (164)

For Meeker, successful evolution encourages communal action to ensure survival:

Its ground rules for participants (including man) are those which also govern literary comedy: organisms must adapt themselves to their circumstances in every possible way, must studiously avoid all-or-nothing choices, must prefer any alternative to death, must accept and encourage maximum diversity, must accommodate themselves to the accidental limitations of birth and environment, and must always prefer love to war—though if warfare is inevitable, it should be prosecuted so as to humble the enemy without destroying him. (166)

Ultimately, in spite of the films' horrific circumstances, they embrace evolutionary narratives. The narratives of both *The Land before Time* and *Jurassic Park* are based in a comic and communal view of survival, even though they both also draw on a tragic and individually driven view that refuses to shed the pioneer role humanity sometimes seems to embrace and that equates survival with extermination of all others.

Roger Ebert finds this evolutionary vision disturbing: "As the backdrop in the series of hazards, the visual look of *The Land before Time* is apocalyptic. All but the last scenes take place in a blasted heath of red skies, parched land, withered trees, barren wastes and thorn thickets" ("The Land before Time"). Ebert asserts that this setting evokes a sense of "grim determinism" and suggests that the film should have "spent more time on natural history and the sense of discovery, and less time on tragedy." A review from *Variety* notes the focus on interdependence once the film's narrative is in play, asserting that the "idea develops that surviving in a changing environment depends on achieving unity among the species," a unity that transforms the rules of nature laid out in Disney films and stresses interdependence rather than species-specific pioneering.

The film's opening highlights this need for interdependence. A series of scenes introduces herbivore species that survive once they achieve unity through evolutionary transformations. A dark underwater scene introduces a fish with froglike appendages eating a red fish and swimming through grasses, illustrating the food chain. Then while turtles swim under a brightening sea, a narrator quickly describes the evolutionary journey that culminated in humanity and then, more important, why herds of dinosaurs ventured west "in search of the Great Valley." According to this narrator, there were two types of dinosaurs. "Some had flat teeth and fed upon the leaves of trees, and those with sharp teeth for eating meat preyed upon the leaf-eaters." Although these types seemed distinctive, their symbiotic relationship became clear, according to the narrator, when "the trees began to die out." Because they were dependent on the leaf-eaters for sustenance, "the mighty beasts who seemed to rule the earth were, in truth, ruled by the leaf," just as the leaf-eaters were. Therefore, according to the narrator, "out of desperation, some of the herds ventured out west in search of the Great Valley, a land still lush and green. It was a journey toward life."

That journey is illustrated by a colony of leaf-eaters protecting their newborns before beginning their search for the Great Valley. After a comic scene of a baby dinosaur coming out of its shell, a variety of herbivores are born, and, according to the narrator, "Some of the young seem born without fear," foreshadowing at least some leaf-eaters' survival. When a storm comes up and the last egg cracks, however, the tenuousness of that survival is illustrated. The narrator explains, "Even hatching could be dangerous." A meat-eater tries to get the egg before an adult knocks it away. The egg rolls and cracks. The adult leaf-eaters name the infant "Littlefoot," and he is dubbed "the last survivor of the herd."

With the last of the leaf-eaters' births complete, the herd must leave on its journey to the Great Valley, where a biotic community is still possible. According to the adult leaf-eaters, the land has been changing. They must walk every day to reach the Great Valley and its life-sustaining leafy trees. Littlefoot's mother shows him a tree star and tells him the Great Valley is filled with food like this. "Some things you see with your eyes. Others you see with your heart," she says of this valley. She explains that "the bright circle must pass over us many times, and we must follow it each day to where it touches the ground" to reach its bounty.

Littlefoot's actions contrast with those of other leaf-eaters and illustrate the interdependent biotic community they seek. He interacts with other species almost immediately, first ramming horns with Cera, a three-horned leaf-eater who seems to embrace separation rather than interdependence: "Three horns never play with long necks," Cera tells Littlefoot. Littlefoot's mother agrees, explaining that "we all keep to our own kind." When Littlefoot asks why, she tells him, "Because we're different. It's always been that way."

Playing with Cera is first constructed as destructive and serves as the catalyst for Littlefoot's and Cera's isolation from their herds. Littlefoot's mother is killed protecting Littlefoot and Cera from a "sharptooth" who attacks them while they play with frog bubbles. Cera is separated from her family during the same episode, which coincides with an earthquake that divides the landscape. Ultimately, Littlefoot and Cera reach the Great Valley only because they work together with other young leaf-eaters, overcoming both the meat-eaters and the cruel environment through which they travel. As Rooter, a spiked leaf-eater, explains after Littlefoot's mother passes away, it is no one's fault. "The great circle of life has begun, but, you see, not all of us arrive together at the end." Littlefoot mourns his mother's loss until he hears her voice reminding him he must journey to the Great Valley that is "past the mountains that burn." With his mother as his guide, Littlefoot can begin his journey.

Littlefoot's journey is also inspired by an evolutionary narrative. According to the narrator, "He had to find his way, or the chain of life would be broken." Because of Rooter's and his mother's encouragement, Littlefoot begins this journey. More significant, orphans from a variety of species join him: Ducky (Judith Barsi), big-mouth swimmer; Petrie (Will Ryan), a flying leaf-eater; Spike, a spike-tailed herbivore; and Cera, the three-horned leaf-eater. The narrator explains, "So the five hungry dinosaurs set off for the Great Valley. There had never been such a herd before. A long neck, a three-horn, a big mouth, a flyer, and a spike-tail all together, all knowing that if they lost their way, they would starve or find themselves in Sharp Tooth's shadow." Together they destroy the sharp-toothed dinosaur and find the Great Valley, cementing the need for interdependence and adaptation in order to survive.

When the leaf-eaters reach the Great Valley and join its

biotic community, the spirit of Littlefoot's mother lights the way. Together they have found "a land of green, of leaves, of life," the narrator says. Children are reunited with parents. Littlefoot finds his grandparents. We see a montage of memories with family and friends. Then, according to the narrator, the leaf-eaters all grow up together in the valley and pass the story of the journey to the next generation. The film ends with a song, "If We Hold On Together," from James Horner, sung by Diana Ross, that emphasizes the need for interdependent relationships. Littlefoot tells his friends, "Now we'll always be together," in a biotic community that accommodates difference for the good of all species rather than only tragic pioneers.

The comic evolutionary journey followed by Littlefoot and his friends contrasts with a tragic evolutionary path that, perhaps, misreads Darwin. David L. Hull discusses the misreading and misinterpretation of both Charles Darwin's and A. R. Wallace's versions of evolution in "Deconstructing Darwin: Evolutionary Theory in Context." According to Hull, "Although the character of Victorian society may have influenced the acceptance of evolutionary theory, it was not the competitive, individualistic theory" that social Darwinists interpret it to be, "but a warmer, more comforting theory" (137).

Evolution is not "red in tooth and claw." Instead, it emphasizes both adaptation and accommodation toward biotic climax communities—comic modes based in community and family—which is the focus of both *The Land before Time* and *Jurassic Park*.

Jurassic Park, however, at first embraces a tragic evolutionary narrative in which human figures attempt to dominate nature as pioneer species. *Jurassic Park*, especially, draws on such a tragic narrative, but the decision its protagonist, Dr. Alan Grant (Sam Neill), makes to build a nontraditional family transforms the tragic pattern begun by Jurassic Park's owner, John Hammond (Richard Attenborough), and catalyzed by computer hacker and thief Dennis Nedry (Wayne Knight).

Animation in *Jurassic Park*

Although much of *Jurassic Park* is live action, the dinosaurs at the center of the film's conflicts were all a product of two styles of animation: stop-motion and computer-generated animation. The film began with a variety of stop-motion animation techniques that brought dinosaurs to life. According to the film's production notes, Spielberg hired the Stan Winston Studio to construct the stop-motion dinosaur figures, "full-size animals who would be both quick and mobile" and authentic with help from paleontologist Jack Horner.

The twenty-foot *Tyrannosaurus rex*, for example, was "constructed from a frame of fiberglass and 3000 pounds of clay" and then "covered with a durable yet delicate latex skin . . . painted by a team of artists who blended a rich palette of colors to bring his body to life." To make sure his movements were also authentic, the production notes explain, the *Tyrannosaurus* was "mounted on a 'dino-simulator,' an imaginative mechanism inspired by hydraulic technology and based on a traditional six-axis flight simulator used by the military." A smaller *Tyrannosaurus* was operated by four puppeteers.

Phil Tippett, an Academy Award–winning animator who improved stop-motion animation with his Go-Motion System, choreographed the dinosaurs' movements and provided a series of "animatics" or storyboards to help Spielberg "prepare and rehearse the highly complex scenes with T-rex and the Velociraptors" (*"Jurassic Park* Production Notes"). Spielberg used miniatures to photograph wide-angle or full-length shots according to Tippett's choreography.

A second form of animation, Computer Generated Images, was also used in some *Jurassic Park* scenes. Industrial Light and Magic's (ILM) crew impressed Spielberg a year into production when they "built the bones and skeleton of a dinosaur in a computer, and from that, they created a walk cycle for the T-rex" (*Jurassic Park* Production Notes). ILM also added a computer-generated dinosaur stampede and "several wide-angle scenes that illustrate a herd of dinosaurs against a sweeping vista."

ILM's work ushered in the most widely used animation form of the twenty-first century, as well, perhaps taking the place of stop-motion and Go-Motion techniques of earlier decades. According to Ellen Poom, a senior animator for the film, "With *Jurassic Park* we tried to use models to do the animation at the start but the movement turned out to be insufficiently fluid to be persuasive, so we did a test and built some dinosaurs that we could scan into the computer" (qtd. in Wells, *The Animated Bestiary* 90).

Tragic Evolutionary Narratives in Jurassic Park

Although CGI may have helped move stop-motion animation to possible extinction, *Jurassic Park*'s narrative demonstrates how community and, perhaps, family, might help us survive. Even though most critics see the film's focus on family as diluting the ethical argument against genetic experimentation, we see this focus as moving the narrative beyond bioethics toward a comic view of evolution, an evolutionary narrative which might, as Leslie Paul Thiele suggests in "Evolutionary Narratives and Ecological Ethics," "inform moral reasoning and facilitate the cultivation of certain moral sentiments [and] might legitimate an ecological ethic" (7–8). Thiele explains, "The point . . . is not to deliver human behavior over to a 'Darwinian science' but to make sure of 'merely philosophical realizations' that can be gleaned from the 'transfer' of certain biological concepts to humanistic concerns. In the end, we do not so much discover values in nature as read values into nature" (8).

Critics of *Jurassic Park* do attempt to read values into the nature on screen, arguing that the family unit waters down Michael Crichton's original argument against genetic engineering in his 1990 novel. Andrew M. Gordon, for example, sees the real stars of the film as the dinosaurs, since the "human characters leave me cold" (203). He also asserts that those human characters obscure the novel's original message. According to Gordon, "*Jurassic Park* is about the contemporary American family" (208). But Gordon claims "Spielberg's concern with fatherhood seems awkwardly grafted onto Crichton's original premise, which was to create believable dinosaurs and then let them run amok to warn about the commercialization of genetic engineering" (2008) and asserts that "Crichton's theme becomes lost as the film turns into yet another Spielbergian endorsement of fatherhood and the nuclear family" (208). Although *Jurassic Park* does attack the commercialization of genetic engineering, just as in Crichton's novel and his earlier *Westworld*, Gordon also suggests this focus on family interferes with the spectacular violence on display.

Stephen Jay Gould takes this criticism even further, arguing, "The dinosaurs are wonderful, but they aren't on the set enough for the time." According to Gould, "The plot line of the human actors reduces to pap and romantic drivel of the worst kind, the very antithesis of the book's grappling with serious themes" (181). Philip Taylor, in his biography of Spielberg, argues, "In many respects, the film contained elements of Spielberg's weaknesses as well as his proven strengths," including the rendering of the animated dinosaurs. According to Taylor, "Indeed, so 'realistic' are the dinosaurs that they tend to steal the film" (141–42).

Nigel Morris in *The Cinema of Steven Spielberg: Empire of Light* highlights a variety of lenses through which to view *Jurassic Park*, including computer animation and digital imagery, intertextuality, psychoanalysis, carnivore carnivalesque, and "'Cola vs. Zola': *Jurassic Park* as Global Phenomenon." Morris's psychoanalytic reading also emphasizes family as it focuses on the Oedipal trajectory. According to Morris, "Contrasting the proxy family [with Grant at its head] against Nedry, embodiment of consumerist, junk-food values and greed associated with Hollywood by the critics, the movie betrays profound ambivalence about its status while naturalizing and ennobling family ideals" (206). Morris asserts that family "stands less for curtailment of Grant's masculine freedom than nostalgic desire to restore and perpetuate frontier community and optimism, represented in America as the antithesis of cultural decadence."

This ambivalence toward the movie's consumer-driven message points to Morris's notion of the film as a "global phenomenon." And connections between humans and dinosaurs—either plant or meat-eaters—highlight his emphasis on the "carnivore carnivalesque" in the film. Although Morris does assert that *Jurassic Park* constructs nature and the dinosaurs that represent it as feminine—a traditional move that can be seen as an excuse to destroy and "rape" the wilderness—he also sees both male and female characters connecting with the dinosaurs on display. Ultimately, however, Morris too notes that the film "allegedly elevate[s] effects over characterisation" (212) and sees Spielberg as either a "manipulative craftsman" or "cinematic artist" (213).

For us, however, *Jurassic Park* follows two evolutionary narrative patterns. The first is driven by a critique of genetic engineering and sees humans as only exploiters of the natural world, a theme many critics find diluted in the translation from novel to film. Dr. Ian Malcolm (Jeff Goldblum) and, to a certain extent, Dr. Ellie Sattler (Laura Dern) initiate and push forward this narrative during the first act of the film. The second pattern, however, which comes into play when John Hammond's grandchildren visit the park, builds toward a comic view of evolution that sees family, accommodation, and adaptation as better responses to nonhuman nature. The last two acts of the film illustrate this narrative. In the second act Dr. Alan Grant transforms from child hater to father figure and protector. In the third act, the family unit is reunited, but nature's life cycle, not human retaliation, ensures their survival.

Tragic and comic evolutionary narratives and their roots in organismic, chaotic, and economic approaches to ecology are broached as the film introduces each of the characters in relation to the film's conflicts. *Jurassic Park* begins and ends on Isla Nublar, an island near Costa Rica where John Hammond has built his dinosaur theme park. Characters that will modify the tragic narrative on display there, however, are introduced with the first conflict of the film: a raptor kills a worker, and the company lawyer Donald Gennaro (Martin Ferrero) hears about it while inspecting an amber mine in the Dominican Republic. Wishing to protect the park's assets, he tells Hammond, "If two experts sign off on the island, the insurance group'll back off" to halt a $20 million lawsuit.

Dr. Alan Grant and Dr. Ellie Sattler are hired as the experts who will join Dr. Ian Malcolm and provide the credibility the theme park needs. Malcolm's role as a chaotician, here aligned with chaotic approaches to ecology, and Grant's disdain for children and for a relationship with Sattler, pointing toward interdependence and an organismic approach to ecology, are introduced almost immediately, as well. The scientists represent comic narratives, then, either rooted in chaotic or organismic approaches to ecology. The park and its owner, however, embrace a tragic evolutionary narrative rooted in economic approaches to ecology that, according to the film's narrative, are doomed to failure.

A second conflict that catalyzes the disruption of Hammond's tragic evolutionary narrative is broached in a café in San José, Costa Rica, where Dennis Nedry agrees to sell fifteen species' embryos from Jurassic Park for $1.5 million. Nedry's decision has catastrophic results, but it also makes possible the movement from a narrative focused on a critique of genetic experimentation to a comic evolutionary narrative focused on community.

Dr. Malcolm provides an argument against Hammond's genetic experimentation early in the scientists' tour of the island and its visitor's center. According to a film the scientists view, all of the plants and dinosaurs they have seen result from cloning based on DNA found in blood samples extracted from prehistoric mosquitoes preserved in amber—petrified tree sap. According to Hammond they plan to maintain control by breeding only females in a lab and by imprinting new hatchlings to human "parents," especially Hammond himself.

Malcolm opposes Hammond's mission as a blow to evolutionary narratives: "John, the kind of control you're attempting is not possible. If there's one thing the history of evolution has taught us, it's that life will not be contained. Life breaks free. It expands to new territories. It crashes through barriers. Painfully, maybe even . . . dangerously, but . . . well, there it is."

Ellie agrees, arguing, "When people try to control things that are out of their power . . . it's antinature." Hammond's attempts to control nature are also rooted in a tragic evolutionary narrative.

Malcolm even disdains the work Hammond has accomplished at Jurassic Park because of its lack of creativity.

According to Malcolm, the park and its creatures "didn't require any discipline to attain it. You read what others had done, and you took the next step. You patented it and packaged it and slapped it on a lunchbox, and now, you're selling it." When Hammond argues that he is preserving species, Malcolm counters, "Hold on—this is no species that was obliterated by deforestation or the building of a dam. Dinosaurs had their shot. Nature selected them for extinction. What you call discovery, I call the rape of the natural world."

Malcolm offers multiple arguments against the experimentation Hammond has put into play, all resting on Hammond's disruption of a comic evolutionary narrative. Hammond disrupts that narrative first by attempting to control nature, exploiting it for his own gain. Such exploitation rests on tragic visions of evolution that see humans as pioneer species "dedicating themselves to survival through the destruction of all our competitors and to achieving effective dominance over other forms of life" (Meeker 162). Malcolm also notes that Hammond has disrupted the narrative further by cloning animals nature had selected for extinction, since, as Meeker explains, "the welfare of individuals is generally subordinated to the welfare of the group." Dinosaurs' extinction, then, can be seen as a means to sustain the welfare of other species, so their return disrupts the evolutionary narrative in play.

Ultimately both Sattler and Grant agree that Hammond can have no real control over either the plants or animals he has cloned. Sattler argues against Hammond's ability to control plant life he has cloned: "You have plants right here in this building, for example, that are poisonous. You picked them because they look pretty, but these are aggressive living things that have no idea what century they're living in and will defend themselves. Violently, if necessary."

And Grant agrees: "Dinosaurs and man—two species

separated by sixty-five million years of evolution—have just been suddenly thrown back into the mix together. How can we have the faintest idea of what to expect?" As Malcolm contends, Hammond's "scientists were so preoccupied with whether or not they could, they didn't stop to think if they should." The mayhem that erupts when Nedry shuts down security around the island demonstrates the dangerous consequences Hammond and the others face because he disrupted the comic evolutionary narrative.

Comic Evolutionary Narratives in *Jurassic Park*

These consequences, however, also provide the catalyst for the second evolutionary narrative, a comic narrative that provides a space for humanity to accommodate and adapt in order to survive as part of the natural world. As Ellie Sattler asserts when faced with the destructive force of unfettered dinosaurs, "I was overwhelmed by this place, but I made a mistake, too. I didn't have enough respect for that power, and it's out now. The only thing that matters now are the things we love: Alan and Lex and Tim. John [Hammond], they're out there where people are dying." Alan Grant, however, must learn that lesson before the family unit is forged. His transformation parallels a comic evolutionary narrative in which heroes succeed only through collaboration.

The distance Grant must travel to gain this knowledge is illustrated by multiple scenes in which he shows disdain for familial connections. In one scene early in the film, Grant even threatens violence when a child scoffs at a *Velociraptor*, calling it a "six-foot turkey." Grant grabs the boy and demonstrates the raptor's hunting prowess with a six-inch retractable razor-like claw, while telling him: "He slashes at you here . . . or here . . . or maybe across the belly, splitting your intestines. The point is, you are alive when they start to eat you. So you know, try to show a little respect." By the end of Grant's demonstration, the boy is nearly in tears, but Grant shows no remorse.

That distaste for children continues when Hammond's grandchildren arrive and are ushered into jeeps for the park tour. In an exchange with Sattler, Grant exclaims, "Kids! You want to have one of those?" and points toward Hammond's grandchildren. And when Sattler says she thinks one of their offspring "could be intriguing," Grant disagrees: "They're noisy; they're messy; they're expensive. . . . They smell. . . . Some of them smell. . . . Babies smell!"

Grant's attitude changes, however, when Nedry's plan disables all electric barriers, leading to an attack on Grant, Gennaro, Malcolm, and the children, Lex (Ariana Richards) and Tim (Joseph Mazzello). While Malcolm is injured and Gennaro is dead, Grant saves the children, willing to sacrifice himself to do so.

While they all huddle together in a tree waiting for dawn, for example, Grant seems to have been adopted into Lex and Tim's family. Now seeing Grant as "Dad," Lex nestles up next to him, and Tim tells him dinosaur jokes. When Lex asks Grant, "What if the dinosaur comes back when we're all asleep?" Grant answers, "I'll stay awake." Lex is skeptical: "All night?" she asks, and Grant agrees, "All night." Most important, he lets a claw like the raptor claw he had used to threaten the boy at his dig fall to the ground, explicitly illustrating his change of attitude toward family.

The next day, while Grant leads Lex and Tim over a fence and toward the safety of the visitor's center, Ellie Sattler volunteers to turn the power back on manually when the system responds slowly to a reboot, so Grant and the children can climb the electrified fence without injury. They all succeed because of their community efforts.

Sattler is able to turn on the power manually because park ranger Robert Muldoon (Bob Peck) fends off raptors on the hunt. Tim is able to jump from the electrified fence because Lex and Grant cheer him on. Grant catches Tim and revives him so they can enter the visitor's center.

Later Lex and Tim work together, as well, escaping from raptors hunting them in the park's cafeteria. They escape into the kitchen and trap one raptor in a freezer before racing out to find Sattler and Grant. Once they are reunited, they all work together to survive. When Sattler cannot reboot the system to secure the doors and fences, Lex, a computer hacker, intervenes, rebooting the system and locking the raptors out of the control room. Lex's hacking repairs the security system, and the phone rings to confirm her success. Ultimately, Sattler, Grant, Lex, and Tim become a family and, along with Malcolm and Hammond, escape the island by helicopter. The message of *Jurassic Park* is explicit: By building community—adapting and accommodating—they have survived so a comic evolutionary narrative can continue.

Conclusion

According to Leslie Paul Thiele, this evolutionary narrative "is the grandest (nonteleological) story at our disposal. It is appropriate that we co-opt it for moral instruction. . . . An ecological ethics situates us within interdependent social and biological relationships and prescribes action to sustain this web of life" (34). Unlike Disney's "web of life," as articulated in films such as *The Lion King* and *Pocahontas*, however, the evolutionary narratives illustrated by *The Land before Time* and *Jurassic Park* do not perpetuate a hierarchical natural order based in a tragic narrative in which pioneer species (races and genders) exploit the natural world and economic approaches to ecology. Instead, the films both point to a

Jurassic Park: Humans confront dinosaurs.

comic narrative in which "the lesson . . . is balance and equilibrium . . . humility and endurance" (Meeker 168). Such a narrative is based in organismic and, to a certain extent, in chaotic approaches to ecology. According to Meeker, such an ethical and comic narrative would mean:

> Human values could no longer be based on the assumption that man [*sic*] is alone at the center of creation; allowance would have to be made for the welfare of all plants, animals, and land of the natural environment. Mankind would have to cultivate a new and more elaborate mentality capable of understanding intricate processes without destroying them. Ecology challenges mankind to vigorous complexity, not passive simplicity. (168)

Perhaps, as Thiele asserts, "the mores that we propagate may persist over millennia with astounding fidelity" (33). Thiele continues, "In this light, propagating mores that facilitate ecological sustainability becomes a very reasonable endeavor indeed." *The Land before Time* and *Jurassic Park* offer a space in which to explore such a proposition.

Over the Hedge: Verne tries to return human stash.

EIGHT

DreamWorks and Human and Nonhuman Ecology

Escape or Interdependence in
Over the Hedge *and* Bee Movie

The Land before Time (1988) and *Jurassic Park* (1993) point the way to two other environmental films with a Spielberg touch, if only because they are products of DreamWorks Animation, the studio associated with the Spielberg name: *Over the Hedge* (2006) and *Bee Movie* (2007). In spite of their shared studio space, however, *Over the Hedge* and *Bee Movie* assert opposing solutions to humans' intervention into and overdevelopment of the natural world. In both a perpetuation and critique of economic approaches to ecology, *Over the Hedge* argues that nonhuman nature must separate from humans and their suburban sprawl in order to survive, avoiding consequences of economic approaches to ecology. *Bee Movie*, on the other hand, asserts that human and nonhuman nature share an interdependent relationship based in both organismic and chaotic approaches to ecology that, once disrupted, may destroy them both. The reason why these films have such conflicting messages may rest in the broad goals and diverse visions of DreamWorks Animation.

DreamWorks Animation SKG, Inc., has been an independent company since 2004, with Paramount Pictures (Viacom) holding exclusive distribution rights to its films through 2012. But the animation studio began as part of the DreamWorks initiative that was first posed by Jeffrey Katzenberg to Steven Spielberg and David Geffen in 1994 after Katzenberg left Disney. Katzenberg brought his animation expertise with him to DreamWorks after success at Disney with films like *The Little Mermaid*, *Beauty and the Beast*, and *The Lion King*, films that renewed Disney's edge in the animation industry. He also brokered the agreement between Disney and Pixar, successes that made it possible for him and his management team to begin an exclusive animation wing for DreamWorks that went independent in 2004.

According to its Web site, "DreamWorks Animation SKG is devoted to producing high-quality family entertainment through the use of computer-generated (CG) animation." The site continues, "With world-class creative talent and technological capabilities, our goal is to release two CG animated feature films a year that deliver great stories, breathtaking visual imagery and a sensibility that appeals to both children and adults." They also "strive to tell great stories that are fun and comedic, told with a level of sophistication and irreverence that appeals to the broadest audience possible and captures the imaginations of all people regardless of age." They plan to transform all of their animated films to 3-D, from *Monsters vs. Aliens* (2009) forward. The studio's focus on computer-generated animation and great stories that capture a wide audience sets it apart from Disney studios, perhaps because irreverence is one of its goals. For example, one of DreamWorks Animation's first films, *Antz* (1998), "plays upon the expectations of its aesthetic and its narrative implications to collapse the anticipated conditions of 'the social' as it is determined within corporate infrastructures." The film advocates for individuality "in the midst of conformist culture and oppressive social hierarchies" through an aesthetic that combines "new geographic conventions" with effects and "uniform practices" (Wells, *Animation and America* 158). *Antz* builds on and moves beyond orthodoxy of classic Disney in an irreverent critique of contemporary American politics and valorization of an alternate worldview that embraces inclusion and rejects marginalization.

Irreverence may take DreamWorks Animation films in a variety of directions, however, addressing issues in sometimes conflicting ways, highlighting varied critiques of environmental practices while promoting an agenda of inclusion. *Antz*, for example, highlights how, according to Z (Woody Allen), the "whole system makes [Z] feel insignificant" as an individual in a communal environment where collective work rules. In the anthill, signs read "Conquer Idleness" and "Time for Training," signifiers of the worker-ant mentality of the hill. But Z, as a unique individual with communal tendencies, urges workers to revolt because they "control the means of production." Ultimately, Z saves the hill's princess and overthrows a tyrannical general wishing to destroy the hill and begin anew with himself in power. In the end, though, Z cannot save the hill or the princess alone. The worker ants must form ladders to save them all from floods caused by the general's treacherous plans. The film, then, advocates for a community that is directed not by fascist dictators but by the proletariat, a "people" who choose their path, even that of a comic-heroic worker ant protecting his species and his princess by following a comic evolutionary narrative. *Antz* then begins with resistance to conformity by force but ends with acceptance of a conformity based in consensus.

The Prince of Egypt (1998), *The Road to El Dorado* (2000), and *Sinbad: The Legend of the Seven Seas* (2003) explore myth in sophisticated ways to meet the needs of a broad contemporary audience concerned with contemporary issues. *The Prince of Egypt*, for example, updates the story of Moses and Rameses to address this contemporary audience in ways Egyptian journalists such as Adel Hammouda called "Jewish revisionist" (qtd. in Wells, *Animation and America* 137) and Michel Shehadeh, director of the Arab Film Festival, argued made the film "a human rights film against oppression" (qtd. in Wells, *Animation and America* 137), negotiating again a resolution to conflicts that end in conformity.

Other DreamWorks Animation SKG films highlight the studio's technological capabilities and commitment to visual spectacle. *Chicken Run* (2000), *Wallace and Gromit in the Curse of the Were-Rabbit* (2005), and *Flushed Away* (2006) are products of DreamWorks Animation's short-lived agreement with British studio Aardman Animations, which produces stop-action cartoons for film and television, and combine compelling stories with a distinctive aesthetic style. *Shrek* (2001) and its three sequels, *Shark Tale* (2004), *Madagascar* (2006), and *Kung*

Fu Panda (2008), highlight DreamWorks Animation's move to completely computer-generated features, again with emphasis on a narrative geared toward a wide audience base, especially because of the fairy-tale allusions scattered throughout the films as comic devices. *Monsters vs. Aliens* introduces the studio's decision to film all future animated features in 3-D.

Spirit: Stallion of the Cimarron (2002), on the other hand, returned the studio to hand-drawn effects in an animated feature asserting an argument for animal rights and Native American sovereignty. Although writing mainly about Disney cartoons, David Whitley draws on *Spirit* as a model environmental cartoon against which animated features such as *Pocahontas* might be compared. According to Whitley, the film "indicate[s] that it is possible to create popular sentimental narratives that are exciting and engaging, yet avoid some of the more obvious pitfalls of *Pocahontas*" (89). Whitley asserts that the film "establishes many of its key values and emotional charge through contrasting the attitudes of Native Americans and white settlers toward nature." As an exploration of white settlers' movement westward, by covered wagon and then by train, "*Spirit* explores critical elements in the myth of the 'Frontier,' which has played such a central role in defining aspirations and goals throughout American history" (89). Whitley demonstrates how the idea of the frontier is interrogated by the film, noting how the railroad destroyed Native Americans, wild horses, and buffalo through its narrative rather than through a didactic voiceover.

But he also discusses how the film represents the interrelationship between human and nonhuman nature. According to Whitley, competing worldviews about our relationship with nonhuman nature "are shown largely through contrasts between the way the Lakota Indians are shown relating to the horse, and [the horse's] treatment under the regime of the cavalry commander and later the overseers of the railroad construction" (91), The Lakota's treatment is constructed as "kinder, based on empathy and identification with the creature." Although Whitley sees this construction as idealized, he also notes that Plains Indians did allow their horses to roam free once they had "accepted humans." *Spirit* highlights the repercussions of modernization but harks back romantically for a wilderness that cannot be recovered. It also not only idealizes Plains Indians but the wild horses at the center of the film, a product of Spanish colonization of the Americas. *Spirit* illustrates a horse's journey through several human cultures: the cavalry, the Lakota, and the railroad, and demonstrates the superior relationship that one of the Lakota, Little Creek (Daniel Studi), has with nonhuman nature. Ultimately, however, Spirit willingly accepts the freedom Little Creek offers him, galloping joyfully away with his mate, Ran.

Unlike *Spirit*, *Over the Hedge* and *Bee Movie* confront contemporary environmental concerns rather than romantically reconstructing an environmental history now out of human control. *Over the Hedge* draws on some of the same arguments made in *Spirit*, demonstrating that "wild" nature thrives best when separate from humans and their domesticated suburbia. *Bee Movie*, on the other hand, asserts a message of interdependence between human and nonhuman nature that calls both to action for mutual survival.

Over the Hedge is drawn from Michael Fry and T. Lewis's comic strip of the same name. The comic strip explores suburbia from the perspective of the animals that lived there before the land was developed and who attempt to save their forest from encroaching developers but get distracted by the comforts of suburban life, from junk food to big-screen televisions. Whereas the comic strip maintains the conflict between suburbia and woodland, highlighting the ambivalence woodland animals might have toward the wonders they find there, the film confronts the conflict between suburban luxury and wilderness life, offering a resolution that validates nonhuman nature over the artificiality of humans and their suburbs, again from the perspective of the forest animals.

According to Joe Strike's outline of the transformation from comic strip to film, the film succeeds because Michael Fry and T. Lewis, the comic-strip creators, were involved throughout the filmmaking process. Yet translating a strip to a feature with a clear resolution oversimplifies the ambivalence woodland animals in the strip have toward their suburban neighbors. Fry and Lewis shopped a film idea around, however, and Fox Films first bought the rights but put the film on the shelf, letting their option expire in 2001. DreamWorks bought the rights and, according to Strike, "The original Fox story pitch . . . was refined into a 'how it all began' tale, recounting RJ's first meeting with Verne and the 'blended family' of animals he looks after." Other changes were made to the animal characters to accommodate movie audiences, but the most blatant change for us is the film's resolution of the conflicts that remain ongoing in the strip and complicate the relationship between human and nonhuman nature.

Directors Tim Johnson and Karey Kirkpatrick and writers Len Blum and Lorne Cameron, however, sought to maintain the point of view of the comic strip, that of the woodland animals. To authenticate this animal point of view, the DreamWorks crew "crawled on [their] bellies through the woods and took pictures," and the cinematography attempts to replicate this perspective. According to Barbara Robertson, "Because the film is told from the animals' point of view, the camera is always at critter height. Anything higher than the animals is an up shot" (14). Filmmakers also visually contrasted the forest from the point of view of the suburban hedge. The forest, then, is presented in a hyperrealistic style, Robertson writes, in which "sunshine dapples the leaves, and flowers bob their head." Suburbia, on the other hand, "looks like Bellagio with colored lights in the sprinklers, but the neighborhood turns harsh when Verne (Garry Shandling) pays a visit."

Nonhuman nature is idealized, as well, however, with animal species working together toward common goals, even when they realistically would be natural enemies. According to Roger Ebert, in *Over the Hedge* "we get an animal population where all the species work together instead of eating each other, and there is even the possibility of interspecies sex, when a human's house cat falls in love with Stella the skunk (Wanda Sykes)." But, as Ebert asserts, in the film "there is also the usual species-ism; mammals and reptiles are first-class citizens, but when a dragonfly gets fried by an insect zapper, not a tear is shed" ("Over the Hedge").

Over the Hedge from its opening highlights the conflict between forest and suburb. The film's protagonist, RJ (Bruce Willis), a junk-food-eating raccoon, steals Vincent's (Nick Nolte), a hibernating bear's, wagon full of junk food, awakening the bear when RJ opens of can of potato chips. In the altercation that follows, the wagon falls off the cliff and is hit by a car. Vincent is angry because he has lost his food through RJ's carelessness, so he gives RJ a week to collect the food and restore his stash.

This suburban scene contrasts with the first view of the forest in which another hibernating animal awakens, a turtle named Verne who senses the melting snow. He leaves his sleeping log and discovers it is spring. He wakes up his animal friends of all species, who have been hibernating with him. The sleeping host of animals have eaten all the stored food during the winter and now must gather more to survive. Verne the turtle shows them the rest of the berries and gives one to each. Instead of living off a stashed load of junk food they must fill the log to the top with food in order to survive another winter, so they begin gathering food in their forest.

The overdevelopment of suburbia, however, begins to penetrate their forest mecca, first because RJ has overheard Verne's goal to fill the log. RJ plans an alternative survival plan that will ultimately repay the bear and save his life. Suburbia also infiltrates their forest home, however, because the suburban development has grown while they slept. As Hammy and the rest of Verne's pack gather nuts, they see a hedge separating them from what they think is the rest of the forest. But when they hear a human voice from behind the hedge, Verne climbs through to investigate and enters a brightly lit human backyard where he sees all the trappings of suburban life: topiary and a swimming pool, a bug zapper, sprinklers, turtle-shaped birdbaths, grills with knives, hoses, and children's outdoor toys. Verne is surprised not only by the excess but also by its implications: half of their forest has been destroyed to build this new human neighborhood.

RJ is there to counteract Verne's dismay, however, offering an alternative survival strategy that will lead them to "the good life" of nacho cheese and sugar. In the human suburb of overconsumption, they can gather their food in a week instead of the typical 237 days. Once they have tasted the junk food RJ offers, the other animals willingly join him, leaving Verne and his antiquated but more natural plan behind.

Suburbia, however, wants nothing to do with wild creatures. Gladys Sharp (Allison Janney), the president of the homeowners' association, is especially dedicated to keeping the suburbs free of all nonhuman life. While the pack gathers human food, Gladys maintains order. RJ introduces the pack to food options in overflowing suburban trashcans.

When Gladys sees the animals, however, she chases them back through the hedge. As head of their forest family, Verne comforts the rest of the animals and leads the chorus of "goodnights" like characters from *The Waltons* (1972). Because RJ has no family he envies this community and, wanting it for himself, further entices the animals to forage for food in suburbia. Instead of helping the hyperactive squirrel, Hammy, gather nuts, RJ introduces Hammy to Girl Scout cookies, attempting to connect him with the human world and to help him fulfill his promise to the bear. Although a Girl Scout attacks Verne with a book and a can of pepper spray, the animals scare the girls away, and RJ steals their wagon and its cookie contents. Despite the dangers to which he exposes them, RJ has converted the animal family to junk-food junkies. A montage sequence shows the animals stealing human food, but when they take a vanload of pizza from Gladys, she calls a "verminator" (Thomas Haden Church). But since they all escape, the animals appoint RJ their new leader.

Verne, however, yearns for a more natural and safe life

and returns the junk food so the family can return to its normal healthy lifestyle in the forest. But a dog and his chain interfere. The wagon and its contents explode in a shower of chips and other food debris. Verne has not returned the family to its more natural state. Instead, because they still crave junk food, RJ and the other animals abandon Verne.

RJ and his new family now embrace the suburban lifestyle. RJ must now replenish the bear's stash in record time, however, so he coerces the family into a dangerous plan to gather a wagon full of junk food at a party thrown by their worst enemy, Gladys. RJ's plan is ingenious and takes all of Gladys's traps into account, but Gladys awakens and calls the verminator who captures all but RJ. RJ rolls away with the food, nearly condemning his forest family to death, but Vincent the bear tells RJ he has done a vicious thing: "You take the food and they take the fall." RJ is transformed and rescues the animals from the verminator and, with their help, fends off the bear.

Over the Hedge ends with nature and culture bifurcated. Forest animals are better off in their forest, away from the dangers of suburbia. Glady's verminator and the animals engage in a comic scene that includes the capture of most of the woodland animals and their escape from both verminator and bear. The scene ends in group harmony in a forest world separate from humans. That separation is best when animals form a community, a family that works together to fill a log, not with junk food but with nuts and berries. Unlike the comic strip, then, the film version of *Over the Hedge* erases ambiguity, leaving no room for interaction between suburbia and the forest beyond its hedgerow.

Bee Movie at first seems to illustrate this same need for

bifurcation, with any interaction between humans and nonhuman nature—in this case bees—not only advised against but outlawed. Jane Lamacraft notes that "the contrast between the hive, humming with contented collaborative endeavor, and the competitive, stressed-out human world, makes you agree with Barry (Jerry Seinfeld): 'No wonder we're not supposed to talk to them. They're insane'" (60). And Barry's interaction with humans reveals a shocking revelation: humans are stealing honey from bees for a profit. Barry takes them to court, suing the human race for their exploitation of all bees. With this premise in place, the film seems geared toward advising the same kind of separation advocated by *Over the Hedge*.

Todd McCarthy of *Variety* agrees, asserting that the film is "a goofy but wispy concept, one hardly developed in ways that charge the emotions or one's sense of justice. Nor does the critter/human dynamic here possess the crucial interdependence that it did, for example, in this summer's *Ratatouille*." But he does point out attempts to enact human/nonhuman interdependence in the film. Peter Travers makes that interdependence explicit when he notes that Barry has more than a platonic relationship with the human, Vanessa (Renee Zellweger), since his "organ of sensation fondles her hand" ("Bee Movie"). And Stephanie Zacharek notes the broader vision of interdependence in the film, that between bee pollinization and plant growth, asserting that "[f]rom an environmentally conscious point of view, the core idea here is sound enough, particularly if you've paid any attention to the recent news stories about how the decreasing bee population threatens to alter the delicate balance of our environment" ("Bee Movie").

For us, the film offers a complex solution to questions

broached in *Over the Hedge*. Although *Over the Hedge* answers "no" to questions regarding human and nonhuman nature's ability to peacefully coexist, *Bee Movie* asserts that bees and humans must live and work together for both species to survive. This is true either individually, as represented by Barry's relationship with Vanessa, or collectively, as illustrated by the drastic loss of plant life when bees go on strike, refusing to pollinate and thus regenerate flowers and other plants around the world.

There is no doubt that bee populations are decreasing rapidly and that their annihilation would have a devastating effect on agriculture. According to Diana Cox-Foster and Dennis vanEngelsdorp in *Scientific American*, in 2007, due to Colony Collapse Disorder (CCD), "a fourth of U.S. beekeepers had suffered . . . losses and . . . more than 30 percent of all colonies had died. The next winter the die-off resumed and expanded, hitting 36 percent of U.S. beekeepers. Reports of large losses also surfaced from Australia, Brazil, Canada, China, Europe and other regions."

These losses may be catastrophic for farmers, Cox-Foster and vanEngelsdorp explain, "because one third of the world's agricultural production depends on the European honeybee, *Apis mellifera*, the kind universally adopted by beekeepers in Western countries." Loss of bees, then, would deplete agricultural products that benefit humans. But because these bees also pollinate other plant species, their depletion could have widespread effects on a biotic community, destroying whole species of flowers and trees.

Researchers see human factors contributing to this loss of bees. Cox-Foster and vanEngelsdorp cite poor nutrition, pesticide exposure, stress-related viruses, and fungicides as factors influencing colony collapse. In order to slow the collapse of bee colonies and to ensure agricultural pollinization, Cox-Foster and vanEngelsdorp assert that beekeepers need to act quickly to minimize disease and ensure good nutrition and less exposure to pesticides for their bee colonies. Farmers, too, should decrease their use of harmful pesticides and herbicides so bees can survive and help maintain a food supply for both humans and bees.

Bee Movie illustrates the catastrophic losses such a lack of pollinization might cause, not because bee colonies have been destroyed by human farming techniques but because bees go on strike. By elucidating this connection between bees and human production, the film also reinforces the need for interdependent relationships between humans and bees, relationships that also draw on both organismic and chaotic approaches to ecology. The film tells this tale of interconnection between human and nonhuman nature through the eyes of Barry, a bumblebee who has just graduated from the equivalent of high school and must choose his job to help keep the hive going. The conceptualization of the process of producing honey works well, with intricate detail, but Barry rebels and joins the pollen jocks instead, leaving the hive to collect pollen for honey processing.

Humorous elements of his first journey out with the pollen jocks show the dangers of connecting personally with the human world and contending with human civilization. The pollen jocks pollinate flowers with pollen power all over New York City but mistake a tennis ball for a flower. Barry rides on a car window with other bugs toward home, flies into a rainstorm, and escapes into an apartment where he is nearly killed by a tennis player, Ken (Patrick Warburton), until Ken's friend, Vanessa, saves the bee because, as she puts it, all life has value to her. Despite a bee law against talking with humans, Barry thanks Vanessa, and they become friends. Dangers of the human world are countered by this personal connection, facilitating a move toward explicit interdependence.

That connection is nearly shattered, however, when Barry learns about humans' exploitation of bees through honey theft. Barry works to legally separate bees from the human world. With Vanessa's help, Barry takes the Ray Liotta Private Select Honey Company to court and wins, shutting down honey production and sending all honey back to the bees. All honey production stops, and bees lie back and grow fat. But without pollination, all flowering plants begin to die.

Once Vanessa points out the dead trees and flowers everywhere, including at her flower shop, Barry responds, realizing that humans and bees must work together interdependently for both species to survive. He must get the hive working again to save the flowers. With Vanessa's help, they hijack a flower-covered float from the Tournament of Roses Parade and take it to the bee community and their pollen jockeys. Once the flowers are pollinated, other plants and flowers respond, demonstrating the symbiotic relationship they share. That relationship is extended to the human world in *Bee Movie*, not only because Barry and Vanessa set up shop together, but also because bees' pollination sustains plants that sustain both human and nonhuman nature. The chaos of bee-colony collapse is now under control in a biotic community grounded in organismic approaches to ecology.

Conclusion

Over the Hedge and *Bee Movie* tackle contemporary environmental issues: overdevelopment and Colony Collapse

Bee Movie: Barry and Vanessa join humans and bees.

Disorder among bees, coming out with divergent solutions to conflicts between human and nonhuman nature. *Over the Hedge* argues for separation between humans and woodland animals from a worldview that critiques economic approaches to ecology. *Bee Movie* illustrates our need for interdependence, especially in order to thrive in a biotic community.

Both movies, however, were produced by the same studio, DreamWorks Animation SKG, a studio that seeks to tell stories that are "fun and comedic with a level of sophistication and irreverence that appeals to the broadest audience possible and captures the imaginations of all people regardless of age." That broad audience also helps DreamWorks Animation SKG capture the box office, raking in profits and contributing to a consumer culture that may contradict the messages it shares.

This contradiction perhaps better connects the studio to the ambivalence of the *Over the Hedge* comic strip than the less ambiguous film. Overall, however, Dream-

Works Animation films, including *Over the Hedge* and *Bee Movie*, offer an alternative to the orthodoxy of classic Disney films by immersing animated characters in a contemporary world tackling contemporary environmental problems. Although resolutions in these DreamWorks films sometimes maintain the nature/culture binary, just as do most contemporary Disney animated features, they also at least tentatively explore how present-day human and nonhuman nature might coexist.

WALL-E: WALL-E and EVE hold hands.

NINE

Pixar and the Case of WALL-E

Moving between Environmental
Adaptation and Sentimental Nostalgia

Although animated films from a variety of studios assert powerful environmental messages such as those of *Happy Feet* (2006) and *The Simpsons Movie* (2007), their sometimes postmodern narratives are told through either a modern or, in the case of most Disney films, orthodox aesthetic. Pixar Studios, on the other hand, attempts to transcend the modern in both narrative and form, interrogating and deconstructing the modern technologies and aesthetics on which animated film is based. In *Animation and America*, for example, Paul Wells asserts that Pixar's films "usefully interrogate the status and impact of the cartoonal 'text'" (152) as a way to comment on the changing manifestation of the American dream.

Pixar films challenge the American notion of individualism on which the pioneer spirit of the frontier was built and suggest that representations of the American dream are relative and are mediated through both cultural knowledge and technological advances. By applying such a cultural and technological relativism, the *Toy Story* films, for example, make possible a postmodern aesthetic to accompany representations of culture and nature as situated. Pixar explores the notion that knowledge is mediated and, hence, nature and culture are situated, illustrating a transition that bridges the modern aesthetic and narrative of most studios with the possibility of a postmodern aesthetic and narrative based in a localized vision of place.

A Bug's Life: Localizing Nature

In *A Bug's Life* (1998), too, norms of the natural order are challenged, not by an idyllic vision like that in Disney's *Bambi* (1942), but by localized opposition to conventional views of nature in both narrative and aesthetic. An ant colony, soon to be ruled by Princess Atta (Julia Louis-Dreyfus), is terrorized by bandit grasshoppers in a direct homage to both *The Seven Samurai* (1954) and *The Magnificent Seven* (1960). The lead grasshopper, Hopper (Kevin Spacey), at first reinforces normal views of natural hierarchies, explaining to Atta, "It's a bug-eat-bug world out there, princess. One of those 'Circle of Life' kind of things. Now let me tell you how things are supposed to work: The sun grows the food. The ants pick the food. The grasshoppers eat the food."

Led by worker ant, Flik (Dave Foley), however, the colony resists this hierarchy and hires an eccentric group of circus insects to oppose the grasshoppers. After combating them with smoke, mirrors, acrobatics, and a mechanical bird, the grasshoppers are finally defeated when Hopper is captured by an actual bird and fed to her young babies, an illustration of another stage in the life cycle. Flik, Princess Atta, and their unusual insect allies have won, so the princess offers an alternative perspective on this cycle of life to the remaining army of grasshoppers: "Nature has a certain order. The ants pick the food. The ants keep the food. The grasshoppers leave."

Aesthetics in this topsy-turvy eco-narrative were made possible by successfully "jump[ing] from the computer-friendly world of plastic toys and static interiors [of *Toy Story*] to the irregular, organic, constantly moving world of wind-blown grass, pebbly terrain, smoke, water, and fire" (Paik 119). According to Karen Paik's *To Infinity and Beyond! The Story of Pixar Animation Studios*, "While Pixar wanted to make a world that felt real, they didn't want to be a copy of the real world" (124). Instead, "they wanted a world that . . . made things seem not photo-real, but hyper-real." Paik asserts that "they were very willing to break rules of nature in service to the story, in order to make the audience relate to and focus on the characters. But they never broke rules of nature that upheld the plausibility of the story and its world."

For example, by providing ants with four instead of six legs, Pixar made them more "appealing" to an audience as representations with human qualities, including community building. In a sense Pixar moves toward a postmodern representation of nature similar to that Dana Phillips asserts is found in Carl Hiassen's novel *Double Whammy* (205–06). In the world of *A Bug's Life*, as Phillips explains it, "Representation has supplanted presence" (206). The hyperrealistic representation Pixar describes serves as a "spectacularization of nature—the doubling of our alleged alienation from it in new and ever more encapsulated forms" (Phillips 209) like photographs of bass in *Double Whammy* and computerized representations of insects in *A Bug's Life*. Place and subjectivity have become fragmented in this postmodern world, but these representations also demonstrate that, as both Phillips and Wendell Berry argue, "Nature is necessary" (Phillips 220).

Berry argues for "a conscious and careful recognition of the interdependence between ourselves and nature that in fact has always existed and, if we are to live, must always exist" (qtd. in Phillips 221). In *A Bug's Life*, representations of nature demonstrate that survival depends on interdependence within the computer-generated insect world and, perhaps, between humans (at least as creators of anthropomorphized bugs) and the natural world, as well.

Finding Nemo and Representation

That same postmodern perspective underlies *Finding Nemo*, as well. As Anthony Lane explains in his review of the film, Pixar "makes art for the age of the iMac." According to Lane, the film's weaknesses are a product of this aesthetic built on technology. As Lane asserts of Pixar, "This time, they have pasted together a thin, sentimental tale that just happens to be the ideal vehicle for the demonstration of an improving medium." For Lane, however, the film seems dull because it focuses on fish, just as *A Bug's Life* highlights an anthill, calling their main characters "insects and fish: the bony extras of the animal kingdom, inexplicably promoted to leading roles."

In spite of this far from appealing review, *Finding Nemo* found numerous critical supporters. Roger Ebert claims "it adds an unexpected beauty, a use of color and form that makes it one of those rare movies where I wanted to sit in the front row and let the images wash out to the edges of my field of vision." Stephen Holden of the *New York Times* asserts, "The humor bubbling through *Finding Nemo* is so fresh, sure of itself and devoid of the cutesy condescension that drips through so many family comedies that you have to wonder what it is about the Pixar technology that inspires the creators to be so endlessly inventive." Yet Salon.com's Stephanie Zacharek sees that inventive technology as problematic because it focuses on representation: "It's all beautiful, all right. But before long I began to feel beaten against the rock of that beauty—*Finding Nemo* smacks of looky-what-I-can-do virtuosity, and after the first 10 minutes or so, it's exhausting." For Zacharek, "*Finding Nemo* is lovely to look at." But she asked herself, "Who cares?"

After Nemo (Alexander Gould) is captured by a human "collector," his father, Marlin (Albert Brooks), searches for and finds him with help from his friend, Dory (Ellen DeGeneres), but the hyperrealistic undersea world Pixar creates takes center stage in reviews. For Paul Wells, however, that hyperrealism transcends mere computer-generated setting and characters and contributes to story. In *The Animated Bestiary*, Wells argues that "*Finding Nemo*, with its opening scenes of a barracuda eating clownfish, sharks seeking food, and interventions by humankind, does most to balance the realism of context with the necessary progress of the characters" (125).

Finding Nemo, then, provides a space to explore representations, constructions of human and nonhuman nature not only in the computer-generated space undersea, but also in a story line that highlights the conflicts within and between nature and culture. These are conflicts that, as in *A Bug's Life*, highlight the need for interdependence, at least among anthropomorphized species in the natural undersea world.

Cars and Transformation of Landscape

Monsters, Inc. (2001) and *The Incredibles* (2004) both seem to critique overuse of technology and, in the case of *Monsters, Inc.*, the resources needed to power it. When screams produce energy, a scare factory becomes gothic torture chamber until Sully (John Goodman) and Mike Wazowski (Billy Crystal) discover that laughter from human children produces twice as much power. The Incredibles' superpowers—perhaps supernatural powers—defeat "Syndrome's" (Jason Lee) technologically driven weapons and again demonstrate that nature and the supernatural transcend cultural constructions like technology.

In *Cars* (2006), on the other hand, technology becomes both culture and nature, taking representation to another level where even cows are replaced by tractors. At the Piston Cup Race that opens the film, the conceit of *Cars* becomes clear. There are no human beings in this world, only anthropomorphized vehicles that, like Lightning McQueen (Owen Wilson), pose for a camera before a race or, like the cars in stands surrounding the track, observe and support the competition. Landscapes are transformed into race tracks in *Cars*, but the film goes further, transforming all human and nonhuman nature into personified cars, tractors, trucks, and other vehicles on four wheels. Even insects look like Volkswagen Beetles, a point that Manohla Dargis of the *New York Times* says is part of "the story's underlying creepiness." Dargis compares the film to *The Terminator* (1984), asserting that *Cars*' director John Lasseter "has done Mr. Cameron [director of *The Terminator*] one better: instead of blowing the living world into smithereens, these machines have just gassed it with carbon monoxide."

For us, however, the major weakness in the film is its nostalgia for what Roger Ebert calls "an earlier America." Ebert validates this message as part of Hollywood's mystique, asserting that "life was better in the old days, when it revolved around small towns where everybody knew each other, and around small highways like Route 66, where you made new friends, sometimes even between Flagstaff and Winona."

A scene between Sally (Bonnie Hunt), Radiator Springs' prosecutor, and Lightning McQueen illustrates the environmental lie such nostalgia broaches. When Sally takes

McQueen out for a drive, she gives him a run for his money through pristine forests, puddles, and leaves into high country with pines near the tops of mountains. They drive through rocky tunnels and see a waterfall in view from a bridge. McQueen gets Volkswagen Beetles in his teeth and exclaims, "Ain't nature grand," not only through a car window but as a car. When they stop at the Wheel Well Motel, the most popular stop on Route 66, we learn that Sally was a Los Angeles lawyer who got fed up, left the big city, and broke down in Radiator Springs where everyone helped her and became her family. She takes McQueen to a view that made her stay, an overlook of an undeveloped desert valley, with rock monuments framing sand and cacti.

The interstate runs through the valley like a snake, but Sally harks back to a time when "the road didn't cut through the land like that interstate. It moved with the land, it rose, it fell, it curved. Cars didn't drive on it to make great time. They drove on it to have a great time." This nostalgia for simpler times when cars were tied to the land instead of to time—saving ten minutes with the bypass—serves as the environmental fallacy of the film, a fallacy proven by the lack of any animal or nonhuman nature on or along the road. In *Cars*, environmental nostalgia for a more environmentally conscious world takes a ludicrous turn in a lifeless world. In WALL-E (2008), on the other hand, nostalgia merges with dystopia and builds a narrative of environmental adaptation that embraces and comments on living nature.

WALL-E: Nostalgia/Dystopia
Two conflicting images of Earth open WALL-E, representations of the film's two visions: nostalgic and dystopic. Nostalgia opens the film. As the camera draws closer to Earth, the music and lyrics from one of *Hello, Dolly!*'s

love songs, "Put On Your Sunday Clothes," accompanies and highlights the cosmos, galaxies, and stars. "Somewhere Out There" amplifies our idealized view of Earth from space. But as we get closer to the landmasses and oceans of Earth, dystopic views intervene. Images of Earth are obscured by brown and gray floating masses of space garbage that become clearer as the shot moves toward a cityscape piled with skyscrapers built from trash. The trash looks like enormous termite hills between vacant buildings. The city is empty and devoid of sound except for the roaring wind until a rolling object appears, playing "Put On Your Sunday Clothes" as it picks up and compacts garbage.

These contrasting visions of Earth introduce the two conflicting ideologies grounding the film's rhetoric, those of Disney and Pixar Studios, and illustrates the approaches to ecology shaping the film's narrative: human ecology that encourages conservation and organismic ecology that demonstrates the need for interdependence. Although produced and released by Disney, WALL-E reflects the postmodern viewpoint of Pixar Animation studios. The creators transform the film and its protagonist, WALL-E, into what Paul Wells calls an "American popular cultural artifact [sic]" that has "become the focus of a significant meta-commentary on American consumer values and social identity" (Animation and America 152). By critiquing consumerism so overtly, WALL-E also critiques Disney's aesthetic and production values throughout much of the film, but it also reinforces a conservative romantic ideology found in classic Disney features from Snow White forward.

The philosophies driving Pixar and Disney both affect the ideology represented in WALL-E. Until the film's end, Pixar's vision resonates in the film and provides a dystopic and mechanistic perspective in which a robot named WALL-E acts as comic hero who empowers an apathetic, indolent, and lethargic human race on a centuries-long luxury solar system "cruise ship" vacation. WALL-E helps transform the hell of Earth into a home through a narrative of environmental adaptation with a clear and cohesive structure that follows an evolutionary pattern focused on place. This "place," the Earth WALL-E transforms, becomes a redefined organismic-based biotic community that includes not only nonhuman and human nature but also humanlike robots that prove more "natural" than the humans they ultimately save.

This dystopic view is made possible because the Pixar philosophy allows a director's vision to take precedence over studio ideology. According to "IGN: The Pixar Philosophy," "The fundamental difference at Pixar, unlike other environments with this melting-pot of collaboration, is that the director is always the final word here no matter where the notes come from, whether they're from the studio, anybody." The director has final decision-making power, and story drives the computer animation, according to Karen Paik, helping Pixar maintain aesthetic and narrative integrity. Andrew Stanton, codirector of *A Bug's Life* and director of both *Finding Nemo* and WALL-E, explains the benefits of this stance in relation to *Nemo*: "In my mind, *Nemo*'s very cohesive with the other films because it was born from the same group. But it's a real big billboard of, 'This is what you get when I drive'" (Paik 225). Stanton's vision shines through in WALL-E, as well. In both *Finding Nemo* and WALL-E, as well as in *A Bug's Life*, nature and the environment take center stage. *A Bug's Life* explores an ant's attempts to save his colony from humanlike grasshoppers; *Finding Nemo* looks at human intervention from under the sea; WALL-E examines environmental exploitation both on Earth's surface and on board its floating cruise ship. The values presented here support Pixar's emphasis on letting the director "drive."

Other values WALL-E illustrates, such as "romantic devotion and monogamy" and "hard work, faithfulness to duty," along with denigrating "passive dependency" (Allen), seem drawn from a Disney scorecard and appeal to both liberal and conservative audiences. Neal Gabler sees Disney animation providing a space in which Disney (in early films) and his viewers "would ultimately find nurturance, love, independence, and authority" (217). Movieguide.org, a "ministry dedicated to redeeming the values of the mass media according to biblical principles," calls WALL-E exemplary. According to the Movieguide review, WALL-E reflects a "strong Christian worldview without mentioning Jesus that tells a story about no greater love has any person than to give up his or her life for his or her neighbor" ("WALL-E Review"). *The New Yorker*'s David Denby calls WALL-E a classic that "demonstrates not just the number but the variety of ideas you need to make a terrific movie."

In spite of the conflicting politics behind these reviews, WALL-E appeals to both liberal and conservative audiences. Liberal audiences seem to be drawn to the blatant environmental message of the film based on its initial critique of overconsumption and the capitalist economy that perpetuate the humans' cruise above the planet. For example, Stephanie Zacharek of Salon.com calls it "an environmental cautionary tale." Cinephiles such as Kirk Honeycutt seemed to react to the homage to silent comedies, as does Peter Travers when he notes how WALL-E and Eve share a relationship that evokes "Charlie Chaplin's Little Tramp and Virginia Cherrill's blind flower girl in *City Lights*."

Conservative Christians feel the film filled a wholesome niche, valorizing values such as conservation. Charlotte Allen, a conservative reviewer for *The Los Angeles Times*, for example, asserts that "if WALL-E is didactic, what it has to teach is profoundly conservative. For starters, the film never even goes near the climate-crusading vocabulary of 'global warming,' 'carbon footprints,' or even 'green.'" Allen suggests instead that "the crime of how humans vacate Earth isn't failure to drive a Prius but strewing detritus." Allen sees this "crime" as rooted in conservatism, claiming, "Conservatives detest litterbugs and other parasites who expect others to clean up after them. WALL-E champions hard work, faithfulness to duty and the fact that even a dreary job like garbage-collecting can be meaningful and fulfilling." According to Allen, the film "isn't denigrating consumerism but passive dependency." And, Allen continues, the film "celebrates Western civilization."

For us, WALL-E presents the most powerful environmental statement made by either Disney or Pixar studios: Humanity must protect Earth and its resources because leaving it behind by spaceship or some other method cannot effectively preserve humankind. Instead, humankind survives as a species only because it is artificially sustained and separate from the natural world it ruined and then rejected until a robot named WALL-E intervened. Like other recent Disney animated films such as *Home on the Range* (2004), *Chicken Little* (2005), or *The Wild* (2006), and dystopic science-fiction movies of the twentieth century, however, WALL-E draws on nostalgia to strengthen its argument. In a merging of human and organismic approaches to ecology, the film asserts not only that humanity has destroyed Earth but that humans—with the help of the robot left to clean up the mess—can and should restore it to its more natural previous state.

Although many reviewers note the nostalgic appeal of the film, none of them align this nostalgia with nature. Instead they highlight WALL-E's nostalgia for human artifacts without connecting them with the natural world. Bob Mondello's NPR review notes WALL-E's homage to Charlie Chaplin's *Modern Times* (1936), stating he is "just as gratified by their look back 70 years to silent movies as [he is] by their look forward 700 years to a silent planet." A. O. Scott declares the film "Chaplinesque in its emotional purity" and notes WALL-E's "collection of treasures, including Zippo lighters, nuts and bolts, and a Rubik's cube" as evidence that "some of that stuff turned out to be useful, interesting, and precious. And some of it may even possess something like a soul." And David Denby calls the film "a work of tragic nostalgia," asserting that "the junk items he finds become fetishes for him. He holds on to plastic forks, hubcaps, and Zippo lighters, and throws away a diamond ring while keeping the felt box." Yet Denby, too, connects this nostalgia only to human artifacts—consumer goods that might be found at Buy N Large, the "box store" that controls Earth and its space station, the Axiom.

For us, on the other hand, WALL-E supports its environmental rhetoric in two ways: It draws on three types of nostalgia that ultimately point to images of nature as both individual and collective eco-memories, and it explores WALL-E's movement from tragic to comic ecological hero. This evolution of environmental adaptation coincides with that of nature, according to ecocritics such as Joseph Meeker.

Nostalgia has been critiqued, reified, and recovered in the past few decades, with a resurgence of research in memory studies complicating negative views of nostalgia built on postmodern views. Postmodern responses to nostalgia critique its move toward essentialism. In her 1988 article, "Nostalgia: A Polemic," Kathleen Stewart engages postmodern cultural critics' views that see nostalgia as a social disease. According to Stewart, "Nostalgia, like the economy it runs with, is everywhere. But it is a cultural practice, not a given content; its forms, meanings, and effects shift with the context—it depends on where the speaker stands in the landscape of the present" (227). Drawing on the work of Roland Barthes, Jean Baudrillard, Walter Benjamin, Pierre Bourdieu, Jonathan Culler, Donna Haraway, Fredric Jameson, and Raymond Williams, Stewart elucidates why nostalgia is such a powerful rhetorical tool, as well. Stewart argues that "on one 'level' there is no longer any place for *anyone* to stand and nostalgia takes on the generalized function to provide some kind (any kind) of cultural form" (227, emphasis Stewart's).

According to Stewart, nostalgia serves as a powerful rhetorical tool that placates and paralyzes the disenfranchised: "Nostalgia is an essential, narrative, function of language that orders events temporally and dramatizes them in the mode of 'that's that happened,' that 'could happen,' that 'threaten to erupt at any moment'" (227). Stewart sees the seductive nature of nostalgia in a postmodern culture as not only culturally situated but reductively negative, resulting in what she calls mirages—either a "grand hotel" of affluence or a "country cottage" of romantic simplicity. For Stewart, then, nostalgia is a negative consequence of attempting to replace postmodern relativism (labeled good) with an essential past based in recovery of a "self" (labeled bad).

From the perspective of these earlier cultural critics, there is a vanishing point of striving and looking for the pure or untouched, unpolluted past, projected into the wilderness of the past of history. But that really is an ideological project. Much of the past, in terms of today's environmental issues, is substantially lost because of population explosion, irrevocable global warming, loss of biodiversity, and unknown effects of pollution. Each year people born will not remember the same past as previous generations did. Our own literatures consider—through the lens of nostalgia—themes such as the vanishing Indian, the disappearance of the buffalo, and the disappearing prairie in relation to Frederick Jackson Turner's recuperative thesis of the frontier, a thesis that promotes progress at any cost, whether it be genocide or the expansion of industrialism in the United States.

More-recent work, especially in anthropology and cultural studies, however, complicates visions of nostalgia as inherently and inescapably bad. In fact, nostalgia may itself prove not only a way to learn from the past but to recuperate real community. In Ethel Pinheiro and Cristiane Rose Duarte's 2004 article, *"Panem et circenses* at *Largo da Carioca,* Brazil: The Urban Diversity Focused on People-Environment Interactions," for example, nostalgia in the form of collective memory and appropriation is what "led *Largo da Carioca* to survive in spite of all the political and urban changes." Pinheiro and Duarte drew on both a historical evolutive approach and participant-observation data. Historical-evolutive research demonstrated that the open plaza maintains functions from Ancient Greece, Egypt, and Mesopotamia, especially those related to performance. Participant observation resulted in interview data that revealed how "people link social activity in the *largo's* physical structure." Answers to a question asking respondents to "choose a word that could explain the place" illustrated the pull of nostalgia—one of the terms given to explain Largo da Carioca. Other terms were related, highlighting outdoor performances, culture, and tradition. The piece is esoteric but reveals the positive impact nostalgia might have, actually affecting the city's shape, ensuring that a people will appropriate a public space for performance and art because their collective memory draws them to it. The power of collective memory—of nostalgia—seems to be manifested in the continuation of Largo da Carioca. In fact, in the context of WALL-E, nostalgia's rhetorical power gains force when contextualized first from a personal standpoint and then collectively, building a community that turns the hell Earth has become into a home.

Nostalgia is manifested in several ways in the film. First WALL-E projects human artifacts through a sentimental and nostalgic lens. Then the film harks back to the innocence and heterosexual romance of Main Street U.S.A. as portrayed in clips and music from *Hello, Dolly!* and homages to other twentieth-century tunes and films. Here the film reinforces Disney's focus on wholesome monogamous heterosexual relationships. But the film also highlights econostalgic images and rhetorical moves such as those in *The Omega Man* (1971), *Silent Running* (1972), and *Soylent Green* (1973), or the more recent *Dark City* (1998) and *An Inconvenient Truth* (2006). In all of these films, images of Earth (or an Earth-like constructed planet) from space introduce a collective nostalgia, a memory of a pristine natural world. In *WALL-E*, as in the films it responds to, the camera zooms down, closer toward the landscape and a city that looks like New York, closely imitating *The Powers of Ten* (1968).

In the city, nostalgia becomes individualized when the last animated intelligent being on Earth, WALL-E (Waste Allocation Load Lifter–Earth-class), appears, his loneliness showing how vast yet empty a world devoid of romantic green nature becomes. There is nature, but it has been corrupted and decimated, leaving Earth for cockroaches, a romantic assumption broached in the film that humans should return when, perhaps, the planet may be better off without us.

WALL-E recalls a variety of apocalyptic science-fiction films but makes most-explicit connections with *Silent Running, Soylent Green, Omega Man,* and *Dark City.* Although *Soylent Green* illustrates the devastating results of not emptiness but overpopulation while highlighting a nostalgic view of Earth's past, it too critiques our destruction of the natural environment. *Dark City* moves us from space to a nostalgic view of a Noir City, but it is nature again that serves as the hero John Murdoch's motivation—to return the city to a more natural state in which life-giving water sustains human and nonhuman nature. *Silent Running* foregrounds a tragic hero who yearns for Earth's pristine forests so much that he sacrifices himself and his friends so the last forest—floating in space—can be saved and preserved by a robot that looks like a double of WALL-E. *WALL-E* also highlights a solitary hero, but that hero, WALL-E, mingles both the singularity of a tragic hero with the community of a comic figure who saves Earth and its former inhabitants from an artificial life. All these films highlight both an individualized and collective nostalgia for an Earth in its most natural state, an Earth, perhaps, unspoiled by humanity.

Cultural Artifacts and a First Level of Nostalgia: WALL-E as Tragic Eco-Hero

WALL-E first introduces nostalgia when he collects cultural artifacts from mountains of debris during his workday. WALL-E is a robot built for cleanup, collecting and compacting garbage to build a new cityscape made of rubbish bricks. He is alone, a tragic hero with only a cockroach as a companion. The vacant Buy N Large shops, banks, and train line they pass demonstrate a loneliness reinforced by the motionless piles of robots like himself along the road, dead "WALL-ES." WALL-E is the sole survivor in this vacant city, and he uses their parts for repairs on himself.

But the city also provides a setting for collective and individual nostalgia for a more natural environment. The people are gone, leaving a silent city in which one robot attempts to clean up centuries of waste after remaining humans escape to a space station with a cruise-ship atmosphere. In homage to the advertisements from the dystopic *Blade Runner* (1982), an electronic billboard commercial that WALL-E passes explains, "Too much garbage in your place? There is plenty of space out in space! BNL StarLiners leaving each day. We'll clean up the mess while you're away."

As if illustrating the commercial message, the camera pans down to show city streets where garbage-brick buildings fill caverns between skyscrapers. Garbage is everywhere in the empty streets. Only one figure moves in this desolate scene, the square robot with "WALL-E" inscribed on his chest that makes garbage bricks to construct these buildings every day. Other nonworking robots and large pieces of machinery bear the name, but WALL-E, the last working robot, turns this arid setting into a memory book, a place where treasures are buried under trash piles and collected in a dilapidated cooler and displayed in a private museum that doubles as WALL-E's home.

In these scenes, WALL-E seems to serve as a tragic hero, which Joseph Meeker defines as "a creature of suffering and greatness . . . [with] enormous . . . capacity for creating and for enduring pain, . . . for employing the power of mind and spirit to rise above the contradictions of matter and circumstance, even though one is destroyed by them" (157). As a tragic hero, WALL-E follows his directive each day, collecting and molding garbage into bricks while seeking to maintain the status quo, discovering artifacts to pay homage to Western culture.

Here he resembles Robert Neville (Charlton Heston) in *The Omega Man* or the Neville character (Will Smith) in *I Am Legend* (2007), seeking to perpetuate his own cultural mecca in a world gone savage. WALL-E first aligns with the Neville of *I Am Legend*, since he too has a sidekick pet—not a dog but a cockroach. Like the Neville of both films, however, WALL-E must barricade himself in his bunker each night, not to escape mutants but another product of nature—wind and dust storms. As a tragic hero, WALL-E is a pioneer, a "highly generalized, flexible, and adaptable creature capable of surviving despite the inhospitable nature of their environments" (Meeker 161). Meeker asserts that "pioneers must be aggressive, competitive, and tough" (161).

In these early scenes, WALL-E does seem to have survived because of a tough exterior. Following his directive, he recharges his solar-powered battery every morning and goes off to work, carrying his cooler on his rounds through the city, turning garbage into bricks and building taller and taller structures with each square. He stops only to collect more artifacts to add to his collections. The piles seem endless, but WALL-E is tireless, working in all conditions, stopping only to admire the treasures he collects, such as the spork he sorts between his set of forks and spoons. And like Neville, WALL-E protects himself from blasts and dust storms in a secure bunker where he stores his collectibles by type and lights up the dark gloom with strings of bright holiday globes.

But this tragic hero seems to have internalized the messages of the artifacts he collects and evolved, gaining characteristics of what Meeker calls a comic hero who is "durable even though he may be weak, stupid, and undignified" (158). WALL-E has evolved from a machine to a more humanoid (and comic) android. Later, with his help, the other robots on the Axiom undergo the same transformation, and vacationing humans transform from mindless consumers to eco-pioneers. According to Meeker, "Comedy is a celebration, a ritual renewal of biological welfare as it persists in spite of any reasons there may be for feeling metaphysical despair" (159). As a comic hero, WALL-E in a later part of the film forms relationships with other robots and with humans that facilitate this renewal.

Instead of highlighting tragedy, then, ultimately *WALL-E*

adheres to a narrative that is embedded in the comic and communal, rather than tragic and individualized, notions of species preservation found in the tragic evolutionary narrative of *The Odyssey* and of "early Darwinism" (Meeker 164). These tragic evolutionary narratives support extermination and warfare rather than accommodation, the results on display in WALL-E's opening shots. According to Joseph Meeker, humans typically embrace a tragic evolutionary narrative as in *The Odyssey* that counters the climax communities of plants and animals, which are "extremely diverse and complicated" (162). But this position comes at a price and may cost humanity its existence. Meeker asserts, "We demand that one species, our own, achieve unchallenged dominance where hundreds of species lived in complex equilibrium before our arrival" (164). This attitude may not only lead to the destruction of other species but of humanity itself.

Humans have embraced a tragic evolutionary narrative in WALL-E that WALL-E at first continues, following his directive. But ultimately the film changes direction, as do climax communities. The evolutionary narrative of WALL-E explores what might happen if humanity did learn from these more stable comic heroes and embrace a biotic community based in organismic approaches to ecology. According to Meeker, "Evolution itself is a gigantic comic drama, not the bloody tragic spectacle imagined by the sentimental humanists of early Darwinism" (164).

WALL-E embraces this focus on adapting to circumstances "in every possible way" (Meeker 164) while adding the element of nature. The film constructs a narrative of environmental adaptation that provides a space for nature and a broader vision of humanity that includes the humanoid robots that teaches them a better way. To build this narrative, the film follows a three-act narrative grounded in nature and versions of nostalgia that evolve from the solitary to the communal: (1) establishing Earth as an inhospitable setting for human and nonhuman nature (except, perhaps, insect and microbes); (2) leaving Earth on an evolutionary journey; and (3) returning to Earth able to transform hell into a home.

Romantic Nostalgia: Adapting to the Inhospitable

WALL-E's comic side emerges in his bunker when he turns on a VCR and scenes from *Hello, Dolly!* come on the screen. Nostalgia for the working parts of Earth and the innocent Main Street of the musical *Hello, Dolly!* drive WALL-E. These are comic elements of community building given the statement that "comedy is the art of accommodation and reconciliation" (Meeker 168). Homages to Charlie Chaplin, Buster Keaton, and Harold Lloyd reinforce this shift in the film. WALL-E's dance with a hubcap hat serves as an entry into a silent comic-film plot with a romantic heroine at its center, not the figure in the *Hello, Dolly!* video, but EVE, a female love interest like those found in Buster Keaton plots, self-sufficient and strong, but ultimately desirable. WALL-E seems to embrace the indefatigable-worker traits of Harold Lloyd characters and the love for a seemingly unattainable woman of Charlie Chaplin's tramp films, all within the Buster Keaton storytelling model—a linear narrative in which WALL-E goes all the way out to the cruise ship and back to rescue and win his girl, a strong female character like the love interest in *The General* (1927).

On one outing, however, WALL-E discovers a different kind of treasure inside a rusty refrigerator, a living, growing plant that broaches another type of nostalgia, that for images of nature. This discovery shifts WALL-E from a tragic individual mode to a communal comic perspective in which he establishes interdependent relationships with other robots and human and nonhuman nature so that all species can survive (Meeker 168).

The introduction of EVE into the desolate landscape provides a source for this interdependent relationship. EVE serves as a romantic female hero like those in Disney films and early silent comedies, but she also signifies a carefree freedom missing from the tragic setting in which WALL-E follows his directive so carefully. In one scene, for example, EVE flies above the waste with grace and speed. Music accentuates the sense of freedom, and the dry landscape contrasts with this lively dance.

After WALL-E sees EVE dance, Louis Armstrong's "La Vie en Rose" hints at WALL-E's sudden feelings for her. He follows her into a grocery store where he is rammed with shopping carts and hears the lyrics "When you kiss me." WALL-E is fascinated. In the early scenes he shares with EVE on Earth, WALL-E seeks EVE's attention as do Keaton, Chaplin, or Lloyd when they work to impress the female love interests in all of their films. In Keaton's films, as in WALL-E, the female protagonist always shares power and demonstrates her autonomy, just as EVE does from her early interactions with WALL-E until their return to Earth from the Axiom.

WALL-E attempts to impress EVE, just like Lloyd's plucky "kid in the city" character in films such as *Safety Last* (1923). Lloyd sends love letters and jewelry to his girl at home. WALL-E shows EVE his nostalgic artifacts, including the *Hello, Dolly!* video. They view the song and dance from the musical—"put on your Sunday clothes"—and WALL-E mimics the dance with his hubcap hat. EVE joins in the dance but is so strong she nearly destroys WALL-E and his home when she emulates him. WALL-E and EVE seem to be moving toward the romance evident on the screen when "And that is love," a line from "Only a Moment," is played as part of the *Hello, Dolly!* sequence. But when WALL-E brings her another "artifact," the plant he found in a refrigerator and stored in a boot, EVE opens up her abdomen, places the plant inside, and shuts down, floating silently. WALL-E has awakened and inspired EVE just as Earth's cultural artifacts had awakened him, but now EVE's directive becomes the priority.

Eco-Memory and Nostalgia:
An Evolutionary Journey

Now images of nature take precedence over romance, but WALL-E is at first unprepared to accept the loss of love it might require. WALL-E is devastated and keeps calling EVE's name after her own directive shuts her down. He attempts to revive her in the sun. He cares for her during a storm, putting umbrellas over her and protecting her from hail. He tries jumper cables to revive her and floats her around with him in a tire boat. He even sits with her on a bench to watch a sunset—like the iconic moment from *Manhattan* (1979). With all the garbage surrounding them, it is an absurd scene.

When EVE's space probe returns and its arm retrieves her, WALL-E races back from his workday and yells her name. He feels so connected with EVE he cannot part from her. He grabs onto the ship's ladder as the ship takes off and plows through old satellites and debris into a quiet and clean space until they reach a brightly lit and massive ship appearing from behind cosmic clouds. The probe enters the Axiom, the cruise ship on display in the ads. This cruise station looks similar to the Earth described in *Silent Running*, one large temperature-regulated mall. Now the paradise of the artificial world depicted in the ads on Earth becomes a nightmare.

In this cruise-ship hell, WALL-E becomes the force of nostalgia, reminding humans and other robots of the value of human relationships such as those in *Hello, Dolly!* and, ultimately, of nonhuman nature. When a human falls out of his floating chair, for example, WALL-E helps him back up and introduces himself. The human—John—talks back, establishing a relationship missing from the isolated video lives humans share. Humans have become such isolated consumers that when a robotic voice tells them that "blue is the new red," all the humans change their costume colors in lock step. But again WALL-E shatters the established order when he opens up a woman's chair controls and turns off her video feed. He introduces himself, and she, too, talks back. Her name is Mary. Two humans now have interacted with WALL-E and changed their pattern of behavior.

WALL-E has already established a relationship with EVE and stays with her as she is ushered to the captain to share her plant discovery. After seven hundred years, EVE, Extraterrestrial Vegetative Extractor, has returned positive for plant life, and "Operation Re-Colonize" can begin. With life returning to the home planet, Axiom will navigate them back to Earth, the manual explains.

Autopilot, the captain's robotic copilot, has a different plan and tells the captain, "We cannot go home." After some coaxing from the captain, AUTO shows another message from Forthright, CEO of Buy N Large, who reveals that Operation Cleanup has failed and toxicity levels are too high to sustain life on Earth. "It will be easier to remain in space," Forthright states. "Do not return to Earth." The plot is now revealed. The Earth, according to Forthright, is past saving and any contrary proof must be destroyed in order for the Axiom to remain in its present place. AUTO is merely following his directive, which is to abandon any attempts to return to Earth.

Eco-Memory and Nostalgia: Culture and Nature Merge to Make Earth a Home

The dirt WALL-E leaves in the captain's hand helps ignite the captain's urge to go home. He is intrigued by the matter in his hand and asks the computer to analyze it. The computer tells him it is soil—earth. Suddenly the captain is nostalgic for images of nature. The captain asks the computer to define Earth, and images of green fields and blue skies come on the screen, just as they do in the opening of *Soylent Green*. Images from D. W. Griffith's *A Corner in Wheat* (1909) show a lone farmer sowing seeds, foregrounding the connection between humans and nature and the possibilities that remain after a corporation has taken control of agricultural industries. The collective eco-memories on display become the captain's individual nostalgic yearnings, all because WALL-E found a plant and brought soil to Axiom's sterile world.

When EVE brings the captain the plant, the captain is thrilled that they can go home. He wants to see what Earth now looks like and turns on a recorded feed of her visit to Earth. It does not look like the computer images. "Where's the blue sky? Where's the grass?" he asks, waxing nostalgic. The computer images, however, also ignite a spark to return the Earth to its earlier more natural state.

WALL-E's tape of *Hello, Dolly!* cements the captain's decision. He knows they must go back. The plant represents the Earth, so the captain must nurture it, as well. The captain waters the plant—it "just needed someone to look after you, that's all. We have to go back!" He implies that Earth, too, needs someone to look after it. WALL-E has awakened the humans and androids from their passive existence so they are drawn to one another and to the Earth they left behind.

Although AUTO attempts to stop the captain, WALL-E, and EVE from returning to Earth, WALL-E fosters relationships with malfunctioning misfit robots, EVE, the captain, and at least two humans and facilitates their return to Earth. Once the rest of the humans awaken from their video-driven lives, they too form interdependent relationships and save one another from collisions. EVE uses a barrier to stop chairs from sliding into rows of humans along a wall. Mary and John save a group of children from crashing into the barrier. AUTO pushes another button to close the process, and WALL-E holds up the mechanism in which they must place the plant. After the captain switches the Axiom to manual power the once-passive humans stand up and pass the plant to EVE and into the Operation Re-Colonize mechanism, setting a course for Earth. WALL-E is nearly crushed, but humans now care about one another and desire to go home.

The return to Earth marks the fruition of the evolutionary journey in WALL-E. EVE has connected so completely with WALL-E that she rushes him to his bunker to repair him, using the parts he had so carefully stored there. After she rebuilds and reenergizes him, he reverts back to a robotic existence, even crushing some of his artifacts to fulfill his directive. Yet even though he does not know EVE, she persists, even after the *Hello, Dolly!* music does not awaken WALL-E's persona. When she follows him out to a garbage pile, touches his hand, and kisses him, however, WALL-E awakens and responds to her, saying her name, just like the prince awakening the princess in Disney's *Sleeping Beauty*. They hold hands, emulating the nostalgic figures in *Hello, Dolly!*

The captain, on the other hand, leads the humans out of the ship to reclaim a different nostalgic memory, that of images of nature viewed on his computer screen and in the plant he carries so carefully with him to Earth. With a crowd of children around him, the captain places the plant in soil—a first act of regeneration—and calls it farming. The camera pans out to reveal other vegetation as it crosses Earth and moves out to space. The film continues into the credits, highlighting the positive consequences of interdependent relationships between human and nonhuman nature: the captain and multiple children and adults farm and fish, building an interconnected civilization, while EVE, WALL-E, and the misfit robots build a family.

WALL-E and EVE's family seems to serve as sustenance for the plant growing beneath them. Its roots deepen, still growing from the boot, and the plant becomes an enormous tree, showing the rejuvenation of nature and the growth of an effective relationship between humans and the natural world. Because of the nostalgia for human artifacts and culture, an eco-memory drives the captain of a cruise ship to return to Earth, leaving the artificial world of the Axiom behind. The rolling end credits reveal a new fertile world emerging from the garbage humans left behind, all made possible because a robot connected with humanity and revived their and their robots' will to remember. It is a happy heterosexual ending. The new pioneers, both human and android, form an alliance to attempt to recover the planet. In this new Eden made possible because of WALL-E and his EVE, even dust storms are eradicated, and a nostalgic image of nature begins to thrive.

Conclusion

In spite of Disney's philosophical influence on the film, WALL-E's vision of nostalgia harks back to the most postmodern of Pixar's films, *Toy Story* and *Toy Story 2*, in which modern narrative meets and embraces a postmodern aesthetic. In *Animation and America*, Paul Wells asserts that Woody and Buzz of the *Toy Story* films "have cultural effects because they anchor and represent the highest quality representation of the transition from the culture of the camera to the dynamics of the digital and the machinations of the mercantile, while encompassing the most important characteristics of each" (169). For Wells, the director's "art is to make this modernity so human" (*Animation*

WALL-E: Captain leads humanity onto Earth.

and America 169), a challenge Pixar's directors meet with all of their films, at least to a certain extent.

These representations become localized and situated from film to film and director to director, but they all, sometimes unintentionally, address conflicts between organic and inorganic, between nature and culture, and between nonhuman and human nature. In *WALL-E*, questions regarding those conflicts remain unanswered. In a nod to the environmental contexts to which they respond, the conflicts remain too complex for a simple solution. Instead, the film draws both on human and organismic approaches to ecology and offers a resolution that requires an ongoing commitment to conservation and interdependence.

The Simpsons Movie: Homer poisons Lake Springfield.

TEN

The Simpsons Movie, Happy Feet, and Avatar

The Continuing Influence of Human, Organismic, Economic, and Chaotic Approaches to Ecology

WALL-E (2008) demonstrates the power of an environmental movement's impact on popular culture, an impact that began with Disney's first animated feature, *Snow White and the Seven Dwarfs* (1937), and continues with contemporary films from a variety of studios, including DreamWorks and Pixar, now owned by Disney. The films we explore not only demonstrate the continuing impact of environmentalism on the animated feature. They also illustrate similar ongoing aesthetic and narrative patterns rooted in twentieth-century approaches to ecology. Although the animated features we explored from 1937 to the present reflect their own cultural and historical contexts, they also continue to follow narrative and aesthetic patterns found in our investigation of animated shorts of the 1930s, 1940s, and 1950s. Perhaps because they are products of either modernist industrial culture or a postmodern culture driven by technology, animated features embedded with environmental messages also continue to reflect the influence of human, economic, organismic, and chaotic approaches to ecology, illustrating aesthetic patterns that encourage separation between human and non-human nature or their interconnection through interdependent relationships.

WALL-E, for example, highlights the need for controlling human intervention (in a pull toward human ecology) and strengthening interdependence (drawing on organismic ecology) while commenting on human exploitation of the natural world. *Ice Age* (2002) and *Ice Age: The Meltdown* (2006), on the other hand, both demonstrate the power of nature over the human (and anthropomorphized animal) world. In *Ice Age*, a wooly mammoth, Manfred (Ray Ramono), and a sloth named Sid (John Leguizamo) escape the coming Ice Age and a pack of saber-toothed tigers with a human child in their protection. They return the baby to its human father and tribe, continuing southward away from the approaching freeze. *Ice Age: The Meltdown* addresses repercussions of massive melting ice and snow: flooding that will destroy animals and their valley unless they again escape the rising water. Both films highlight the battle with the elements found in early Felix the Cat cartoons from the 1930s, a narrative and aesthetic pattern that continues and, perhaps, draws on economic approaches to ecology.

Three other contemporary feature-length enviro-toons from two different studios illustrate criticism of human exploitation of the natural world but approach that criticism in varied ways that either include or exclude non-human nature: *Happy Feet* (2006), *The Simpsons Movie* (2007), and *Avatar* (2009).

In a nod toward both tenets of the animal rights movements and organismic approaches to ecology, Warner Brothers' *Happy Feet* demonstrates the need to control human intervention and nurture the natural world in its critique of treatment of glacial oceans and their wildlife through Mumble's journey with his "happy feet."

Grounded in human approaches to ecology, Fox Films' *The Simpsons Movie* focuses on one environmental catastrophe, toxic-waste dumping in Lake Springfield and multiple attempts to contain the waste and save the rest of the planet. Little reference is made to nonhuman nature in the film, however, and final violent attempts to contain Springfield's toxicity are thwarted in a spectacular act of comic heroism that supersedes the film's environmental message.

Also from Fox Films, *Avatar* makes the most blatant comment on humans' exploitation of the environment, arguing against "fair use" and economic approaches to ecology that promote the overconsumption of resources, especially the mining of a profitable mineral, unobtainium. Humans have left their own dying Earth to rip the mineral from the core of another planet, Pandora, where its people, the Na'vi, illustrate how to build effective interdependent relationships with nonhuman nature in a biotic community that sustains them all.

Organismic and Human Approaches to Ecology in *Happy Feet*

Harking back to the species-survival message of *Fox Pop*, *Happy Feet* is, according to an *Onion A.V. Club* review by Tasha Robinson, "a gorgeously rendered marvel that pulls out all the stops to wow its viewers" while maintaining "its integrity with a smart and surprisingly deep story." Employing long takes and a moving camera, the film provides "heightened elegance and precision as well as a strong sense of space" and effective use of motion-capture techniques, according to *Variety*'s Todd McCarthy. But the film also attempts to convey two perhaps conflicting themes that Jordan Harper in his *Village Voice* review defines as "be yourself" and "we must regulate the overfishing of the Antarctic oceans." Harper suggests that these dual themes dilute the film's message, but we see the environmental theme overshadowing the individualist motif Harper describes, providing environmental messages grounded in organismic and human ecology coupled with tenets of the animal rights movement.

Happy Feet highlights nature from the beginning with shots of northern lights that look like the Milky Way. The camera moves toward a globe from space, as in films from *Dark City* to *An Inconvenient Truth* and WALL-E. The helicopter-mounted camera pans onto an icy surface, revealing a community of penguins to individualize this view of the natural world. In this idealized animated world, however, penguins sing "heart songs" that demonstrate their inner essence and connect them with other members of their species. In this opening scene two of the penguins, Norma Jean (Nicole Kidman) and Memphis (Hugh Jackman), mate by singing a duet of "You Don't Have to Be Rich," eventually hatching the egg that incubates the film's protagonist, Mumble (Elijah Wood).

From this point, the film broadcasts at least two social and potentially environmental messages. The first serves as a catalyst for Mumble's journey to the human world. Because Mumble is born with different skills than the other penguins, dancing rather than singing like his parents, he teaches them a lesson of acceptance and tolerance rooted in organismic ecology after demonstrating the folly of their choice to ostracize him.

The second combines tenets of the animal rights movement with human approaches to ecology. Penguins will starve if humans continue to overfish and pollute the seas. Because they blame the diminishing sea life on Mumble and his inability to sing, the penguin community banishes him. Mumble discovers a large Caterpillar earthmover near the shore that suggests some other reason for the penguins' lack of food. He recruits a group of smaller penguins and their oracle, Lovelace (Robin Williams), slowly being strangled by plastic from a six-pack burrowing into his neck, to discover both the reason for the diminishing fish supplies and the species behind the huge machine.

Ultimately Mumble and his entourage discover the cause for their famine, what elephant seals call the "annihilator," humans that even eat whales. At a shipyard, they discover the source of the fish shortage: unrestrained fishing and waste disposal. But since Mumble and the others are powerless to stop this large force, Mumble swims after the ship to appeal "to its better nature" and is, according to the narrator, "carried endlessly across vast oceans to worlds unknown."

When he climbs on shore, however, Mumble is captured and placed in a penguin habitat. But he finds a way to save himself and his fellow penguins from starvation. While trapped in the zoo, Mumble dances in front of a glass window. And when a little girl dances along with him, a crowd watches in amazement. The humans all think Mumble communicates with them through his tapping so, as a sentient being, he and his fellow penguins are seen as valuable enough to save. They have the same rights as humans and deserve to survive. After placing a locator on his leg, human captors take him back to his icy home.

The film's conclusion resolves both social issues. Mumble is accepted back into his now more tolerant "biotic" penguin family. And, in a narrowly focused environmental outcome, ocean fishing is curbed to ensure penguins survive after humans follow Mumble's locator and again respond to his dancing. Mumble's transmitter has brought them there. Mumble explains that the alien humans put the food chain out of whack, and now humans want to help. All the penguins dance and sing. Humans watching from a snowy hill exclaim, "Are they trying to tell us something? We're messing with their food chain. Abandon all marine harvesting!" Now fishing will cease because these humans cannot imagine a world without penguins, a resolution that may disregard greater environmental problems such as global warming but at least points toward the need for maintaining both human and nonhuman nature, a significant starting point perhaps drawn more from both the animal rights movement and a conservation movement grounded in human approaches to ecology.

Human Approaches to Ecology versus Comedy in *The Simpsons Movie*

The Simpsons Movie, on the other hand, recalls a sing-along cartoon from 1948, *Little Brown Jug*, because of its blatantly environmental message with a foundation in human ecology and an ending that may eclipse those ecological leanings. *Little Brown Jug* demonstrates how a stream can become polluted by human waste, in this case from a cider mill producing hard cider. Although humorously showing animals getting drunk when they drink water from the stream, the cartoon also depicts the stream's changing color as the cider spills into it. And the pollution is caused by negligence that results in overproduction. The animals produce so much cider that the kegs break, spilling over into the stream. In *The Simpsons Movie*, the environmentally driven conflict arises when Homer Simpson (Dan Castellaneta) adopts a pig. The pig serves as the catalyst for environmental catastrophe because Homer pours the pig's waste into Lake Springfield despite EPA warnings, causing what Nathan Rabin of *The Onion A.V. Club* calls "an ecological disaster of extinction-level proportions."

Lake Springfield is so polluted that its acid content destroys the band Green Day's barge and sinks them. The town is on notice. It must clean up its lake, or the EPA will intervene. Waste dumping is prohibited in Springfield's lake, and a barrier is erected. But Homer breaks that barrier and by accident, when he sees a sign for free doughnuts, dumps the pig waste in the lake instead of at an environmentally sound site. Environmental disaster takes center stage immediately after the pig waste hits the water. Lake Springfield turns black, and a squirrel grows multiple eyes when it falls in the toxic water.

Instead of attempting a clean-up effort, however, in the context of a Simpsons film, the EPA suggests containing the toxic lake by placing a dome over both the lake and the city of Springfield. Everyone will be trapped there. When the town finds out it is Homer's fault they attack the Simpsons' home. A sinkhole in their yard provides an outlet for the Simpsons, through which they escape to Alaska.

When the EPA's first efforts fail because citizens madly attempt to escape the dome, the EPA offers another suggestion. Again instead of cleaning up the lake, they suggest blowing up the city of Springfield and creating a new Grand Canyon (as Tom Hanks asserts in a public-service announcement). Safe in Alaska, Homer first refuses to stop the bombing, but when Marge (Julie Kavner) and the children leave him, he has a change of heart, returns to Springfield, and, with help from Bart (Nancy Cartwright) and his newfound motorcycle skills, destroys the bomb before it wipes out Springfield.

The town rebuilds, and Homer continues his goofy adventures to the end of the film, leaving the ecological problems unresolved. In fact, the film suggests that neither the town nor the government can or will solve them. Instead, the film plays up pollution for the sake of comedy, merely "seizing on an environmental theme," according to Brian Lowry's *Variety* review, and perhaps erasing any possible environmental message on display. A. O. Scott of the *New York Times* sees the rendition of the themes as part of the expectations for a summer blockbuster movie: "Arnold Schwarzenegger, who has been elected president of the United States; the elite forces of the Environmental Protection Agency; and the near-destruction of Springfield" ("We'll Always Have Springfield"). Still, the toxic Lake Springfield serves as the catalyst for the fun, drawing on pollution-control tenets of human approaches to ecology.

Technology Meets Organismic Approaches to Ecology in *Avatar*

Avatar, on the other hand, seems to reflect the same focus on interdependence found in *Molly Moo Cow and the Butterflies*. As in *Molly Moo Cow*, nonhuman nature must combat exploitation to maintain interdependent relationships, not between a cow and her butterflies, as in *Moo Cow*, but between the Na'vi people and the humans who invade their world to extract unobtainium beneath their home tree. Although 40 percent of the film is live action, the other 60 percent relies on photo-realistic CGI using motion-capture technology, linking the film explicitly with animated shorts and features that came before it.

Like the first animated feature, *Snow White*, *Avatar* awes its audience with the effects produced by groundbreaking technologies. It is, according to Roger Ebert, "a technical breakthrough" that "like *Star Wars* . . . employs a new generation of special effects." Multiplane animation technology used in *Snow White* transformed the "more than 1,500,000 individual pen-and-ink drawings and water-color paintings" (Boone) to produce "depth, a sense of perspective and distance hitherto seen only in 'live action' pictures," according to Andrew R. Boone's 1938 *Popular*

Science article. Boone describes the "novel picture-taking device" used to produce this effect, which looks like a printing press and "consists of four vertical steel posts, each carrying a rack along which as many as eight carriages may be shifted both horizontally and vertically. On each carriage rides a frame containing a sheet of celluloid, on which is painted part of the action or background."

With the addition of Technicolor film stock, the images of *Snow White* were breathtaking, just as the world produced for *Avatar* inspires awe. Using motion-capture technology, James Cameron transferred live-action movements to CGI. He also created a new "picture-taking device" for the film to create better 3-D effects, "a filming rig that is more advanced than anything that has gone before," Bobbie Johnson explains in a *Guardian* article. According to Johnson, "The setup consists of a number of stereoscopic cameras that each use a pair of lenses built to mimic human eyes." These techniques create a spectacularly breathtaking world in which conflicts between ecological values are resolved.

Pandora, the world produced for *Avatar*, embraces interdependence and a biotic community. The Na'vi people of Pandora remain connected to plants and animals of their world. Their hair, for example, forms a bond with the horselike creatures they ride and the banshees they fly. At night, plants light their way. Pods close up to form hammocks for sleeping. As Dr. Grace Augustine (Sigourney Weaver) explains, they have a "deep connection . . . to the forest." Dr. Augustine teaches them that each tree has 104 connections to each of the other trees, more connections than those in the human brain. To emphasize the interdependent nature of these connections, the Na'vi believe all the energy in these connections is borrowed and must be returned.

Embracing fair-use policies and economic approaches

Happy Feet: Mumble and the other penguins dance for a human audience.

to ecology, human invaders disrupt these interdependent connections when they invade Pandora to extract unobtainium, a mineral that is most abundant beneath the Na'vi's home tree. With help from Jake Sully (Sam Worthington), a former Marine now gone native as an avatar, and a natural world fighting for its life, the human invaders are defeated, leaving Pandora to the Na'vi and a few chosen avatar humans.

The film's narrative, however, is derivative, "a weak patchwork of [Cameron's] other films," according to *Onion A.V. Club* reviewer Scott Tobias. These other films include *Terminator 2: Judgment Day* (1991) and *Aliens* (1986). Tobias also cites the influence of films with similar references to Native Americans (see *Dances with Wolves* [1990]), rainforest annihilation (see *Ferngully* [1992] and *The Emerald Forest* [1985]), and battles over resources (see *Tank Girl* [1995], *Total Recall* [1990], *Pale Rider* [1985], and countless anti-mining and anti-oil-drilling films). Stephanie Zacharek of Salon.com writes, "For a movie that stresses how important it is for us to stay connected with nature, to keep our ponytails plugged into the

Avatar: Piercing the heart of the "vampire" exploiting
Pandora's resources.

life force, *Avatar* is peculiarly bloodless." Although technology does overshadow the blatant environmental message on display, its *Dances With Wolves*–like pull toward
interdependence attests to the continuing influence of environmental history, especially a biotic community manifested in Aldo Leopold's land ethic and organismic approaches to ecology.

Conclusion

These three films to some extent draw on current environmental issues for narrative and aesthetic considerations,
but in the end they favor, perhaps, comic happy endings.
But they also attest to the continuing influence of twentieth-century approaches to ecology, demonstrating that
themes driven by human, organismic, economic, and, to a
certain extent, chaotic approaches to ecology still resonate
in twenty-first-century animated features.

Content, then, seems to have changed since the 1930s,
'40s, and '50s only in relation to the species under at-

tack (ocean fish and penguins), the type of pollution needing control (toxic waste), and the mineral extraction that needs to end (unobtainium). Animated films with environmental politics either overtly or covertly underlying their narrative and aesthetic patterns seem to have maintained their popularity since 1937 and the first animated feature from Disney. Only the cultural and historical context behind the environmental message seems to have changed.

Conclusion

Animation's Movement to Green?

Our study of animated features from a variety of American studios demonstrates that enviro-toons from shorts to animated features, beginning with *Snow White* (1937) through the present, continue to reflect twentieth-century approaches to ecology. These approaches to ecology manifest themselves in the particular aesthetic and narrative patterns that separate humans from the natural world, connect them with it in interdependent relationships, or provide opportunities to critique humans' treatment of the environment in multiple ways.

We believe this exploration has also begun to broach answers to several questions regarding the origins and impact of enviro-toons: Does the studio producing the enviro-toon affect the environmental message on display? Has the content of enviro-toons changed in response to changes in historical and cultural context? Have these enviro-toons changed in relation to changes in the environmental movement? Have these films had an impact on viewers, changing their views on environmental issues, as did Al Gore's *An Inconvenient Truth*? And has the environmental movement affected how animated features are produced?

Although the studios producing these enviro-toons sometimes influence, to a certain extent, the environmental messages on display (see, for example, Fleischer Brothers versus Disney), studios may also produce enviro-toons grounded in different visions of environmentalism. Examples are DreamWorks Animation, with its emphasis on irreverent story, and Pixar, with its emphasis on the individual director's vision. *Over the Hedge* (2006) and *Bee Movie* (2007), both DreamWorks Animation films, convey differing visions of ecology manifested in contrasting narratives and aesthetics. The first film emphasizes the need for separation between nonhuman and human nature, and the second asserts that interdependent relationships between nonhuman and human nature are essential for survival. Pixar's *Finding Nemo* (2003) and WALL-E (2008) also convey conflicting environmental messages, again emphasizing either a need for separation (*Nemo*) or interdependence (WALL-E).

Historical and cultural context, however, do affect which issues are tackled by enviro-toons. For example, the 1942 Warner Brothers short *Fox Pop* critiques "fur farming" and the commercialization of wearing animal pelts for status. *Happy Feet* (2006), also from Warner Brothers, critiques overfishing and its effects on nonhuman nature. Both *Little Brown Jug* and *The Simpsons Movie* critique water pollution, but whereas the 1948 Paramount short *Little Brown Jug* critiques polluting a river with hard cider, the 2007 Twentieth Century Fox feature *The Simpsons Movie* interrogates toxic-waste pollution in Lake Springfield. Like *Mr. Bug Goes to Town* (1941) from the Fleischer Brothers, DreamWorks Animation's *Bee Movie* emphasizes interdependence between human and nonhuman nature. But the conflict in *Bee Movie* revolves around humanity's need for bee pollinization rather than both human and nonhuman nature's need for a rooftop "garden" in the city that transcends the modernist development below.

Enviro-toons also reflect the evolution of the environmental movement, with animated features from the 1990s forward providing illustrations of the most recent approach to ecology, chaotic—and conveying more blatant calls to environmental action such as those found in the *Captain Planet* (1990) series. In Steven Spielberg's *Jurassic Park* (1993), for example, chaos theory and, perhaps, chaotic approaches to ecology are broached by the character Dr. Ian Malcolm, a chaotician. Although chaos theory and chaotic approaches are under dispute (see, for example, Klaus Rohde and Peter P. Rohde, "Fuzzy Chaos"), their appearance in a film from 1993 demonstrates the continuing impact of environmental history and the evolution of the environmental movement on the content of animated features.

Enviro-toons, however, seem to have less clear influence on the environmental activism of their viewers. Although some audience members on both the left and the right called for a boycott of WALL-E merchandise to protest Disney's hypocrisy in its critique of megacorporations like itself, few viewers seemed to respond to the call. The WALL-E Web site sells its own merchandise, including figures, DVDs, and games but makes no reference at all to environmental concerns. The *Happy Feet* website does contain an "environmental" link, but it connects to a page where site users can create *Happy Feet* cards, not participate in environmentally conscious projects. Some audience members watching *Happy Feet* may have changed one behavior, however, and now encourage others to cut up plastic rings of six-packs. The Captain Planet Foundation, on the other hand, does promote environmental causes, with a Down to Earth Day festival for kids, grant money to fund hands-on educational projects, and programs to plant organic gardens and establish outdoor classrooms. Primarily, however, animated features promote entertainment and consumption, not only of the films themselves but also of the many products that accompany them. The content of animated features may be lauded by the Environmental Media Association, but the call to action is diluted by the ongoing call to buy.

On the other hand, the environmental movement has had an effect on how animated features are produced, with production practices at a variety of studios at least appearing to move toward green policies. Since 2004, for example, there have been a growing number of articles and Environmental Media Association Awards foregrounding environmentally sound film and television production practices (Corbett and Turco 11). Even in publications such as *The Hollywood Reporter* and *Variety*, there has been an increase in stories centered on the environmental content of productions. The Environmental Media Association (EMA) Awards now not only include categories related to content of films and television shows with environmental messages, but also (since 2004) include "a separate category for environmental 'process' improvements based on EMA's Green Seal checklist." In 2006, *Ice Age: The Meltdown* and *An Inconvenient Truth* won awards for environmental content. Productions from 10,000 B.C. to *The Dukes of Hazzard* won Green Seal Awards for best environmental practices, and corporate offices such as Dualstar and United Talent Agency (UTA) won Green Seal Awards for industry corporate offices.

The UCLA Institute Report notes that the number of environmental messages highlighted in films and film-industry publications has increased significantly from 2002 to the present (Corbett and Turco 40), an increase we see as a hopeful reason to explore films in relation to the environmental messages they present; however, the film and television industry continues to contribute to environmental degradation, not only in Los Angeles but around the world. Corbett and Turco note the "environmental impacts of filmmaking, which involve energy consumption, waste generation, air pollution, greenhouse gas emission, and physical disruptions on location" (5). Although our book focuses primarily on environmental content, especially content that is both obscured and revealed when read through an ecocritical lens, we also see the need to interrogate both content and production practices in relation to ecology. Studios producing animated films seem to be moving in the green direction and have prompted a move to digital filmmaking that will continue this trend for live-action films.

The Walt Disney Studio, for example, launched Disneynature with the premiere of *Earth* on Earth Day 2009 and planted a tree in the Brazilian rain forest for each ticket sold during the first five days of screenings. Disney also changed its packaging standards, using 100 percent recyclable material for all DVDs and Blu-Rays and created an environmental steward to work on each film to help implement "best environmental practices throughout all departments on a live-action shoot" as outlined in its Environmental Production Resource Guide. Disney has taken multiple steps to decrease its carbon footprint, according to the Disney Corporation's annual enviro-report, including preserving 8,500 acres of the Everglades, establishing the Disney Worldwide Conservation Fund to fund conservation projects around the world, and developing Disney's Environmentality Challenge, an environmental youth-education program engaging 1.5 million children in projects benefiting the environment.

Fox Entertainment Group also implemented an environmental guide, the FOX Green Guide, available at

FOXGreenGuide.com, with information about how to implement eco-friendly production practices and to buy from green vendors. According to Elizabeth Kaltman, "X-MEN *Origins: Wolverine* set a strong example for environmentally friendly film production, diverting 94 percent of its waste from landfills by implementing recycling programs in production offices and on set." Kaltman also lauds 24, the first carbon-neutral television series. Fox, then, has taken steps to "green" at least a few of its live-action films and television series.

NBC Universal, Paramount, and Sony also have implemented "green" programs, from switching to biodiesel fuels to encouraging further recycling. According to Kaltman, Universal City Studios was awarded a 2008 Smart Business Recycling Award by Los Angeles County for its outstanding waste reduction efforts. With future green productions in mind, Warner Brothers constructed a new, "green" sound stage for film and television production, following the U.S. Green Building Council's LEED guidelines (Kaltman). In addition to further recycling, Warner Brothers has expanded its solar-energy capabilities.

The production process followed by *An Inconvenient Truth*'s filmmakers serves as an apt example. The film is, according to the official Web site's blog, the first carbon-neutral documentary: "Paramount Classics, Participant Productions, and NativeEnergy have joined forces to offset 100% of the carbon dioxide emissions from air and ground transportation and hotels for production and promotional activities associated with the documentary" (*An Inconvenient Truth*). The Internet Movie Database's writes that funds from carbon-offsets "will go towards helping build new Native American, Alaskan Native Village, and farmer-owned renewable energy projects, creating sustainable economies for communities in need and diversifying our energy supply."

246

The film's executive producer, Jeff Skoll, who collaborated with NativeEnergy to offset carbon-dioxide emissions, says, "These renewable energy projects offer options that will decrease our demand for fossil fuels and otherwise would likely not happen without these kinds of investments." Albert Gore contributes a portion of the profits from both the movie and its accompanying book to a bipartisan educational campaign to combat global warming. Gore's documentary, as well as recent film productions such as *Syriana* (2005), also a carbon-neutral film, illustrate one way Hollywood's film industry can "go green" not only in film content but also in production practices. The turn away from film to digital production will enhance this environmental turn. Other companies have also adopted NativeEnergy's mission. Filmgreener. com, for example, advocates for green filmmaking and environmentally conscious films. And Ecoset Consulting provides expertise for establishing an environmentally sound film set.

That turn to digital also highlights the inherently more environmentally friendly filmmaking process followed by animation studios. Thanks to the current success of digital 3-D films such as *Up* (2009) and *Monsters vs. Aliens* (2009), projected with video digital projectors, it is envisioned that more theaters will make the transition from film projection to video projection. The goal is that all theatrical projectors will be digital video. This goal of transforming all theaters to digital video projection will mean the end of film in the production process. Computer-generated video production and exhibition, like that produced by Pixar's RenderMan, ends the chemical element in producing film prints, eliminates the need to create and deliver thousands of prints for exhibition, and ends the need to destroy the prints after their theatrical runs.

This transformation also means savings of millions of

dollars on every major release while also substantially reducing the carbon footprint that creating, delivering, and exhibiting films has caused since their invention in the late nineteenth century. With studio practices becoming more environmentally sound and environmental messages becoming more audience-friendly, digital films such as WALL-E can reach a wide audience, crossing not only age groups but classes, religions, and political stances with a potentially lighter carbon footprint.

As we write, the rapid technological changeover from film to digital projection is reaching high speed. The changeover to digital eliminates celluloid, chemical processing, and the physical delivery of thousands of film prints per major feature release. This greening of film distribution and exhibition had been jump-started by the 3-D success of *Avatar* (2009) ($2.75 billion in worldwide ticket sales) and *Alice in Wonderland* (2010) ($1 billion in worldwide ticket sales). Since 3-D is now a major draw for audiences, theaters have been forced to adapt quickly by phasing in digital projection at a far higher rate than previously anticipated. IMAX Theatres, for example, have completely transitioned to digital projection. A majority of theaters worldwide will soon be projecting feature films digitally, now that box-office potential for 3-D has become a financial reality. This success now creates far more beneficial environmental results throughout the process of filmmaking and film viewing. The digital age will reduce the carbon footprint of film companies in ways that are still being calculated.

This book, then, demonstrates the ongoing focus on environmental issues in animated films from 1937 forward. Although the content of enviro-toons reflects various approaches to ecology in relation to corresponding narrative and aesthetic patterns and that content mirrors the films' historical and cultural contexts and, to a certain extent,

Snow White and the Seven Dwarfs: The first animated film illustrates interdependence between humans and nature.

their studios' or director's visions, few enviro-toons seem to encourage environmental activism, despite their sometimes explicit, even "preachy," environmentalist-driven content.

Future studies might further examine historical and cultural contexts in relation to the film industry and its evolving production practices. Most important, however, such studies might explore this wider gap between environmental content and environmentalist activism. We end this book, then, with at least one area of concern: How can enviro-toons make the jump from environmentalist messages couched in entertaining animated features to tools of the environmental movement? And, perhaps more important, should this jump even be attempted?

Filmography

The Adventures of Ichabod and Mister Toad. Dir. James Algar,
Clyde Geronimi. Perf. Bing Crosby, Basil Rathbone,
Eric Blore. Walt Disney Pictures, 1949. DVD.

Aladdin. Dir. Ron Clements, John Musker. Perf. Scott Weinger,
Robin Williams. Walt Disney Pictures, 1992. DVD.

Alice in Wonderland. Dir. Clyde Geronimi, Hamilton Luske,
Wilfred Jackson. Perf. Kathryn Beaumont, Verna Felton,
Bill Thompson. Walt Disney Pictures, 1951. DVD.

Alice in Wonderland. Dir. Tim Burton. Perf. Johnny Depp,
Mia Wasikowska. Walt Disney Pictures, 2010.

Alice Gets in Dutch. Dir. Walt Disney. Perf. Virginia Davis.
Walt Disney Pictures, 1924. Web. 1 May 2009.

Alice's Wonderland. Dir. Walt Disney. Perf. Virginia Davis.
Walt Disney Pictures, 1923. Web. 1 May 2009.

Aliens. Dir. James Cameron. Perf. Sigourney Weaver. Twentieth
Century Fox, 1986. DVD.

American Pop. Dir. Ralph Bakshi. Perf. Ron Thompson.
Columbia Pictures, 1981. DVD.

An American Tail. Dir. Don Bluth. Perf. Erica Yohn, Phillip
Glasser. Amblin Entertainment, 1986. DVD.

Anchors Aweigh. Dir. George Sidney. Perf. Frank Sinatra,
Kathryn Grayson. Metro-Goldwyn-Mayer, 1945. DVD.

The Ant Bully. Dir. John Davis. Perf. Julia Roberts, Nicolas Cage, Meryl Streep. Warner Brothers Pictures, 2006. DVD.

Antz. Dir. Eric Darnell, Tim Johnson. Perf. Woody Allen, Dan Aykroyd. DreamWorks SKG, 1998. DVD.

April Maze. Dir. Otto Messner. Sullivan Studios, 1930. DVD.

Arachnophobia. Dir. Frank Marshall. Perf. Jeff Daniels, John Goodman. Amblin Entertainment, 1990. DVD.

The Aristocats. Dir. Wolfgang Reitherman. Perf. Phil Harris, Eva Gabor. Walt Disney Productions, 1970. DVD.

Atlantis: The Lost Empire. Dir. Gary Trousdale, Kirk Wise. Perf. Michael J. Fox. Walt Disney Pictures, 2001.

Avatar. Dir. James Cameron. Perf. Sam Worthington, Zoe Saldana, Sigourney Weaver. Twentieth Century Fox, 2009. DVD.

Bambi. Dir. David Hand. Perf. Donnie Dugan, Will Wright, Tim Davis, Ann Gillis, Sterling Holloway. Walt Disney Pictures, 1942. DVD.

Barnyard: The Original Party Animals. Dir. Steve Oedekerk. Perf. Kevin James, Courteney Cox. Paramount Pictures, 2006. DVD.

Beauty and the Beast. Dir. Gary Trousdale, Kirk Wise. Perf. Paige O'Hara, Robbie Benson. Walt Disney Pictures, 1991. DVD.

Bedknobs and Broomsticks. Dir. Robert Stevenson. Perf. Angela Lansbury, David Tomlinson. Walt Disney Pictures, 1971. DVD.

Bee Movie. Dir. Steve Hickner, Simon J. Smith. Perf. Jerry Seinfeld, Renee Zellweger. DreamWorks, 2007. DVD.

Blade Runner. Dir. Ridley Scott. Perf. Harrison Ford, Rutger Hauer. Warner Brothers Pictures, 1982.

Boobs in the Woods. Dir. Robert McKimson. Warner Brothers Studios, 1950. DVD.

Brother Bear. Dir. Aaron Blaise, Robert Walker. Perf. Joaquin Phoenix, Jeremy Suarez. Walt Disney Pictures, 2003. DVD.

Brotherhood of Man. Dir. Robert Cannon. United Productions of America, 1945. DVD.

A Bug's Life. Dir. John Lasseter, Andrew Stanton. Perf.
Dave Foley, Phyllis Diller, Julia Louis-Dreyfus, Kevin
Spacey. Pixar Animation Studios (Walt Disney Pictures),
1998. DVD.

Captain Planet and the Planeteers. Dir. Jim Duffy et al. Perf.
David Coburn, LeVar Burton. Turner Broadcasting
System, 1990–96. DVD.

Car of Tomorrow. Dir. Tex Avery. Perf. June Foray. Metro-
Goldwyn-Mayer, 1951. DVD.

Cars. Dir. John Lasseter. Perf. Owen Wilson, Paul Newman,
Bonnie Hunt. Walt Disney Pictures (Pixar Animation
Studios), 2006. DVD.

Chicken Little. Dir. Mark Dindal. Perf. Zach Braff, Patrick
Stewart, Amy Sedaris. Walt Disney Pictures, 2005. DVD.

Chicken Run. Dir. Peter Lord, Nick Park. Perf. Phil Daniels,
Lynn Ferguson, Mel Gibson. DreamWorks, 2000. DVD.

Chip an' Dale. Dir. Jack Hannah. Disney Studios, 1947. DVD.

Cinderella. Dir. Wilfred Jackson, Hamilton Luske,
Clyde Geronimi. Perf. Ilene Woods, Eleanor Audley,
Verna Felton. Walt Disney Pictures, 1950. DVD.

Close Encounters of the Third Kind. Dir. Steven Spielberg. Perf.
Richard Dreyfuss, Francois Truffaut, Teri Garr. Columbia
Pictures, 1977. DVD.

Coal Black and de Sebben Dwarfs. Dir. Bob Clampett. Warner
Brothers, 1943. DVD.

Cool World. Dir. Ralph Bakshi. Perf. Kim Basinger,
Gabriel Byrne, Brad Pitt. Paramount Pictures, 1992. DVD.

Coonskin. Dir. Ralph Bakshi. Perf. Barry White,
Charles Gordone. Ruddy Productions, 1975.

A Corner in Wheat. Dir. D. W. Griffith. Perf. Frank Powell,
Grace Henderson. Biograph, 1909. DVD.

Dances with Wolves. Dir. Kevin Costner. Perf. Kevin Costner.
MGM Home Entertainment, 1990. DVD.

Dangerous When Wet. Dir. Charles Walters. Perf.
Esther Williams, Fernando Lamas. Metro-Goldwyn-
Mayer, 1953. VHS.

Dark City. Dir. Alex Proyas. Perf. Rufus Sewell, William Hurt, Kiefer Sutherland, Jennifer Connelly. New Line Cinema, 1998. DVD.

The Daydreamer. Dir. Jules Bass. Perf. Tallulah Bankhead, Victor Borge, Patty Duke. Embassy Pictures Corporation (Videocraft International), 1966. VHS.

Dinosaur. Dir. Eric Leighton, Ralph Zondag. Perf. D. B. Sweeney, Alfre Woodard. Walt Disney Pictures, 2000. DVD.

Dragon Around. Dir. Jack Hannah. Walt Disney Pictures, 1954. DVD.

Duck Amuck. Dir. Chuck Jones. Warner Brothers Studios, 1953. DVD.

The Dukes of Hazzard. Dir. Jay Chandrasekhar. Perf. Johnny Knoxville, Seann William Scott, Alice Grecyn. Warner Brothers, 2005. Television.

Dumbo. Dir. Ben Sharpsteen. Perf. Edward Brophy, Sterling Holloway, Cliff Edwards. Walt Disney Pictures, 1941. DVD.

The Emerald Forest. Dir. John Boorman. Perf. Powers Booth, Meg Foster. MGM Home Entertainment, 1985. DVD.

Enchanted. Dir. Kevin Lima. Perf. Amy Adams, Patrick Dempsy, James Marsden, Susan Sarandon. Walt Disney Pictures, 2007. DVD.

E.T.: The Extraterrestrial. Dir. Steven Spielberg. Perf. Henry Thomas, Dee Wallace. Amblin Entertainment, 1982. DVD.

Farm of Tomorrow. Dir. Tex Avery. Perf. Daws Butler, June Foray. Metro-Goldwyn-Mayer, 1954. DVD.

Ferngully: The Last Rainforest. Dir. Bill Kroyer. Perf. Tim Curry, Samantha Mathis. Twentieth Century Fox, 1992. DVD.

Finding Nemo. Dir. Andrew Stanton. Perf. Alexander Gould, Albert Brooks, Ellen DeGeneres, Willem Dafoe. Pixar Animation Studios, 2003. DVD.

Flowers and Trees. Dir. Bert Gillett. Disney Studios, 1932. DVD.

Flushed Away. Dir. David Bowers, Sam Fell. Perf. Hugh Jackman, Kate Winslet. DreamWorks Animation, 2006. DVD.

Fog Line. Dir. Larry Gottheim. Canyon Cinema, 1970. DVD.

The Fox and the Hound. Dir. Ted Berman, Richard Rich. Perf. Mickey Rooney, Kurt Russell. Walt Disney Pictures, 1981. DVD.

Fox Pop. Dir. Chuck Jones. Warner Brothers, 1942. DVD.

Fritz the Cat. Dir. Ralph Bakshi. Perf. Skip Hinnant. Steve Krantz Productions, 1972. DVD.

Gay Purr-ee. Dir. Abe Levitow. Perf. Judy Garland, Robert Goulet, Red Buttons. United Productions of America (Warner Bros. Pictures), 1962. DVD.

The General. Dir. Clyde Buckman, Buster Keaton. Perf. Marion Mack, Buster Keaton. United Artists, 1927. DVD.

Gerald McBoing Boing. Dir. Robert Cannon. Perf. Marvin Miller.
United Productions of America, 1951. DVD.

Gertie the Dinosaur. Dir. Winsor McCay. Perf. Winsor McCay. McCay, 1914. DVD.

The Girl Next Door. Dir. Richard Sale. Perf. Dan Daley, June Haver. Twentieth Century Fox Films, 1953. VHS.

Gone with the Wind. Dir. Victor Fleming. Perf. Thomas Mitchell, Barbara O'Neil, Vivien Leigh. Selznick International Pictures (Metro-Goldwyn-Mayer), 1939. DVD.

The Graduate. Dir. Mike Nichols. Perf. Dustin Hoffman, Anne Bancroft. Embassy Pictures Corporation, 1967. DVD.

Grand Canyonscope. Dir. Charles Nichols. Disney Studios, 1955. DVD.

Gulliver's Travels. Dir. Dave Fleischer, Willard Bowsky. Perf. Jessica Dragonette, Lanny Ross. Fleischer Studios, 1939. DVD.

Happy Feet. Dir. George Miller. Perf. Robin Williams, Elijah Wood, Brittany Murphy. Warner Brothers, 2006. DVD.

Hare Conditioned. Dir. Chuck Jones. Warner Brothers, 1945. DVD.

Heavy Traffic. Dir. Ralph Bakshi. Perf. Joseph Kaufmann, Beverly Hope Atkinson. American International Pictures, 1973. DVD.

Hell-Bent for Election. Dir. Chuck Jones. United Productions of
America, 1944. DVD.

Hello, Dolly! Dir. Gene Kelly. Perf. Barbra Streisand, Walter
Matthau. 20th Century Fox, 1969. DVD.

Hercules. Dir. Ron Clements, John Musker. Perf. Tate Donovan.
Walt Disney Pictures, 1997. DVD.

Home on the Range. Dir. Will Finn, John Sanford. Walt Disney
Pictures, 2004. DVD.

The Hunchback of Notre Dame. Dir. Gary Trousdale, Kirk
Wise. Perf. Jason Alexander. Walt Disney Pictures, 1996.
DVD.

I Am Legend. Dir. Francis Lawrence. Perf. Will Smith. Warner
Brothers, 2007. DVD.

Ice Age. Dir. Chris Wedge. Perf. Ray Romano, John Leguizamo,
Denis Leary. Blue Sky Studios (Twentieth Century Fox
Animation), 2002. DVD.

Ice Age, the Meltdown. Dir. Carlos Saldanha. Perf. Ray
Romano, John Leguizamo, Denis Leary. Blue Sky Studios
(Twentieth Century Fox Animation), 2006. DVD.

An Inconvenient Truth. Dir. Davis Guggenheim. Perf. Al Gore.
Paramount, 2006. DVD.

The Incredible Mr. Limpet. Dir. Arthur Lubin. Perf. Don Knotts,
Carole Cook. Warner Brothers Pictures, 1964. DVD.

The Incredibles. Dir. Brad Bird. Perf. Craig T. Nelson, Holly
Hunter. Pixar Animation Studios (Walt Disney Pictures),
2004. DVD.

Jaws. Dir. Steven Spielberg. Perf. Roy Scheider, Richard
Dreyfuss. Universal, 1975. DVD.

The Jungle Book. Dir. Wolfgang Reitherman. Perf. Phil Harris,
Sebastian Cabot. Walt Disney Productions, 1967. DVD.

Jurassic Park. Dir. Steven Spielberg. Perf. Sam Neill, Laura
Dern. Amblin Entertainment, 1993. DVD.

King Kong. Dir. Merian C. Cooper, Ernest B. Schoedsack. Perf.
Fay Wray, Robert Armstrong. RKO Radio Pictures, 1933.
DVD.

Kung Fu Panda. Dir. Mark Osborne, John Stevenson. Perf. Jack

Black, Dustin Hoffman. DreamWorks Animation, 2008. DVD.

Lady and the Tramp. Dir. Hamilton Luske, Clyde Geronimi, Wilfred Jackson. Perf. Barbara Luddy, Larry Roberts, Peggy Lee. Walt Disney Pictures, 1955. DVD.

The Land before Time. Dir. Don Bluth. Perf. Judith Barsi, Gabriel Damon. Amblin Entertainment, 1988. DVD.

The Last Unicorn. Dir. Jules Bass, Arthur Rankin Jr. Perf. Alan Arkin, Jeff Bridges, Mia Farrow. Rankin/Bass Productions (Incorporated Television Company), 1982. DVD.

Lilo and Stitch. Dir. Dean DeBlois, Chris Sanders. Perf. Daveigh Chase, Chris Sanders. Walt Disney Pictures, 2002. DVD.

The Lion King. Dir. Roger Allers, Rob Minkoff. Perf. Jonathan Taylor Thomas, Matthew Broderick. Walt Disney Pictures, 1994. DVD.

Little Brown Jug. Dir. Seymour Kneitel. Famous Studios, 1948. DVD.

The Little Mermaid. Dir. Ron Clements, John Musker. Perf. Rene Auberjonois, Jodi Benson. Walt Disney Pictures, 1989. DVD.

Little Nemo. Dir. Winsor McCay, J. Stuart Blackton. Perf. Winsor McCay. Vitagraph Company of America, 1911. DVD.

Lumber Jerks. Dir. Friz Freleng. Warner Brothers, 1955. DVD.

M. Dir. Fritz Lang. Perf. Peter Lorre. Vereinigte Star-Film GmbH (Criterion Collection), 1931. DVD.

Madagascar. Dir. Eric Darnell, Tom McGrath. Perf. Ben Stiller, Chris Rock, David Schwimmer. DreamWorks SKG, 2005. DVD.

Mad Monster Party? Dir. Jules Bass. Perf. Phyllis Diller, Ethel Ennis. Embassy Pictures Corp., 1967. VHS.

Manhattan. Dir. Woody Allen. Perf. Woody Allen, Diane Keaton. United Artists, 1979. DVD.

The Many Adventures of Winnie the Pooh. Dir. John Lounsbery, Wolfgang Reitherman. Perf. Sebastian Cabot, Junius Matthews. Walt Disney Pictures, 1977. DVD.

Mary Poppins. Dir. Robert Stevenson. Perf. Julie Andrews, Dick Van Dyke. Walt Disney Pictures, 1964. DVD.

Modern Times. Dir. Charles Chaplin. Perf. Charles Chaplin. United Artists, 1936.

Molly Moo Cow and the Butterflies. Dir. Burt Gillett, Tom Palmer. Van Bueren Studios, 1935. DVD.

Monsters, Inc. Dir. Pete Docter. Perf. John Goodman, Billy Crystal, Mary Gibbs. Pixar Animation Studios (Walt Disney Pictures), 2001. DVD.

Monsters vs. Aliens. Dir. Rob Letterman, Conrad Vernon. Perf. Reese Witherspoon, Seth Rogen. DreamWorks Animation, 2009. DVD.

Mr. Bug (Hoppity) Goes to Town. Dir. Dave Fleischer. Perf. Kenny Gardner, Gwen Williams, Jack Mercer. Fleischer Studios (Paramount Pictures), 1941. DVD.

Mr. Deeds Goes to Town. Dir Frank Capra. Perf. Gary Cooper, Jean Arthur. Frank Capra Productions (Columbia Pictures Corporation), 1936. DVD.

Mulan. Dir. Tony Bancroft, Barry Cook. Perf. Miguel Ferrer, Harvey Fierstein. Walt Disney Pictures, 1998. DVD.

My Favorite Duck. Dir. Chuck Jones. Warner Brothers, 1942. DVD.

My Neighbor Totoro. Dir. Hayao Miyazaki. Perf. Noriko Hidaka, Chika Sakamoto. Tokuma Japan Communications Co. Ltd. (Studio Ghibli), 1988. DVD.

Nausicaa of the Valley of the Wind. Dir. Hayao Miyazaki. Perf. Sumi Shimamoto, Mahito Tsujimura. Hakuhodo (Studio Ghibli), 1984. DVD.

Neptune Nonsense. Dir. Burt Gillett, Tom Palmer. Van Beuren Studios, 1936. DVD.

The Nightmare before Christmas. Dir. Henry Selick. Perf. Danny Elfman. Buena Vista (Walt Disney Studios Home Entertainment), 1993. DVD.

No Hunting. Dir. Jack Hannah. Disney Studios, 1954. DVD.

The Oblongs. Dir. Joe Horn et al. Perf. Laraine Newman, Will Ferrell. Warner Brothers Television, 2001–2002. DVD.

The Omega Man. Dir. Boris Sagel. Perf. Charlton Heston. Warner Brothers, 1971. DVD.

One Hundred and One Dalmatians. Dir. Wolfgang Reitherman, Hamilton Luske, Clyde Geronimi. Perf. Rod Taylor, Betty Lou Gerson, Lisa Davis, Ben Wright, Cate Bauer. Walt Disney Pictures, 1961. DVD.

1001 Arabian Nights. Dir. Jack Kinney. Perf. Jim Backus, Kathryn Grant, Dwayne Hickman. United Productions of America, 1959. DVD.

Out of Scale. Dir. Jack Hannah. Disney Studios, 1951. DVD.

Out on a Limb. Dir. Jack Hannah. Disney Studios, 1950. DVD.

Over the Hedge. Dir. Tim Johnson, Karey Kirkpatrick. Perf. Bruce Willis, Garry Shandling. DreamWorks Animation, 2006. DVD.

Pale Rider. Dir. Clint Eastwood. Perf. Clint Eastwood, Carrie Snodgrass, Michael Moriarty. Warner Brothers, 1985. DVD.

Peter Pan. Dir. Clyde Geronimi, Wilfred Jackson. Perf. Bobby Driscoll, Kathryn Beaumont. Walt Disney Pictures, 1953. DVD.

Pete's Dragon. Dir. Don Chaffey. Perf. Helen Reddy, Jim Dale. Walt Disney Productions, 1977. DVD.

Pinocchio. Dir. Hamilton Luske, Ben Sharpsteen. Perf. Dickie Jones, Christian Rub. Walt Disney Pictures, 1940. DVD.

Pocahontas. Dir. Mike Gabriel, Eric Goldberg. Perf. Irene Bedard, Mel Gibson. Walt Disney Pictures, 1995. DVD.

Porky Chops. Dir. Arthur Davis. Warner Brothers, 1949. DVD.

Powers of Ten. Dir. Charles Eames, Ray Eames. Perf. Phil Morrison. International Business Machines, 1968. DVD.

The Prince of Egypt. Dir. Brenda Chapman, Steve Hickner. Perf. Val Kilmer, Ralph Fiennes. DreamWorks SKG, 1998. DVD.

Raiders of the Lost Ark. Dir. Steven Spielberg. Perf. Harrison Ford, Karen Allen. Paramount/Lucasfilm, 1981. DVD.

Ratatouille. Dir. Brad Bird. Perf. Patton Oswalt, Ian Holm. Pixar Animation Studios (Walt Disney Pictures), 2007. DVD.

The Reluctant Dragon. Dir. Alfred Werker, Hamilton Luske. Perf. Robert Benchley, Barnett Parker, Billy Lee. Walt Disney Productions, 1941. DVD.

The Rescuers. Dir. John Lounsbery, Wolfgang Reitherman. Perf. Bob Newhart, Eva Gabor. Walt Disney Pictures, 1977. DVD.

The Rescuers Down Under. Dir. Hendel Butoy, Mike Gabriel. Perf. Bob Newhart, Eva Gabor. Walt Disney Pictures, 1990. DVD.

The Road to El Dorado. Dir. Bibo Bergeron et al. Perf. Kevin Kline, Kenneth Branagh. DreamWorks SKG, 2000. DVD.

Robin Hood. Dir. Wolfgang Reitherman. Perf. Brian Bedford, Monica Evans. Walt Disney Productions, 1973. DVD.

Rooty Toot Toot. Dir. John Hubley. Perf. Thurl Ravenscroft. United Productions of America, 1951. DVD.

Rugrats Go Wild. Dir. John Eng, Norton Virgien. Perf. Elizabeth Daily, Nancy Cartwright, Kath Soucie. Klasky-Csupo, 2003. DVD.

Safety Last! Dir. Fred C. Newmeyer. Perf. Harold Lloyd, Mildred Davis. Hal Roach Studios (Pathe Exchange), 1923. DVD.

A Scanner Darkly. Dir. Richard Linklater. Perf. Keanu Reeves, Winona Ryder. Warner Independent Pictures, 2006. DVD.

The Seapreme Court. Dir. Seymour Kneitel. Famous Studios, 1954. DVD.

The Secret of NIMH. Dir. Don Bluth. Perf. Derek Jacobi, Elizabeth Hartman, Arthur Malet. Aurora (Mrs. Brisby Ltd.), 1982. DVD.

Shark Tale. Dir. Bibo Bergeron, Vicky Jenson. Perf. Will Smith, Robert De Niro, Renee Zellweger. DreamWorks Animation, 2004. DVD.

Shrek. Dir. Andrew Adamson, Vicky Jenson. Perf. Mike Myers, Eddie Murphy, Cameron Diaz. DreamWorks Animation, 2001. DVD.

Silent Running. Dir. Douglas Trumbull. Perf. Bruce Dern. Universal Pictures, 1972. DVD.

The Simpsons. Dir. Mark Kirkland et al. Perf. Dan Castellaneta, Julie Kavner, Nancy Cartwright, Yeardley Smith. Twentieth Century Fox, 1989–. DVD.

The Simpsons Movie. Dir. David Silverman. Perf. Dan Castellaneta, Julie Kavner, Nancy Cartwright, Yeardley Smith. Twentieth Century Fox Films, 2007. DVD.

Sinbad: The Legend of the Seven Seas. Dir. Patrick Gilmore, Tim Johnson. Perf. Brad Pitt, Catherine Zeta-Jones. DreamWorks Animation, 2003. DVD.

Sleeping Beauty. Dir. Clyde Geronimi. Perf. Mary Costa, Bill Shirley. Walt Disney Pictures, 1959. DVD.

Snow-White. Dir. Dave Fleischer. Perf. Cab Calloway. Fleischer Studios, 1933. DVD.

Snow White and the Seven Dwarfs. Dir. David Hand. Disney, 1937. DVD.

Some Like It Hot. Dir. Billy Wilder. Perf. Marilyn Monroe, Tony Curtis, Jack Lemmon. Ashton Productions (The Mirisch Corporation), 1959. DVD.

Song of the South. Dir. Harve Foster, Wilfred Jackson. Perf. Ruth Warrick, Bobby Driscoll. Walt Disney Productions, 1946. DVD.

Soylent Green. Dir. Richard Fleischer. Perf. Charlton Heston, Edward G. Robinson. Metro-Goldwyn-Mayer (MGM), 1973. DVD.

Spinning Mice. Dir. Burt Gillett, Tom Palmer. Van Bueren Studios, 1935. DVD.

Spirit: Stallion of the Cimarron. Dir. Kelly Asbury, Lorna Cook. Perf. Matt Damon, James Cromwell. DreamWorks Animation, 2002. DVD.

Star Wars. Dir. George Lucas. Perf. Mark Hamill, Harrison Ford, Carrie Fisher. Twentieth Century Fox Films/LucasFilm, 1977. DVD.

The Story of a Mosquito. Dir. Winsor McCay. Perf. Winsor McCay. Vitagraph, 1912. DVD.

The Sword in the Stone. Dir. Wolfgang Reitherman. Perf. Rickie Sorelson, Carl Swenson. Walt Disney Pictures, 1963. DVD.

Syriana. Dir. Stephen Gaghan. Perf. Kayvan Novak, George Clooney. Warner Brothers Pictures, 2005. DVD.

Tank Girl. Dir. Rachel Talalay. Perf. Lori Petty. MGM Home Entertainment, 1995. DVD.

The Tantalizing Fly. Dir. Max Fleischer. Perf. Max Fleischer. Bray Studios, 1919. DVD.

Tarzan. Dir. Chris Buck, Kevin Lima. Perf. Tony Goldwyn, Minnie Driver. Walt Disney Pictures, 1999. DVD.

10,000 B.C. Dir. Roland Emmerich. Warner Brothers, 2008.

The Terminator. Dir. James Cameron. Perf. Arnold Schwarzenegger, Linda Hamilton. Hemdale Film/Orion Pictures, 1984.

Terminator 2: Judgment Day. Dir. James Cameron. Perf. Arnold Schwarzeneggar, Linda Hamilton, Edward Furlong, Robert Patrick. Columbia/TriStar, 1991. DVD.

Total Recall. Dir. Paul Verhoeven. Perf. Arnold Schwarzenegger. Twentieth Century Fox Home Entertainment, 1990. DVD.

Toy Story. Dir. John Lasseter. Perf. Tom Hanks, Tim Allen. Pixar Animation Studios (Walt Disney Pictures), 1995.

Toy Story 2. Dir. John Lasseter. Perf. Tom Hanks, Tim Allen. Pixar Animation Studios (Walt Disney Pictures), 1999.

The Tree's Knees. Dir. Hugh Harman, Rudolf Ising. Warner Brothers, 1930. DVD.

Tron. Dir. Steven Lisberger. Perf. Jeff Bridges. Walt Disney Pictures, 1982. DVD.

Tweet Tweet Tweety. Dir. Friz Freleng. Warner Brothers Studios, 1951. DVD.

24. Dir. John Cassar et al. Perf. Kiefer Sutherland, Mary Lynn Rajskub. Twentieth Century Fox Television, 2001. Television.

Two Guys from Texas. Dir. David Butler, Friz Freleng. Perf. Dennis Morgan, Jack Carson. Warner Brothers Pictures, 1948. VHS.

UP. Dir. Pete Docter. Perf. Edward Asner. Pixar Animation (Walt Disney Pictures), 2009. DVD.

Volcano. Dir. Dave Fleischer. Fleischer Brothers Studios, 1942. DVD.

Waking Life. Dir. Richard Linklater. Perf. Wiley Wiggins. 20th Century Fox Films, 2001. DVD.

Wallace and Gromit and the Curse of the Were Rabbit. Dir. Steve Box and Nick Park. Perf. Peter Sallis, Ralph Feinnes,

Helena Bonham Carter. DreamWorks Animation, 2005.
DVD.

WALL-E. Dir. Andrew Stanton. Perf. Ben Burtt, Elyssa Knight.
Pixar/Disney, 2008. DVD.

The Waltons. Dir. Earl Hamner Jr. Perf. Jon Walmsley, Mary
Beth McDonough. Warner Brothers Television, 1972.

Westworld. Dir. Michael Crichton. Perf. Yul Brynner, Richard
Benjamin. Metro-Goldwyn-Mayer, 1973. DVD.

Who Framed Roger Rabbit. Dir. Robert Zemeckis. Perf. Bob
Hoskins, Christopher Lloyd, Joanna Cassidy. Amblin Entertainment (Touchstone Pictures), 1988. DVD.

The Wild. Dir. Steve "Spaz" Williams. Perf. Kiefer Sutherland,
James Belushi. Walt Disney Pictures, 2006.

The Wild Thornberrys Movie. Dir. Cathy Malkasian, Jeff
McGrath. Perf. Lacey Chabert, Tom Kane. Paramount
Pictures, 2002. DVD.

Willy McBean and His Magic Machine. Dir. Arthur Rankin Jr.
Perf. Larry D. Mann, Billie Mae Richards. Dentsu Motion
Pictures (Videocraft International), 1965. VHS.

The Wizard of Oz. Dir. Victor Fleming. Perf. Judy Garland.
Metro-Goldwyn-Mayer, 1939. DVD.

X-Men Origins: Wolverine. Dir. Gavin Hood. Perf. Hugh Jackman. Twentieth Century Fox Film Corp., 2009.

Works Cited

Allan, Robin. *Walt Disney and Europe: European Influences on the Animated Feature Films of Walt Disney*. Bloomington: Indiana University Press, 1999. Print.

Allen, Charlotte. "WALL-E Doesn't Say Anything." *Los Angeles Times* 13 July 2008. Web. 1 June 2009.

Artz, Lee. "The Righteousness of Self-Centered Royals: The World according to Disney Animation." *Critical Arts*. 1 Jan. 2004. Web. 2 April 2009.

A.W. "'The Adventures of Ichabod and Mr. Toad' Sees the Return of Disney to Realm of Pure Animation." *New York Times* 10 Oct. 1949: 18. Print.

Barrier, Michael. *The Animated Man: A Life of Walt Disney*. Berkeley: University of California Press, 2007. Print.

———. *Hollywood Cartoons: American Animation in Its Golden Age*. New York: Oxford University Press, 1999. Print.

Bendazzi, Giannalberto. *One Hundred Years of Cinema Animation*. Trans. Anna Taraboletti-Segre. Bloomington: Indiana University Press, 1994. Print.

Bennet, Michael W., and David Teague, eds. *The Nature of Cities: Ecocriticism and Urban Environments*. Tucson: University of Arizona Press, 1999. Print.

Boon, Andrew R. "The Making of Snow White and the Seven Dwarfs." *Popular Science* Jan. 1938. Web. 3 May 2010.

Bordwell, David, and Kristin Thompson. *Film Art: An Introduction.* 9th ed. New York: McGraw-Hill, 2009. Print.

Cabarga, Leslie. *The Fleischer Story.* New York: DaCapo Press, 1988. Print.

Callahan, Dan. "The Fox and the Hound." *Slant* 13 Oct. 2006. Web. 12 May 2009.

Callicott, J. Baird. "Animal Liberation and Environmental Ethics: Back Together Again." *The Animal Rights/Environmental Ethics Debate: The Environmental Perspective.* Ed. Eugene C. Hargrove. Albany: SUNY University Press, 1992. 249–61. Print.

Canby, Vincent. "Disney's 'Rescuers' Cheerful Animation." *New York Times* 7 July 1977. Web. 15 May 2009.

———. "Old Style Disney." *New York Times* 10 July 1981. Web.

Carmichael, Deborah A., ed. *The Landscape of the Hollywood Western: Ecocriticism in an American Film Genre.* Salt Lake City: University of Utah Press, 2006. Print.

Carr, David. "Is Animation Funnier Than Live Action?" *New York Times* 6 July 2003: 2:18. Print.

Carson, Rachel. *Silent Spring.* Cambridge MA: Riverside Press, 1962. Print.

Cartmill, Matthew. "The Bambi Syndrome." *Natural History* 102.6 (June 1993): 6–10. Print.

———. *A View to a Death in the Morning: Hunting and Nature through History.* Cambridge: Harvard University Press, 1996. Print.

Chambers, Bill. "The Fox and the Hound." *Film Freak Central.* Web. 12 May 2009.

Chaw, Walter. "*Mad Monster Party?* Review." *Film Freak Central.* 8 June 2008. Web. 15 May 2009.

Cohen, Karl F. *Forbidden Animation: Censored Cartoons and Blacklisted Animators in America.* Jefferson NC: McFarland & Co., 1997. Print.

Corbett, Charles J., and Richard P. Turco. "Film and Television Industry." *Southern California Environmental Report Card*, 2006. 5–11, 40. Print.

Cox-Foster, Diana, and Dennis vanEngelsdorp. "Solving the Mystery of the Vanishing Bees." *Scientific American* 31 Mar. 2009. Web. 1 June 2009.

Cronon, William. "The Trouble with Wilderness; or, Getting Back to the Wrong Nature." *Uncommon Ground: Rethinking the Human Place in Nature*. New York: Norton, 1995. 69–90. Print.

Crowther, Bosley. "Disney's Cartoon Adaptation of 'Alice in Wonderland' Arrives at Criterion." *New York Times* 30 July 1951: 12. Print.

———. "Disney's 'Lady and the Tramp' at Roxy." *New York Times* 24 June 1955: 17. Print.

———. "The Screen: Six Newcomers Mark Holiday." *New York Times* 23 Feb. 1950: 33. Print.

———. "Walt Disney's Cartoon, 'Dumbo,' a Fanciful Delight, Opens at the Broadway—'You'll Never Get Rich,' with Fred Astaire and Rita Hayworth, Is Seen at the Music Hall—New Film at Palace." *New York Times* 24 Oct. 1941: 27. Print.

Dargis, Manohla. "'Cars' Is a Drive down a Lonely Highway." *New York Times* 9 June 2006. Web. 9 Oct. 2009.

Denby, David. "Past Shock: *The Dark Knight* and WALL-E." *The New Yorker* 21 July 2008. Web. 1 June 2009.

DreamWorks Animation SKG, Inc. Web. 1 May 2009.

Ebert, Roger. "*Avatar*." *Chicago Sun-Times* 11 Dec. 2009. Web. 17 May 2010.

———. "*The Fox and the Hound*." *Chicago Sun-Times* 1 Jan. 1981. Web. 12 May 2009.

———. "*The Land before Time*." *Chicago Sun-Times* 18 Nov. 1988. Web. 15 May 2009.

———. "*Over the Hedge*." *Chicago Sun-Times* 19 May 2006. Web. 20 May 2009.

———. "*The Secret of NIMH*." *Chicago Sun-Times* 1 Jan. 1982. Web. 20 May 2009.

————. "*Snow White and the Seven Dwarfs.*" *Chicago Sun-Times* 14 Oct. 2001. Web. 12 Apr. 2009.

Erickson, Hal. *Television Cartoon Shows: An Illustrated Encyclopedia, 1949 through 2003*. Jefferson NC: McFarland, 2005. Print.

Friedman, Lester D., and Brent Notbohm. *Steven Spielberg: Interviews*. Jackson: University Press of Mississippi, 2000. Print.

Fromm, Harold. "Ecocriticism: The Greening of Literary Studies." MLA Conference, San Francisco, 1991. Web. 9 Oct. 2008. www.asle.org/site/resources/ecocritical-library/intro/forum/dodd

Furniss, Maureen. *Art in Motion*. London: John Libbey, 1998. Print.

Gabler, Neal. *Walt Disney: The Triumph of the American Imagination*. New York: Alfred A. Knopf, 2006. Print.

Giroux, Henry A. *The Mouse That Roared: Disney and the End of Innocence*. Lanham MD: Rowman and Littlefield, 1999. Print.

Glotfelty, Cheryll, and Harold Fromm, eds. *The Ecocriticism Reader: Landmarks in Literary Ecology*. Athens: University of Georgia Press, 1996. Print.

Goldman, Ilene S. "Gertie the Dinosaur." *St. James Encyclopedia of Pop Culture* 29 Jan. 2002. Web. 1 Mar. 2008.

Goldschmidt, Rick. *The Enchanted World of Rankin/Bass*. Issaquah WA: Tiger Mountain Press, 1997. Print.

Goldschmidt, Rick, and Mark Sykora. *The Enchanted World of Rankin/Bass* 15 Nov. 2005. Web. 1 Dec. 2008. www.rankinbass.com

Gordon, Andrew M. *Empire of Dreams: The Science Fiction and Fantasy Films of Steven Spielberg*. Lanham MD: Rowman & Littlefield, 2008. Print.

Gottlieb, Robert. *Forcing the Spring: The Transformation of the American Environmental Movement*. Washington DC: Island Press, 2005. Print.

Gould, Stephen Jay. "Dinomania." *The Films of Steven Spiel-*

berg: Critical Essays. Ed. Charles L. P. Silet. Lanham MD:
Scarecrow Press, 2002. 171–88. Print.

Grady, Pam. "*Anchors Aweigh Review.*" *Reel.com.* Web. 1 May
2009.

Hajdu, David. *Ten Cent Plague: The Great Comic-Book Scare
and How It Changed America.* New York: Farrar, Straus
and Giroux, 2008. Print.

Hanke, Ken. "The Last Unicorn." *Mountain Express* 8 Aug.
2007. Web. 15 May 2009.

Hargrove, Eugene C., ed. *The Animal Rights/Environmental
Ethics Debate: The Environmental Perspective.* Albany:
SUNY University Press, 1992. Print.

Harmetz, Aljean. "Ex Disney Animators Try to Outdo Their
Mentor." *New York Times* 14 July 1982: C17. Print.

Harper, Jordan. "*Happy Feet* Review." *The Village Voice* 7 Nov.
2006. Web. 17 May 2010.

Hayakawa, S. I. "Introduction: The Revision of Vision." *Language of Vision.* By Gyorgy Kepes. Chicago: P. Theobald,
1951. 8–10. Print.

Henderson, Eric. "The Aristocats." *Slant* 4 Feb. 2008. Web. 1
Apr. 2009.

Hiaasen, Carl. *Double Whammy.* New York: Grand Central
Publishing, 1989. Print.

Hinson, Hal. "The Land before Time." *Washingtonpost.com* 18
Nov. 1988. Web. 15 May 2009.

Holden, Stephen. "*Finding Nemo* Review: Vast Sea, Tiny Fish,
Big Crisis. *New York Times* 30 May 2003. Web. 1 May
2010.

Hull, David L. "Deconstructing Darwin: Evolutionary
Theory in Context." *Journal of the History of Biology*
38.1 (2005): 137–52. Print.

An Inconvenient Truth. Climatecrisis.net. Web. 1 May 2006.

"IGN: The Pixar Philosophy." *Movies.IGN.com* 2 Aug. 2008.
Web. 15 May 2009.

Ingram, David. *Green Screen: Environmentalism and Hollywood Cinema.* Exeter, England: University of Exeter Press,
2000. Print.

Johnson, Bobbie. "The Technological Secrets of James Cameron's New Film *Avatar*." *The Guardian*. 20 Aug. 2009. Web. 3 May 2010.

"Jurassic Park Production Notes." *Ibiblio: The Public's Library* 1992. Web. 20 Mar. 2010.

Kaltman, Elizabeth. "Major Film Studios Roll Out the Green Carpet." *Motion Picture Association of America*. 22 Apr. 2009. Web. 1 Oct. 2009.

Kepes, Gyorgy. *Language of Vision*. Chicago: P. Theobald, 1951. Print.

Klein, Norman M. *Seven Minutes: The Life and Death of the American Animated Cartoon*. New York: Verso, 1993. Print.

Kovarik, William. "Environmental History Timeline." *Environmental History* Apr. 2008. Web. 1 May 2010.

Lamacraft, Jane. "Bee Movie." *Sight and Sound* 18.1 (2008): 59–60. Print.

"The Land before Time Review." *Variety* 1 Jan. 1988. Web. 1 May 2009.

Langer, Mark. "Institutional Power and the Fleischer Studios: The 'Standard Production Reference.'" *Cinema Journal* 30.2 (1991): 3–22. Print.

———. "Regionalism in Disney Animation: Pink Elephants and Dumbo." *Film History* 4.4 (1990): 305–21. Print.

Leopold, Aldo. *Sand County Almanac*. New York: Oxford University Press, 1949. Print.

Lowry, Brian. "*The Simpsons Movie* Review." *Variety* 24 July 2007. Web. 17 May 2010.

Lutts, Ralph H. "The Trouble with Bambi: Walt Disney's Bambi and the American Vision of Nature." *Forest & Conservation History* 36.4 (1992): 160–71. Print.

MacDonald, Scott. *The Garden in the Machine: A Field Guide to Independent Films about Place*. Berkeley: University of California Press, 2001. Print.

Maher, Neil M. *Nature's New Deal: The Civilian Conservation Corps and the Roots of the American Environmental*

Movement. New York: Oxford University Press, 2008. Print.

Maltin, Leonard. *The Disney Films*. 4th ed. New York: Jessie Film, 2000. Print.

———. *Of Mice and Magic: A History of American Animated Cartoons*. New York: McGraw-Hill, 1980. Print.

Markstein, Don. "Gerald McBoing Boing." *Toonpedia*. Web. 15 Apr. 2009.

———. "*Mad Magazine*." *Toonpedia* 8 June 2008. Web. 15 Apr. 2009.

Marx, Leo. *The Machine in the Garden: Technology and the Pastoral Ideal in America*. New York: Oxford University Press, 1964. Print.

Maslin, Janet. "The Last Unicorn: An Animated Fable." *New York Times* 19 Nov. 1982. Web. 1 May 2009.

May, Theresa J. "Beyond Bambi: Toward a Dangerous Ecocriticism in Theater Studies." *Theater Topics* 17.2 (2007): 95–110. Print.

McCarthy, Todd. "*Bee Movie* Review." *Variety* 28 Oct. 2007. Web. 15 May 2010.

———. "*Happy Feet* Review." *Variety* 10 Nov. 2006. Web. 17 May 2010.

Meeker, Joseph W. "The Comic Mode: The Biology of Comedy." *The Ecocriticism Reader*. Ed. Cheryll Glotfelty and Harold Fromm. Athens: University of Georgia Press, 1996. 155–69. Print.

Merchant, Carolyn. *American Environmental History: An Introduction*. New York: Columbia University Press, 2007. Print.

Midgley, Mary. "The Mixed Community." *The Animal Rights/ Environmental Ethics Debate: The Environmental Perspective*. Ed. Eugene C. Hargrove. Albany: SUNY University Press, 1992. 211–25. Print.

Mondello, Bob. "WALL-E: Speaking Volumes with Stillness and Stars." *NPR.org* 27 June 2008. Web. 1 June 2009.

Morris, Nigel. *The Cinema of Steven Spielberg: Empire of Light*. London: Wallflower Press, 2007. Print.

"Mr. Bug Goes to Town." The Film Society of Lincoln Center 1 Jan. 2006. Web. 1 Jan. 2009.

"Mr. Bug Goes to Town." *Time* 1941. Web. 1 Sept. 2006.

Murray, Robin L., and Joseph K. Heumann. *Ecology and Popular Film: Cinema on the Edge.* Albany: SUNY Press, 2009. Print.

Null, Christopher. "The Incredible Mr. Limpet." *Filmcritic.com.* 27 Sept. 2002. Web. 1 Jan. 2009.

Osborn, Fairfield. *Our Plundered Planet.* Boston: Little, Brown, 1948. Print.

Paik, Karen. *To Infinity and Beyond! The Story of Pixar Animation Studios.* San Francisco: Chronicle, 2007. Print.

Phelps, Norm. *The Longest Struggle: Animal Advocacy from Pythagoras to Peta.* New York: Lantern, 2007. Print.

Phillips, Dana. "Is Nature Necessary?" *The Ecocriticism Reader: Landmarks in Literary Ecology.* Ed. Cheryll Glotfelty and Harold Fromm. Athens: University of Georgia Press, 1996. 204–24. Print.

Pinheiro, Ethel, and Cristiane Rose Duarte. "*Panem et circenses* at *Largo da Carioca*, Brazil: The Urban Diversity Focused on People-Environment Interactions." *Anthropology Matters Journal* 6.1 (2004). Print.

Rabin, Nathan. "*The Simpsons Movie* Review." *A.V. Club* 27 July 2007. Web. 17 May 2010.

Raglon, Rebecca, and Marion Scholtmeijer. "'Animals Are Not Believers in Ecology': Mapping Critical Differences between Environmental and Animal Advocacy Literatures." *Isle: Interdisciplinary Studies in Literature and Environment* 14.2 (2007): 121–40. Print.

Richards, Ellen Swallow. "Human Ecology and the Habits of Sanitation in the Modern Urban Environment." *So Glorious a Landscape: Nature and the Environment in American History.* Ed. Chris J. Magoc. Wilmington DE: Scholarly Resources, 1907, 2002. 142–44. Print.

Robertson, Barbara. "Seduced by Suburbia." *Animation* 20.6 (2006): 12–14. Print.

Robinson, Tasha. "*Happy Feet* Review." *A.V. Club* 16 Nov. 2006. Web. 17 May 2010.

Rohde, Klaus, and Peter P. Rohde. "Fuzzy Chaos: Reduced Chaos in the Combined Dynamics of Several Independently Chaotic Populations." *The American Naturalist* 158.5 (2001): 553–56. Print.

Ross, Deborah. "Escape from Wonderland: Disney and the Female Imagination." *Marvels and Tales: Journal of Fairy-Tale Studies* 18.1 (2004): 53–66. Print.

Rothman, Hal. *Saving the Planet.* Chicago: Dee, 2000. Print.

Salten, Felix. *Bambi: A Forest Life.* New York: Aladdin, 1988. Print.

Sanello, Frank. *Spielberg: The Man, the Movies, the Mythology.* Dallas: Taylor, 1996. Print.

Schmidt, Robert H. "Why Do We Debate Animal Rights?" *Wildlife Society Bulletin* 18.4 (1990): 459–61. Print.

Scott, A. O. "*WALL-E.*" *New York Times* 27 June 2008. Web. 1 Dec. 2008.

———. "We'll Always Have Springfield." *New York Times* 27 July 2008. Web. 17 May 2010.

Shabecoff, Philip. *Fierce Green Fire: The American Environmental Movement.* Washington DC: Island Press, 2003. Print.

Silet, Charles L. P., ed. *The Films of Steven Spielberg: Critical Essays.* Lanham MD: Scarecrow Press, 2002. Print.

Simon, Ben. "The Incredible Mr. Limpet." *Animated Views* 28 Sept. 2002. Web. 1 Jan. 2009.

Singer, Peter. *Animal Liberation.* New York: Avon Books, 1975. Print.

Smoodin, Eric. *Animating Culture: Hollywood Cartoons from the Sound Era.* New Brunswick NJ: Rutgers University Press, 1993. Print.

Stewart, Kathleen. "Nostalgia—A Polemic." *Cultural Anthropology* 3.3 (1988): 227–41. Print.

Strike, Joe. "*Over the Hedge*: Making the Leap from Newsprint to Pixels." *Animation World* 19 May 2006. Web. 1 May 2009.

Taylor, Philip. *Steven Spielberg: The Man, His Movies, and Their Meaning*. 3rd ed. New York: Continuum, 1999. Print.

Thiele, Leslie Paul. "Evolutionary Narratives and Ecological Ethics." *Political Theory* 27.1 (1999): 6–38. Print.

Thompson, Howard. "Movie Review: *Mad Monster Party?* (1968)." *New York Times* 8 Mar. 1969. Web. 1 May 2009.

T.M.P. "*Johnny Eager*, starring Lana Turner, Robert Taylor at Capitol—*Mr. Bug Goes to Town* Opens at Loews State." *New York Times* 20 Feb. 1942: 21. Print.

Tobias, Scott. "*Avatar*: An IMAX 3D Experience." *A.V. Club* 17 Dec. 2009. Web. 17 May 2010.

Travers, Peter. "Bee Movie." *Rolling Stone* 1 Nov. 2007. Web. 1 May 2009.

———. "*WALL-E*." *Rolling Stone* 10 July 2008. Web. 1 May 2009.

Vogt, William. *Road to Survival*. New York: W. Sloane, 1948. Print.

Waage, Frederick O. *Teaching Environmental Literature: Materials, Methods, Resources*. New York: MLA, 1985. Print.

"*WALL-E* Review." *Movieguide.org*. Web. 1 May 2009.

"The Walt Disney Company 2008 Corporate Responsibility Report." 2008. Web. 1 May 2009.

Warren, Mary Anne. "The Rights of the Nonhuman World." *The Animal Rights/Environmental Ethics Debate: The Environmental Perspective*. Ed. Eugene C. Hargrove. Albany: SUNY University Press, 1992. 185–210. Print.

Watts, Steven. *The Magic Kingdom: Walt Disney and the American Way of Life*. Boston: Houghton, 1997. Print.

Weinman, Jaime. "A Good Enviro-toon." *Something Old, Nothing New: Thoughts on Popular Culture and Unpopular Culture* 6 Sept. 2004. Web. 10 Oct. 2005.

Wells, Paul. *The Animated Bestiary: Animals, Cartoons, Culture*. New Brunswick NJ: Rutgers University Press, 2009. Print.

———. *Animation: Genre and Authorship*. New York: Wallflower, 2002. Print.

————. *Animation and America*. New Brunswick NJ: Rutgers
    University Press, 2002. Print.
Whitley, David. *The Idea of Nature in Disney Animation*.
    Hampshire, England: Ashgate, 2008.
Wilson, Alexander. *The Culture of Nature: North American
    Landscape from Disney to the Exxon Valdez*. Blackwell,
    Oxford: 1992. Print.
Wood, Naomi. "Domesticating Dreams in Disney's *Cinderella*."
    The Lion and the Unicorn 20.1 (1996): 25–49. Print.
Youngblood, Gene. *Expanded Cinema*. New York: Dutton,
    1970. Print.
Zacharek, Stephanie. "*Avatar*: Dances with Aliens." *Salon.com*
    18 Dec. 2009. Web. 17 May 2010.
————. "*Bee Movie*." *Salon.com* 2 Nov. 2007. Web. 1 May
    2009.
————. "*Finding Nemo*." *Salon.com* 8 June 2003. Web. 1 May
    2009.
————. "*WALL-E*." *Salon.com* 27 June 2008. Web. 1 May 2009.

Index